RECORDED PLAYS

*Indexes to Dramatists,
Plays, and Actors*

RECORDED PLAYS

Indexes to Dramatists, Plays, and Actors

compiled by

Herbert H. Hoffman

American Library Association
Chicago and London 1985

Cover design by Marcia Rasmussen

Composed in Manuscript 819 and
    in OCR-B 806 on an Olympia
    "Eurotronic" typewriter.
    Display type, Goudy, composed
    by Pearson Typographers.

Printed on 55-pound Glatfelter,
    a pH-neutral stock, and bound
    in Bamberger Iris cloth
    by Edwards Brothers, Inc.

Library of Congress Cataloging in Publication Data
Hoffman, Herbert H.
    Recorded plays.

    1. Drama--Audio-visual aids--Indexes.
2. Drama--Discography--Indexes. 3. Drama--
Film and video adaptations--Indexes. 4. Dramatists--
Indexes. 5. Actors--Indexes. I. Title.
PN1701.5.H64 1985   016.80882   85-19190
ISBN 0-8389-0440-8

Printed in the United States of America.

Contents

Preface

Drama, if it is not the oldest of the performing arts, certainly has a
long history. At the same time it is a very vital modern art form. Of
all literary genres the play has always made the most powerful statement,
has touched more people than any other form. From Euripides to Shakespeare
to Chekhov and beyond, the playwright has rivaled the philosopher and the
scientist in the importance of what he has had to say. And the audience
shows no signs of dwindling. This is in part because it is not only what
a play says but how it is said. One can read the playwright's text, of
course, but only when combined with the actor's art does the play become
living, gripping theater. Recordings of great performances, therefore,
must be considered among the special treasures of world literature.

RECORDED PLAYS was designed to guide poeple to performances and readings
of plays that have been recorded on phonodiscs, audio cassettes or tapes,
video cassettes, and 16mm film. Altogether there are 1,844 entries for a
total of approximately 700 different works by 284 playwrights, distributed
by their native languages as follows:

English	127	Russian	14	Latin	2
French	43	Uzbek	6	Norwegian	2
German	40	Greek	4	Georgian	1
Spanish	19	Yiddish	4	Swedish	1
Italian	18	Japanese	2	Ukrainian	1

With very few exceptions, only recordings produced since the advent of
the standard longplaying album have been considered.

Among the users of RECORDED PLAYS will be students of literature and of
foreign languages; actors and directors; radio and television stations;
teachers in schools and colleges who want to bring drama to life for their
classes; librarians who need to know what is available in this genre
and who must tell others where to find things; and all persons who would
like to be entertained or inspired by a dramatic performance on a level
of intensity that cannot usually be attained in a mere private reading
of the text.

RECORDED PLAYS is divided into three parts. The main part is an author
index arranged by playwrights' names. Here the plays are described bibli-
ographically, with actors' names whenever that information was available,
and with identification numbers of the recordings. Most of the recordings
are stand-alone works, containing one play.

Also included are some 270 anthologies or collections of several plays
or parts of plays. The majority of the recordings listed are 33 1/3
rpm LP phonodiscs. Other recording speeds and other media have
been designated by suitable symbols explained in the list of
abbreviations. Each entry in the author index is numbered and stands
for one performance. If the same performance is marketed in different
formats or on different labels, they are clustered and combined into
one entry. Unless stated otherwise recordings are in the English
language.

The second part is a title index. Here the plays are listed
alphabetically by their original titles, with cross references from
translated titles as necessary. All title index entries are referenced
to entry numbers in the author index.

The third part is an actor index, also referenced to entry numbers
in the author index. Over 2,500 names are listed in the actor index.

So, if you want to see if a recording exists of Arthur Miller's
"Death of a Salesman" you can consult the author index directly. If
a reader is unsure of the author, the title index shows that there is
such a play by Miller and that four recordings have been indexed, under
entry numbers 554 through 557. One of these performances (554) stars
Lee Cobb in the leading role, another (555) has Thomas Mitchell
playing the part. If you would like to know what else Thomas Mitchell
has recorded turn to the actor index. The actor index shows that
Mitchell can also be heard on different discs and cassettes in
Shakespeare's "Julius Caesar", in "King Lear", in "Twelfth Night", and
in various excerpts on an ARIEL recording.

At the end of the actor index follows a list of anthologies, defined
as recordings that contain full performances of or selected scenes from
more than one play. If, for example, you were to look for a recording
of Pierre Franck's "Faiseur" the author index tells you to look "in
anth. ADES 7003". Checking the list of anthologies you learn that you
must look for a set of two phonodiscs entitled Hommage à Charles Dullin.

Many of the recordings indexed are in print and can be obtained from
their producers if not from dealers. A directory of recording companies
with addresses, if known, has been added at the end of the book. Recordings that are out of print or whose producers have merged or gone
out of business are still important, of course, because they remain
available in libraries.

Part of the information included in this index was gathered from
secondary sources. It was not always possible to double check details
such as label numbers; the identity of actors or the correct spelling
of their names; or whether a certain performance was identical to a
performance released under a different name. For example, an actor might
have been given on a cassette only as "Edwards". There was no way to
determine if this was Alan, Hilton, Maurice, Meredith, or Rob Edwards,
or perhaps still another person by that name. The compiler has always
made separate index entries in doubtful cases and hopes that index users
will overlook ambiguities that occasionally result.

Herbert H. Hoffman

Abbreviations

ac	audio cassette
anth.	anthology, defined as any recording that contains more than one play
at	audio tape reel
exc.	excerpt, selection, or abbreviated arrangement of a play
orig.	in the original (language, as stated)
pd	phonodisc, 33 1/3 rpm
pd45	phonodisc, 45 rpm (or other speed, as indicated)
vc 1/2	video cassette, 1/2 inch tape (or other width, as indicated)
vt	video tape reel

Author Index

Achard, Marcel
  1 JEAN DE LA LUNE (orig. French)
     Marcel Achard; M. Simon; J. Mar-
     tinelli; M. Renaud; P. Syrac.
     DECCA 163.801/2, also DECCA DE
     100.125/6 (2 pd)
  2 JEAN DE LA LUNE (exc., orig.
     French)
     M. Simon. In anth. COLUMB
     ESJF 1
  3 MARLBOROUGH S'EN VA-T-EN GUERRE
     (orig. French)
     Read by the author. LVA 21
  4 PATATE (exc., orig. French)
     M. Teynac; P. Dux; F. Delahalle;
     S. Pitoeff; S. Daumier; M.
     Achard. PHIL B 77.913
  5 VOULEZ-VOUS JOUER AVEC MÔA?
     (orig. French)
     Read by the author. LVA 24

Aeschylus
  6 AGAMEMNON (exc., in English)
     Paul Roche. NORTON 23114
  7 AGAMEMNON (exc., in French)
     Fechter; Chamarat. In anth.
     HACH 320E899
  8 CHOEPHOROI (exc., in English as
     THE LIBATION BEARERS)
     MICHMED 9368 (vc, also 16mm
     film)
  9 CHOEPHOROI (exc., in French as
     CHOEPHORES)
     Dacqmine; Chamarat. In anth.
     HACH 320E899
 10 CHOEPHOROI (exc., in Italian as
     COEFORE)
     V. Gassmann; Vera Gherarducci;
     Paolo Carlini; Arnoldo Foà;
     Memo Benassi; Nado Gazzolo. In
     anth. CETRA CLC 0855

 11 EUMENIDES (exc., in English)
     MICHMED 9369 (vc, also 16mm
     film)
 12 ORESTEIA (in English)
     Players Inc. LC T 3297 (at)
 13 PERSAI (in German as DIE PERSER)
     Annie Rosar. ODEON O 80779
 14 PERSAI (exc., in German as DIE
     PERSER)
     Elisabeth Flickenschildt. In
     anth. DEUTGR 2570 013
 15 PERSAI (exc., in French as LES
     PERSES)
     Morane; Deschamps. In anth.
     HACH 320E899
 16 PERSAI (exc., in Italian as I
     PERSIANI)
     Vittorio Gassmann; E. Aldini;
     C. Montagna; A. Cucari. In
     anth. CETRA CLC 0824
 17 PERSAI (exc., in Modern Greek)
     Katina Paxinou; Alexis Minotis.
     In anth. CAED TC 1127 (pd),
     also CDL 51127 (ac)
 18 Miscellaneous exc.
     Read by John F. C. Richards.
     In anth. FOLKW 9984
 19 Miscellaneous exc.
     In anth. SUPERSC I 141 (ac)

Aiken, Conrad
 20 COMING FORTH BY DAY OF OSIRIS
     JONES
     American National Theatre and
     Academy. In anth. LC T 3281 (at)
 21 KID
     American National Theatre and
     Academy. In anth. LC T 3281 (at)

Albee, Edward
  22 DELICATE BALANCE
        Katharine Hepburn as Agnes; Lee
        Remick as Julia; Joseph Cotten
        as Harry; Paul Scofield as
        Tobias; Kate Reid as Claire;
        Betsy Blair as Edna. CAED TRS
        360 (3 pd), also CDL 5360(3 ac)
  23 FAM AND YAM
        American National Theatre and
        Academy. LC T 3602 (at)
  24 LISTENING
        Irene Worth; Maureen Anderman;
        James Ray. In anth. MINN
        29121/5
  25 WHO'S AFRAID OF VIRGINIA WOOLF?
        Uta Hagen as Martha; Arthur
        Hill as George; George Grizzard
        as Nick; Melinda Dillon as
        Honey. COLUMB DOL 287 (4 pd),
        also CDOS 687 (4 ac)
  26 ZOO STORY
        Mark Richman; William Daniels.
        SPOA SA 808 (pd), also 7149(ac)

Aleichem, Sholom
  27 HIGH SCHOOL
        Morris Carnovsky; Howard Da
        Silva; Ruby Dee; Gilbert Green;
        David Pressman; Pearl Somner.
        In anth. TIKVA T 28
  28 Miscellaneous exc. (in Yiddish)
        In anth. BRUNO BR 50196

Alfieri, Vittorio
  29 MIRRA (exc., orig. Italian)
        Carlo D'Angelo; Lucilla Mor-
        lacchi. In anth. CETRA
        LPZ 2058
  30 ORESTE (exc., orig. Italian)
        Carlo D'Angelo; Lucilla Mor-
        lacchi. In anth. CETRA
        LPZ 2058
  31 SAUL (exc., orig. Italian)
        Carlo D'Angelo; Lucilla Mor-
        lacchi. In anth. CETRA
        LPZ 2058
  32 SAUL (exc., orig. Italian)
        G. Giacobbe as Micol; O.
        Fanfani as Abner; E. Ta-
        rascio as Saul; F. Grazi-
        osi as David; G. Chazalet-
        tes as Gionata. In anth.
        EIA DSM 116

**Alvarez Quintero, Serafín &
Joaquín**
  33 GILITO (orig. Spanish)
        Josefina Claudio as Pura;
        Rafael Bartolomei as Gilito;
        José Díaz as Don Juan; Nor-
        berto Kerner as Manuel; Ismael
        Diaz Tirado as Rafael. In
        anth. SMC 1032
  34 MAÑANA DEL SOL (orig. Spanish)
        Lola Alba as Doña Laura;
        Marta María Gonsálvez as Petra;
        Antonio Moreno as Don Gonzalo;
        Miguel Pastor Mata as Juanito;
        Victoriano Evangelio as Bar-
        quillero. SPOA 851 (pd), also
        50-5 (ac)

Anderson, Maxwell
  35 WINTERSET
        Burgess Meredith; John Carra-
        dine. BUDGET (vc)

Angelo Beolco, detto Il Ruzzante
  36 RITORNO DEL REDUCE (orig. Italian)
        Vittorio Gassmann; E. Aldini;
        C. Montagna; A. Cucari. In
        anth. CETRA CLC 0824

Anouilh, Jean
  37 ANTIGONE (orig. French)
        Read by the author. LVA 1
  38 ARDELE; OU, LA MARGUERITE (orig.
        French)
        Read by the author. LVA 10
  39 CÉCILE; OU, L'ÉCOLE DES PÈRES
        (orig. French)
        Read by the author. LVA 6
  40 CONSPIRATION DE L'HURLEBERLU
        (orig. French)
        SONOPR Théatrorama 1 (3 pd)
  41 FOIRE (orig. French)
        Read by the author. LVA 19
  42 MÉDÉE (orig. French)
        Read by the author. LVA 31
  43 MÉDÉE (in English as MEDEA)
        Madeline Sherwood. LC T 4276(at)
  44 MÉDÉE (exc., in Ukrainian as
        MEDEA)
        Wira Lewycka as Medea. LEWYCKY
        GL 1

Anouilh, Jean, and Laudanbach,
Roland
45 PETITE MOLIÈRE (exc., orig.
French)
Jean-Louis Barrault; M. Re-
naud; C. Anouilh; R. Lombard.
VEGA T 31 SP 8002

Aristophanes
46 EIRENE (exc., in French as LA
PAIX)
Charles Dullin. In anth. ADÈS
7003 (2 pd)
47 EKKLESIAZOUSAI (in French as
L'ASSEMBLÉE DES FEMMES)
Nerval; D. Benoit; Hardy. In
anth. HACH 320E909
48 LYSISTRATE (in English as LYSIS-
TRATA)
Hermione Gingold as Lysistrata;
Stanley Holloway as Commissioner;
Miriam Karlin as Women's Chorus
Leader; Edward Atienza as Men's
Chorus Leader; Patricia Rout-
ledge as Kalonike; Timothy Bate-
son as Kinesias; Elvi Hale as
Myrrhine; Tarn Bassett as Lampi-
to; Trevor Martin as Spartan;
Patricia Somerset as Woman;
Jerry Verno; Douglas Muir; John
Saunders; Gillian Lind; Dandy
Nichols; Avril Elgar. CAED
TRS 313 (2 pd), also CDL 5313
(2 ac)
49 ORNITHES (exc., in French as LES
OISEAUX)
Charles Dullin. In anth. ADÈS
7003
50 ORNITHES (in French as LES OISEAUX)
Moulinot; Furet; Rochefort;
Parédès; Virlojeux. In anth.
HACH 320E909
51 SPHEKES (in French as LES GUÊPES)
Parédès; Maurin; Virlojeux;
Rochefort. In anth. HACH
320E909
52 Miscellaneous exc.
Read by John F. C. Richards. In
anth. FOLKW 9984
53 Miscellaneous exc.
In anth. SUPERSC I 141

Arniches y Barrera, Carlos
54 FIERA DORMIDA (orig. Spanish)
Antonio García Quijada as Ma-
nolo; Lola del Pino as Bruna;
Lola Villaespesa as Amparo;
José Manuel Martin as Felipe;
Nela Conjíu as Charito; En-
rique Rincón as Quique; Ara-
celi Fernández Baizán as Consu-
elito; Victoriano Evangelio as
Dr. Metodio; Domingo de Moral
as Sr. Neme.   SPOA 844 (pd),
also 49-6 (ac)

Aubrey
55 BRIEF LIVES
Roy Dortrice. MM LP 48

Bacigalupo, Nicoló
56 MANEZZI PE' MAIÂ NA FIGGIA
(orig. Italian)
Gilberto Govi; Rina Govi;
Nelda Meroni; Gian Fabio Fosco;
Jole Lorena; Ariano Praga;
Luigi Dameri. CETRA LPB 35035
(pd), also MC 66 (ac)

Bacon, Frank. Jt. auth. with
Smith, Winchell, q.v.

Bahr, Hermann
57 KONZERT (orig. German)
DEUTGR 43060

Bakhmanov, Bakhram
58 YURAK SIRLARI (orig. Uzbek; translated title: Heart's Secrets)
Khamza Drama Theatre.
MK D 011669-74 (3 pd)

Bale, John
59 KYNGE JOHAN
Stephen Murray as Kynge Johan;
Gladys Young as Widow England.
In anth. DOVER 99717-0-N

Barry, Julian
60 LENNY
Cliff Gorman as Lenny. BLUE
BTS 9001

Barry, P. J.
  61 HERITAGE: AN AMERICAN FOLK TALE
    ABOUT THE LINCOLN WOMEN
      American National Theatre and
      Academy. LC T 6381 (at)

Bauman, M.
  62 Miscellaneous exc., in Yiddish
    In anth. BRUNO BR 50196

Baxter, James K.
  63 JACK WINTER'S DREAM
      Bernard Beeby as Jack Winter;
      Alan Jarvin as Will Trevelyan;
      Roy Leywood as Preacher Lowry;
      William Austin as Charlie Bird;
      Patrick Smith as Ballarat Jake;
      Dorothy Munro as Jennie Bird.
      KIWI SID 40

Beaumarchais, Pierre-Augustin
Caron de
  64 BARBIER DE SÉVILLE (orig. French)
      Micheline Boudet as Rosine;
      Jean Weber as Almaviva; Jean
      Piat as Figaro; André Brunot as
      Bartholo; Robert Pizani as Ba-
      sile; Darry Cowl as Valet.
      LONDON TW 91058/9, also DECCA
      163.565/6 (2 pd)
  65 BARBIER DE SÉVILLE (exc., orig.
    French)
      Rouvel; Roux; Crémieux; Patu-
      rel; Mazzotti. BOR SSB 121
  66 BARBIER DE SÉVILLE (exc., orig.
    French)
      J. Weber; J. Piat; A. Brunot;
      R. Pizani. DECCA 455.575 (pd45)
  67 BARBIER DE SÉVILLE (exc., orig.
    French)
      P. Desboeuf; J. Bertheau; L.
      Arbessier; A. Moya. LUM
      LD 1.283/4 (2 pd45)
  68 MARIAGE DE FIGARO (orig. French)
      J. Meyer; L. Seigner; G.
      Chamarat; G. Descrières; H.
      Rollan; A. de Chauveron; M.
      Boudet; Y. Gaudeau; M. Grellier.
      PAT DTX 303-5 (3 pd)
  69 MARIAGE DE FIGARO (orig. French)
      Comédie Française. GMS DISC
      7077-79 (3 pd)
  70 MARIAGE DE FIGARO (exc., orig.
    French)
      Piat. In anth. HACH 320.914

  71 MARIAGE DE FIGARO (exc., orig.
    French)
      Jean Deschamps. In anth. HACH
      460E803/5 (3 pd)
  72 MARIAGE DE FIGARO (exc., orig.
    French)
      J. Bertheau; P. Desboeuf; A.
      Moya. LUM LD 1.285/6 (2 pd45)
  73 MARIAGE DE FIGARO (exc., orig.
    French)
      Jean-Louis Barrault; Made-
      leine Renaud. In anth. SPOA
      715 (pd), also 48-6 (ac)

Beaumont, Francis, and Fletcher,
John
  74 KNIGHT OF THE BURNING PESTLE (exc.)
      Peter Gray. In anth. PEARL
      SHE 525

Beckett, Samuel
  75 EN ATTENDANT GODOT (in English as
    WAITING FOR GODOT)
      Bert Lahr; E. G. Marshall; Kurt
      Kasznar; Alvin Epstein; Lu-
      chino Solito de Solis. CAED
      TRS 352 (2 pd), also CDL 5352
      (2 ac); also COLUMB 02L-238
      (2 pd)
  76 ENDGAME
      Lester Rawlins; Gerald Hiken;
      P. J. Kelly; Nydia Westman.
      EVERG EV 400 (2 pd), also EVR
      003
  77 ENDGAME (exc.)
      Frank Doherty. In anth SAGA
      PSY 30003
  78 KRAPP'S LAST TAPE
      Read by Donald Davis. SPOA
      788 (pd), also 7148 (ac)
  79 KRAPP'S LAST TAPE (in German as
    DAS LETZTE BAND)
      Martin Held. DEUTGR 2570 001
  80 OH LES BEAUX JOURS (in English as
    HAPPY DAYS)
      Irene Worth; George Voscovec.
      CAED TRS 366 (2 pd), also CDL
      5232 (2 ac)
  81 OH LES BEAUX JOURS (exc., orig.
    French)
      Madeleine Renaud; Jean-Louis
      Barrault. ADÈS 16,024

Behan, Brendan
    82 HOSTAGE
        Diana Webster as Meg Dillon;
        M. Patten as Pat; Sheila Coonan
        as Old Ropeen; James Cahill
        as Rio Rita; Arthur French as
        Princess Grace; Margalo Bur-
        nett as Colette; Julie Harris
        as Teresa; Geoff Garland as
        Leslie. COLUMB CDS 729, also
        DOL 329 (3 pd); also OS 6772;
        also SPECSERV COS 6771-2 (3 pd)
    83 QUARE FELLA
        Arthur O'Sullivan; Frank O'
        Dwyer; Brendan Caldwell; Ea-
        monn Kelly; Thomas Studley;
        John Stephenson; Lionel Day;
        Niall Toibin; Chris Curran;
        Connor Farrington; Eamonn
        Keane; Joseph O'Dea; George
        Greene; Brendan Burke; Leo
        Leyden; Liam Devally; Noel
        Lynch; Charles McCarthy.
        SPOWRD SW A-24 (2 pd)

Behrman, S. N.
    84 BIOGRAPHY
        Faye Emerson. CENT 010-2282 (ac)

Benavente, Jacinto
    85 INTERESES CREADOS (orig. Spanish)
        Asunción Sancho as Silvia;
        Josefina Santaularia as Doña
        Sirena; Amparo Gómez as Colom-
        biña; Julia Berry as Señora de
        Polichinela; Asunción Pascual
        as Laura; Ana Sillero as Rise-
        la; Manuel Dicenta as Crispín;
        Félix Navarro as Leandro; Alfon-
        so Muñoz as Doctor; José Brugu-
        era as Polichi; Avelino Cánovas
        as Arlequín; Antonio Puga as
        Capitán; José Guijarro as Pan-
        talón; José Luis Heredia as
        Hostelero; Emilio Matos as
        Secretario. GMS D 7140/41 (2 pd)
    86 MAQUERIDA (orig. Spanish)
        Ana Adamuz; Carmen Lombarte;
        Luis Orduna. GMS D 7142/3; also
        REGAL LSX 101/2 (2 pd)

Bennett, Alan
    87 FORTY YEARS ON
        DECCA (3 pd)

Bernhard, Thomas
    88 MACHT DER GEWOHNHEIT (orig. Ger-
        man)
        Bernhard Minetti; Fritz Lichten-
        hahn; Hans Peter Hallwachs;
        Bruno Dallansky; Anita Lochner.
        DEUTGR 2752 007 (2 pd)

Berrigan, Daniel
    89 TRIAL OF THE CATONSVILLE NINE
        Ed Flanders; Douglass Watson;
        Leon Russom; Anthony Costello;
        Peter Strauss; Gwen Arner; Don-
        ald Moffat; Richard Jordan;
        Nancy Malone; David Spielberg;
        William Schallert; Mary Jackson;
        Jason Bernard; John S. Batters-
        by; Lou Fant; Harv Selsby; Kev-
        in Tighe. CAED TRS 353 (2 pd),
        also CDL 5353 (2 ac)

Bersezio, Vittorio
    90 MISERIE 'D MONSSU TRAVET (orig.
        Italian)
        Erminio Macario; F. Barbero;
        M. Brusa; W. D'Eusebio; I. Er-
        betta; O. Fagnano; R. Lori; V.
        Lottero; M. Malaspina; B.
        Marchese; A. Rossi. CETRA
        LEL 146

Besier, Rudolf
    91 BARRETTS OF WIMPOLE STREET (exc.)
        Katharine Cornell; Anthony
        Quayle. CAED TC 1071
    92 BARRETTS OF WIMPOLE STREET (exc.)
        Katharine Cornell; Brian Aherne.
        In anth. DECCA DL 9009

Bhasa
    93 VISION OF VASAVADATTA (in English)
        Institute for Advanced Studies
        in the Theatre Arts. LC T 4154
        (at)

Björnson, Björne
    94 BERGLIOT
        In anth. TONO X 25033

Böll, Heinrich
    95 POSTKARTE (orig. German)
        BERLET ISBN 0-699-07623-4
        (16mm film)

Bolt, Robert
  96 MAN FOR ALL SEASONS
        Paul Scofield as Sir Thomas
        More; Wendy Hiller; Leo McKern;
        Robert Shaw; Orson Welles; Su-
        sannah York; Nigel Davenport;
        John Hurt; Corin Redgrave;
        Colin Blakely; Cyril Luckham;
        Vanessa Redgrave. RCA VDM 116,
        also RB 6712/3 (2 pd)
  97 MAN FOR ALL SEASONS (exc.)
        PROTHM 1EP3 (ac)

Bosselet, Jacqueline
  98 SCÈNES DE LA VIE FRANCAISE (orig.
     French)
        Jean-Philippe Gaussens as Mi-
        chel; Marie-Noëlle Ruckwied as
        Brigitte; Jacqueline Bosselet as
        Mère; Jean-Gabriel Gaussens as
        Père. SPOA SA 841

Brecht, Bertolt
  99 AUFHALTSAME AUFSTIEG DES ARTURO
     UI (exc., in French as LA RÉSIS-
     TIBLE ASCENSION D'ARTURO UI)
        Jean Vilar; G. Wilson. In
        anth. ADÈS TS 30 LA 552
  100 AUSNAHME UND DIE REGEL (in English
      as THE EXCEPTION AND THE RULE)
        Paul E. Richards as Merchant;
        Joseph Chaikin as Coolie; Sam
        Greene as Guide; Frank Grose-
        close as Judge; Jeanette Hodge
        as Widow; Willard Bond as
        Judge; William Shorr as Leader
        of the Caravan; Charles Sulli-
        van as Policeman; Ron Vaad as
        Innkeeper; Eric Bentley, Narra-
        tor. FOLKW 9848
  101 ELEPHANTENKALB (in English as THE
      ELEPHANT CALF, OR, THE PROVABILITY
      OF EVERY CONTENTION)
        Logan Ramsey; James Antonio.
        ASCH FL 9831
  102 FURCHT UND ELEND DES DRITTEN
      REICHES (exc., orig. German)
        Therese Giehse. In anth.
        DEUTGR 2571 011 (pd), also
        3321 011 (ac); also in 168 094
  103 GEWEHRE DER FRAU CARRAR (orig.
      German)
        Helene Weigel as Frau Carrar;
        Ekkehard Schall as José; Erwin
        Geschonnek as Pedro; Erich

Franz; Regine Lutz; Norbert
        Christian; Angelica Hurwicz;
        Friedrich Gnass; Harry Gill-
        mann; Joseph Noerden. PLÄNE
        860 081
  104 MANN IST MANN (in English as MAN'S
      A MAN)
        John Heffernan as Galy Gay;
        Jenny Egan as Widow Begbick;
        Michael Granger as Bloody Five;
        Maurice Edwards as Uriah Shel-
        ley; Eric Bentley, Narrator.
        SPOA 870
  105 MUTTER COURAGE UND IHRE KINDER
      (orig. German)
        Helene Weigel as Mutter Coura-
        ge; Angelika Hurwicz as Kat-
        trin; Ekkehard Schall as Eilif;
        Heinz Schubert as Schweizer-
        kas; Willi Schwabe; Gerhart
        Bienert; Ernst Busch. DEUTGR
        860 122/4 (3 pd)
  106 Miscellaneous exc.
        Therese Giehse; Gisela May.
        In anth. DEUTGR 2755 005

Büchner, Georg
  107 DANTON'S TOD (exc., orig. Ger-
      man)
        Rolf Boysen; Charles Brauner;
        Heinz G. Lück; Bernhard Mi-
        netti; Will Quadflieg; Viola
        Wahlen; Ruth Niehaus; Louise
        Martini; Karl Merkatz; Hans
        Ulrich. DEUTGR 140 024, also
        2571 012
  108 DANTON'S TOD (exc., orig. German)
        Elisabeth Flickenschildt. In
        anth. DEUTGR 2570 013
  109 DANTON'S TOD (exc., orig. german)
        Helmut Griem. In anth. TELEF
        STSC 13.454
  110 WOYZECK (in English)
        John Rowe as Woyzeck; Kate
        Binchy as Mistress. BBC ECN
        165 (ac)

Buero Vallejo, Antonio
  111 MENINAS (orig. Spanish)
        Read by the author. In anth.
        AGUILAR GPE 11 102

Calderón de la Barca, Pedro
    112 ALCALDE DE ZALAMEA (orig. Span-
        ish)
            Rafael Calvo as Figueroa;
            Alejandro Ulloa as Pedro Crespo;
            Luís Torner as Notary; Fran-
            cisca Ferrándiz as Isabel;
            María Rollan as Ines; Enrique
            del Cerro as Juan Crespo;
            Francisco Camacho as Soldier;
            José Poveda as King Philip II;
            Emilio Menendez as Sergeant;
            Carmen Pradillo as Chispa; Pe-
            dro Gil as Captain; Miguel
            García as Rebolledo. CAED
            TC 2003 (2 pd), also CDL
            52003 (3 ac)
    113 ALCALDE DE ZALAMEA (exc., in
        French as L'ALCADE DE ZALAMÉA)
            C. Minazzoli; J. Vilar; J.
            Guiomar; J-F. Rémi; G. Riquier.
            ADÈS TS 25 LA 538
    114 ALCALDE DE ZALAMEA (exc., in
        French as L'ALCADE DE ZALAMÉA)
            Jean Vilar. In anth. ADÈS TS
            30 LA 552
    115 DAMA DUENDE (in English as THE
        PHANTOM LADY)
            Institute for Advanced Studies
            in the Theatre Arts. LC T
            4557 (at)
    116 DEVOCIÒN DE LA CRUZ (in French
        as DÉVOTION A LA CROIX)
            Comédie Française. CHA TH 6
    117 VIDA ES SUEÑO (orig. Spanish)
            Alejandro Ulloa as Segis-
            mundo; Francisca Ferrándiz as
            Rosaura; Miguel García as
            Clarin; Emilio Menendez as
            Clotaldo; Pedro Gil as Astolfo;
            Carmel Pradillo as Estrella;
            Rafael Calvo as Basilio. CAED
            TC 2001 (2 pd), also CDL 52001
            (2 ac)
    118 VIDA ES SUEÑO (orig. Spanish)
            Teófilo Martínez; Angel Balta-
            nás. GMS D 7114/5 (2 pd)
    119 VIDA ES SUEÑO (exc., in French
        as LA VIE EST UN SONGE)
            Charles Dullin. ADÈS 7003/4
            (2 pd)

Carroll, Paul Vincent
    120 COGGERERS
            American National Theatre and
            Academy. LC T 3071 (at)

Casona, Alejandro
    121 MANCEBO QUE CASO CON MUJER BRAVA
        (orig. Spanish)
            José Díaz as Patronio; Rafa-
            el Bartolomei as Mancebo; Is-
            mael Diaz Tirado as Padre del
            Mancebo; Mercedes Varnez as
            La Moza; Norberto Kerner as
            Padre de La Moza; Josefina
            Claudio as Madre de La Moza.
            In anth. SMC 1032

Cervantes Saavedra, Miguel de
    122 CUEVA DE SALAMANCA (orig. Span-
        ish)
            Manuel Durán as Pancracio; Eva
            Llorens as Leonarda; Maria Te-
            resa Navarro as Cristina; Al-
            berto Castilla as Estudiante;
            Felipe Rodriguez as Sacristán;
            Miguel Buisán as Barbero. In
            anth. SPOA 862 (pd), also 50-6
            (ac)
    123 HABLADORES (orig. Spanish)
            Manuel Durán as Sarmiento;
            Alberto Castilla as Roldán;
            Eva Llorens as Beatriz; M. T.
            Navarro as Inés; Miguel Buis-
            án as Alguacil. In anth.
            SPOA 863 (pd, also ac)
    124 VIEJO CELOSO (orig. Spanish)
            Eva Llorens as Doña Lorenza;
            M. T. Navarro as Cristina;
            Gloria Durán as Hortigosa;
            Alberto Castilla as Compadre;
            Miguel Buisán as Alguacil.
            In anth. SPOA 862 (pd), also
            50-6 (ac)

Chekhov, Anton
    125 CHAIKA (exc., in Italian as IL
        GABBIANO)
            Vittorio Gassmann; E. Aldini;
            C. Montagna; A. Cucari. In
            anth. CETRA CLC 0824
    126 CHAIKA (exc., in English as THE
        SEA GULL)
            Edith Evans; Torin Thatcher;
            Ivan Simpson. In anth. DECCA
            DL 9009

Chekhov, Anton, cont'd.
  127 CHAIKA (exc., in English as THE
       SEA GULL)
          Robert Culp. LIST 4012R (pd),
          also 412CX (ac); also MAGICT
          CTG 4012
  128 DYADYA VANYA (orig. Russian)
          MK D 07915-20
  129 DYADYA VANYA (in English as
       UNCLE VANYA)
          Laurence Olivier as Doctor;
          Michael Redgrave as Younger
          Brother; Joan Plowright as
          Sister; Sybil Thorndike; Rose-
          mary Harris; Lewis Casson;
          Fay Compton; Robert Lang; Max
          Adrian. CAED TRS 303 (2 pd),
          also CDL 5303 (2 ac)
  130 DYADYA VANYA (in English as
       UNCLE VANYA)
          Same cast as entry 129.
          PHIL PHS 2-701 (2 pd), also
          AL 3448-9

  131 DYADYA VANYA(exc., in English as
       UNCLE VANYA)
          Laurence Olivier; Michael Red-
          grave; Rosemary Harris; Joan
          Plowright. FFHS ISBN 0-699-
          03298-9 (16mm film)
  132 DYADYA VANYA (exc., in English as
       UNCLE VANYA)
          Robert Culp as Voynitsky; Hiram
          Peckins as Vladimirovitch;
          Jo Hamilton as Yelena Andreyevna;
          Sherry Selfors as Sofya Alexan-
          drovna; Elayna Carroll as Marya
          Vassilevna Voynitsky; Lawrence
          Chelsi as Mihail Lvovitch As-
          trov. LIST 4003R (pd), also 403
          CX (ac); also MAGICT CTG 4003
  133 IVANOV (in English)
          John Gielgud as Ivanov; Vivian
          Leigh as Anna; Ethel Griffies
          as Marriage Broker. RCA 199,
          also VDM 109
  134 JUBILEJ (orig. Russian)
          MK D 6523-4, also S 6567-8
  135 LEBEDINAYA PESNYA (in English as
       SWAN SONG)
          Read by Eli Wallach. DAVINCI
          DRC 205
  136 PREDLOZHENIYE(orig. Russian)
          Vakhtangov Theatre, Moscow.

          MK ND 909-10
  137 PREDLOZHENIYE (orig. Russian)
          M. Derjavin; T. Blazhina; V.
          Koltsov. SSSR D 909
  138 TRI SESTRY (orig. Russian)
          Moscow Art Theatre. MELOD
          D 9647-52 (3 pd)
  139 TRI SESTRY (in English as THREE
       SISTERS)
          Siobhan McKenna as Olga; Zena
          Walker as Masha; Caroline John
          as Irina; Cyril Cusack as
          Tchebutykin; James Donald as
          Vershinin; Alec McCowen as Ku-
          ligin; John Stride as Prozo-
          rov; Evi Hall as Natasha.
          CAED TRS 325 (3 pd), also CDL
          5325 (2 ac)
  140 TRI SESTRY (in English as THREE
       SISTERS)
          TIMLIF (vc 3/4)

Childress, Alice
  141 Miscellaneous exc.
          Read by the author. PAC (2 ac)

Claudel, Paul
  142 ANNONCE FAITE À MARIE (exc.,
       orig. French)
          Maria Casares; Jacques Dac-
          mine. In anth. FEST FRL 1531,
          also FLDX 49
  143 ANNONCE FAITE À MARIE (exc.,
       orig. French)
          Danièle Delorme as Violaine;
          Antoine Taffin as Pierre de
          Craon; Michel Etcheverry as
          Anne Vercors; Germaine Delbat
          as Mère; Loleh Bellon as Mara;
          Jean Negroni as Narrator; An-
          dré Oumansky as Jacques Hury.
          GMS D 7130; also UNI PM 30004
  144 ANNONCE FAITE À MARIE (exc.,
       orig. French)
          Feuillère; Nerval; Winter;
          Barrault; Chamarat; Desailly.
          In anth. HACH 320E866
  145 CHRISTOPHE COLOMB (orig. French)
          LONDON TW 91084-5 (2 pd)
  146 OTAGE (orig. French)
          Compagnie Doublier. CHA TH 3
  147 OTAGE (exc., orig. French)
          Feuillère; Nerval; Claude Win-
          ter; Barrault; Chamarat; De-

sailly.   In anth. HACH 320E866
148 PARTAGE DE MIDI (orig. French)
    Edwige Feuillère; Natalie Nerval;
    Claude Winter; Jean-Louis Bar-
    rault; George Chamarat; Jean De-
    sailly.   In anth. HACH ES 320
    E 866
149 SOULIER DE SATIN (exc., orig.
    French)
    Jean-Louis Barrault.   In anth.
    HACH 320E866
150 SOULIER DE SATIN (exc., orig.
    French)
    Nerval.   In anth. HACH 320E914
151 Miscellaneous exc., orig. French
    In anth. HACH 320E924

Cocteau, Jean
152 AIGLE À DEUX TÊTES (exc., orig.
    French)
    Edwige Feuillère as Reine; Jean
    Marais as Stanislaus.   In anth.
    HACH 320E874
153 BACCHUS (exc., orig. French)
    Jean-Louis Barrault; Jean Desai-
    lly.   In anth. PHIL P 76715R
154 MACHINE INFERNALE (in English as
    THE INFERNAL MACHINE)
    Margaret Leighton as Jocasta;
    Jeremy Brett as Oedipus; Diane
    Cilento as Sphinx; Alan Webb as
    Tiresias; Miriam Karlin as
    Theban Matron; Patrick Magee as
    Oracle; Charles Gray as Anubis;
    Paul Curran; James Cairncross;
    Trevor Martin.   CAED TRS 321
    (3 pd), also CDL 5321 (3 ac)
155 MACHINE INFERNALE (exc., orig.
    French)
    Read by the author.   In anth.
    CAED TC 1083 (pd), also CDL
    51083 (ac)
156 MACHINE INFERNALE (exc., orig.
    French)
    Jeanne Moreau; Jean Marais.
    In anth. FEST FLDX 70; also in
    anth. GMS D 7084
157 MARIÉS DE LA TOUR EIFFEL (orig.
    French)
    Groupe des Six.   ADÈS 15.501,
    also 14.007
158 MARIÉS DE LA TOUR EIFFEL (exc.,
    orig. French)
    Read by the author.   In anth.
    LVA 13

159 MÉDÉE (exc., orig. French)
    Read by the author.   In anth.
    LVA 13
160 ORPHÉE (orig. French)
    Read by the author.   LVA 8
161 ORPHÉE (exc., orig. French)
    Jean-Pierre Aumont as Orphée;
    Michel Bouquet as Heurtebise;
    Monique Mélinand as Eury-
    dice.   In anth. HACH 320E874
162 PARENTS TERRIBLES (orig. French)
    Read by the author.   LVA 2
163 PARENTS TERRIBLES (exc., orig.
    French)
    Yvonne de Bray; Jean Marais.
    In anth. FEST FRL 1530, also
    FLDX 70; also in anth. HACH
    320E874; also in anth. GMS
    D 7084
164 VOIX HUMAINE (orig. French)
    Simone Signoret.   CNI 48802
165 VOIX HUMAINE (orig. French)
    G. Morlay.   DECCA 163622;
    also LONDON TW 91102
166 VOIX HUMAINE (orig. French)
    B. Bovy.   PAT DTX 288
167 VOIX HUMAINE (in English as
    THE HUMAN VOICE)
    Ingrid Bergman.   CAED TC 1118
    (pd), also 51118 (ac)
168 VOIX HUMAINE (in German as DIE
    GELIEBTE STIMME)
    Hildegard Knef.   DEUTGR
    2571 013
169 Miscellaneous exc., orig. French
    Bovy; Le Poulain; Charon;
    Crémieux; Périer; Dermit; Ca-
    sarès.   In anth. PAT C 161-
    11.311/13 (3 pd)

Congreve, William
170 LOVE FOR LOVE
    Laurence Olivier as Tattle;
    Joyce Redman as Mrs. Fore-
    sight.   RCA VDS 112, also VDM
    112 (3 pd)
171 WAY OF THE WORLD
    Helen Burns as Foible; Ed-
    ward Hardwicke as Anthony Wit-
    woud; Hazel Hughes as Lady Wish-
    fort; Robert Lang as Edward
    Mirabell; John Moffat as Fain-
    all; Gabrielle Laye as Betty;
    Peter Penry-Jones as Messenger;
    David Ryall as Petulant; Lewis

Congreve, William, cont'd.
  WAY OF THE WORLD, cont'd.
    Jones as Coachman; Fre-
    derick Pyne as Servant; Sheila
    Reid as Mrs. Fainall; Jane Wen-
    ham as Mrs. Marwood; Geraldine
    McEwan as Millamant; Jane Lapo-
    taire as Mincing; Edward Pether-
    bridge as Waitwell; Suzanne Va-
    sey as Peg. CAED TRS 339 (3 pd),
    also CDL 5339 (3 ac)
  172 WAY OF THE WORLD (exc.)
    Edith Evans as Mrs Millamant &
    as Lady Wishfort; John Gielgud
    as Mirabell; Pauline Jameson as
    Mrs. Marwood; Jane Wenham as
    Mrs. Fainall; Jessie Evans as
    Foible; Peter Williams as Sir
    Wilfull Witwoud; Maureen Quin-
    ney as Peg. In anth. ANGEL
    35213; also in anth. EMI HLM
    7108
  173 WAY OF THE WORLD (exc.)
    Max Adrian; Claire Bloom;
    Anthony Quayle. In anth. CAED
    TC 4002, also CDL 54002
  174 WAY OF THE WORLD (exc.)
    In anth. FOLKW 9841/2
  175 WAY OF THE WORLD (exc.)
    Robert Culp. LIST 4006 (pd),
    also 406 CX (ac)

Connelly, Marc, and Elser, Frank
  176 FARMER TAKES A WIFE
    CENT 010-1902 (at)
  177 FARMER TAKES A WIFE (exc.)
    Henry Fonda; Julie Harris;
    Marc Connelly; Katharine
    Cornell; Brian Aherne; Edith
    Evans; Torin Thatcher; Ivan
    Simpson; Donald Buka; Olive
    Dunbar; Tallulah Bankhead.
    In anth. DECCA DL 9009

Corneille, Pierre
  178 ATTILA (exc., orig. French)
    Marguerite Perrin as Honorie;
    Jean-Paul Moulinot as Attila.
    In anth. HACH ES LAE 3310
  179 CID (orig. French)
    Monique Chaumette as Infante;
    Silvia Monfort as Chimène; Mona
    Dol as Elvire; Laurence Con-
    stant as Leonor; André Schlesser
    as Page; Roger Mollien as Don

    Sanche; Georges Riquier as
    Don Alonse; Jean Vilar as Roi
    D. Fernand; Georges Wilson as
    Compte; Gérard Philipe as
    Don Rodrigue; Philippe Noiret
    as Don Arias; Jean Deschamps
    as Don Diègue. HACH ESH 320
    E 806/7 (2 pd)
  180 CID (exc., orig. French)
    Sellers; Vaneck; Cuny; Topart;
    Caussimon; Negroni. BOR SS B
    100; also SPOA SSB 100
  181 CID (exc., orig. French)
    Gérard Philipe; Maria Casarès.
    In anth. FEST FLD 166; also
    in anth. GMS D 7065
  182 CID (exc., orig. French)
    Gérard Philipe as Rodrigue;
    Françoise Spira as Chimène.
    In anth. HACH LAE 3.310
  183 CID (exc., orig. French)
    Philipe. In anth. HACH 320914
  184 CID (exc., orig. French)
    Jean Yonnel; Jean Debucourt;
    André Falcon; Jean Davey; Ber-
    nard Noël; Thérèse Marney.
    PERIOD FRL 1503; also PLEI
    T 542
  185 CID (exc., orig. French)
    C. Nollier; M. Escande; G.
    Descrières; Balpétré; A.
    Gaillard. PHIL E1E9.146
    (pd45)
  186 CINNA (orig. French)
    Jean Deschamps; André Ou-
    mansky; François Maistre;
    Christine Ferson. HACH 320
    E 887/888 (2 pd)
  187 CINNA (exc., orig. French)
    Jean Vilar. In anth. ADÈS
    TS 30 LA 552; also in anth.
    SPOA 924
  188 CINNA (exc., orig. French)
    Philipe. HACH ES 190E852
  189 CINNA (exc., orig. French)
    Ferson; Oumanski; Maistre;
    Deschamps. HACH ES 190E989
  190 CINNA (exc., orig. French)
    A. Balpétré; H. Buthion;
    A. Haber; F. Robiane; M.
    Roland; J. Souchon. PLEI
    P 3.099
  191 DON SANCHE D'ARAGON (exc., orig.
  French)
    Jean Deschamps as Carlos;

George Riquier as Manrique.
In anth. HACH LAE 3310

192 HORACE (orig. French)
Comédie Française. GMS DISC
7055-57 (3 pd)

193 HORACE (orig. French)
Jean Desailly as Tulle; Jean
Deschamps as Horace; Fernand
Ledoux as Vieil Horace; Ber-
nard Noël as Valère; Pierre
Vaneck as Curiace; Catherine
Sellers as Camille; Maria Mau-
ban as Sabine; Françoise Ro-
say as Julie; Lucien Agostini
as Procule; Roger Pech as
Flavian. HACH ESH 320.830/31
(2 pd)

194 HORACE (orig. French)
M. Escande; J. Marchat; P.-E.
Deiber; A. Falcon; D. Noël; T.
Marney; G. Martinet. PAT
DTX 293/5 (3 pd)

195 HORACE (orig. French)
Jean Chevrier as Horace; Jean
Davy as Vieil Horace; André
Falcon as Curiace; Paul-Emile
Deiber as Valère; Véra Korène
as Camille; Germaine Rover as
Julie. PERIOD FRL 1501

196 HORACE (exc. , orig. French)
Négroni; Cuny; Trintignan;
Tamar. BOR SSB 113; also SPOA
SSB 113

197 HORACE (exc., orig. French)
Zanie Campan as Camille; Pierre
Vaneck as Curiace; Jean Des-
champs as Horace. In anth.
HACH ES LAE 3310

198 HORACE (exc., orig. French)
Ledoux; Deschamps; Vaneck;
Noël; Mauban; Rosay. HACH ES
190E873

199 HORACE (exc., orig. French)
Ledoux; Deschamps; Sellers.
HACH ES 190E874

200 HORACE (exc., orig. French)
Sellers. In anth. HACH
320.914

201 HORACE (exc., orig. French)
PAT EA 10.031

202 HORACE (exc., orig. French)
J. Chevrier; A. Falcon; J.
Davy; P.-E. Deiber; V. Ko-
rène; G. Rouer. PLEI T 543

203 IMITATION DE JÉSUS-CHRIST (exc.,
orig. French)
Jean Deschamps. In anth. HACH
ES LAE 3310

204 MÉDÉE (exc., orig. French)
Marguerite Perrin. In anth.
HACH ES LAE 3310

205 NICOMÈDE (orig. French)
Page; Monfort; Etcheverry;
Toja; Ledoux; Deiber. HACH
ESH 320.946

206 NICOMÈDE (exc., orig. French)
Magre; Basile; Terzieff;
Falcon. BOR SSB 119

207 NICOMÈDE (exc., orig. French)
Georges Riquier as Prusias;
Jean Deschamps as Nicomède.
In anth. HACH ES LAE 3310

208 POLYEUCTE (orig. French)
Page; Deiber; Bouquet; Guers.
HACH ESH 320.917

209 POLYEUCTE (orig. French)
Jean Yonnel as Polyeucte;
Maurice Escande as Sévère;
Maurice Chambreuil as Félix;
Paul-Emile Deiber as Néarque;
Jacque Eyser as Albin; Annie
Ducaux as Pauline. PERIOD
FRL 1507

210 POLYEUCTE (exc., orig. French)
Klein; Vaneck; Destoop;
Caussimon; Eine; Delbon;
Farabet. BOR SSB 120

211 POLYEUCTE (exc., orig. French)
Roger Mollien as Sévère;
Marcelle Ranson as Pauline;
Jean Deschamps as Polyeucte.
In anth. HACH LAE 3310

212 POLYEUCTE (exc., orig. French)
In anth. HACH 320E812

213 POLYEUCTE (exc., orig. French)
J. Yonnel; M. Escande, Chambreuil; Deiber; Eyser; A. Ducaux. PLEI T 527

214 RODOGUNE (exc., orig. French)
Edwige Feuillère as Cléo-
pâtre; Nadine Basile as Rodogune; Jacques Destoop as
Antiochus; Alain Feydeau as
Séleucus; Pierre Asso as Ti-
magène; Catherine Prasteau
as Récitante. BOR SSB 123

215 SURÉNA (exc., orig. French)
Marcelle Ranson as Eurydice;

Corneille, Pierre, cont'd.
    SURÉNA, cont'd.
        Jean-Paul Moulinot as Suréna.
        In anth. HACH LAE 3310
    216 Miscellaneous exc.
        In anth. HACH 320.924

Courteline, Georges
    217 ARTICLE 330 (orig. French)
        In anth. RODALE RO 3
    218 PAIX CHEZ SOI (orig. French)
        Emile de Hervin as E. Trielle;
        Catherine Clouzot as V. Trielle.
        In anth. SPOA SA 786
    219 PEUR DES COUPS (orig. French)
        Emile de Hervin as Lui; Cathe-
        rine Clouzot as Elle. In anth.
        SPOA SA 786

Coward, Noel
    220 BLITHE SPIRIT
        Rex Harrison as Charles Con-
        domine; Kay Hammond as Spirit;
        Constance Cummings as Second
        Wife; Margaret Rutherford as
        Madame Arcati; Joyce Carey;
        Hugh Wakefield; Jacqueline Clark.
        LEARNC ISBN 0-699-36805-7
        (16mm film)
    221 BLITHE SPIRIT (exc.)
        Noel Coward; Margaret Leighton.
        In anth. CAED TC 1069 (pd),
        also CDL 51069 (ac)
    222 BRIEF ENCOUNTER
        Noel Coward; Margaret Leighton.
        In anth. CAED TC 1069, also CDL
        51069 (ac)
    223 CONVERSATION PIECE
        Lily Pons as Melanie; Noel Cow-
        ard as Paul; Cathleen Nesbitt
        as Lady Julia Charteris; Ethel
        Griffies as Duchess of Beneden;
        Norah Howard as Rose; Richard
        Burton as Marquis of Sheere;
        Rex Evans as Duke of Beneden;
        Eilèen Turner as Sophie Otford;
        Dorothy Johnson as Martha James.
        COLUMB SL 163 (2 pd)
    224 PRESENT LAUGHTER (exc.)
        Noel Coward; Margaret Leighton.
        In anth. CAED TC 1069 (pd), also
        in anth. CDL 51069 (ac)
    225 PRESENT LAUGHTER (exc.)
        Paul Scofield; Patricia Rout-
        ledge; Miriam Margolyes.

TALK TTC NCW 02
    226 PRIVATE LIVES (exc.)
        Noel Coward; Gertrude Lawrence.
        In anth. RCA LCT 1156
    227 PRIVATE LIVES (exc.)
        Paul Scofield; Fenella Fiel-
        ding; Miriam Margolyes. TALK
        TTC NCW 01
    228 RED PEPPERS (exc.)
        Noel Coward; Gertrude Law-
        rence. In anth. RCA LCT 1156
    229 SHADOW-PLAY (exc.)
        Noel Coward; Gertrude Law-
        rence. In anth. RCA LCT 1156

Crowley, Mart
    230 BOYS IN THE BAND
        Kenneth Nelson; Frederick
        Combs; Cliff Gorman; Keith
        Prentice; Laurence Luckin-
        bill; Reuben Greene; Peter
        White; Robert La Tourneaux;
        Leonard Frey.   A & M SP
        6001 (2 pd)

Csokor, Franz Theodor
    231 DRITTER NOVEMBER, 1918 (orig.
        German)
        Fred Hennings; Stefan Skodler;
        Helmut Janatsch. AMADEO
        AVRS 1008

Dadiani, Shalva
    232 RIGHT INTO THE HEART (exc., in
        orig. Georgian)
        Marjanishvili Drama Theatre,
        Tbilisi. MK D 14509/10

Dann, Sam
    233 SALLY, GEORGE, AND MARTHA
        Matinee Theatre. LC T 6787
        (at)

D'Annunzio, Gabriele
    234 CITTÀ MORTA (exc., orig. Italian)
        Inna and Emma Gramatica. In
        anth. CETRA CLC 0856
    235 FIACCOLA SOTTO IL MOGGIO (exc.,
        in orig. Italian)
        Irma and Emma Gramatica. In
        anth. CETRA CLC 0856
    236 FIGLIA DI IORIO (exc., in orig.
        Italian)
        Irma and Emma Gramatica. In
        anth. CETRA CLC 0856

Daudet, Alphonse
  237 ARLÉSIENNE (in orig. French)
      Comédie Française.   LONDON
      LL 1489-90 (2 pd)

De Rojas, Fernando
  238 CELESTINA (exc.)
      Elisabeth Flickenschildt.
      In anth. DEUTGR 2570 013

Denger, Fred
  239 LANGUSTEN (in orig. German)
      Annie Rosar.   PREISR 3008

Dostoyevsky, Fyodor
  240 DYADYUSHKIN SON (exc., in orig.
      Russian)
      O. Knipper-Chekhova; N.
      Khmelyov. In anth. MK D
      00015187-8

Draper, Ruth
  241 3 GENERATIONS IN A COURT OF DO-
      MESTIC RELATIONS
      Performed by author. In anth.
      SPOA 779
  242 ACTRESS
      Performed by author. In anth.
      SPOA 805
  243 CHILDREN'S PARTY
      Performred by author. In anth.
      SPOA 799
  244 CHURCH IN ITALY
      Performed by author. In anth.
      SPOA 798
  245 DOCTORS AND DIETS
      Performed by author. In anth.
      SPOA 805
  246 ENGLISH HOUSE PARTY
      Performed ba author. In anth.
      SPOA 798
  247 ITALIAN LESSON
      Performed by author. In anth.
      SPOA 779
  248 ON A PORCH IN A MAINE COAST VILL-
      AGE
      Performed by author. In anth.
      SPOA 799
  249 SCOTTISH IMMIGRANT
      Performed by author. In anth.
      SPOA 779
  250 SOUTHERN GIRL AT A DANCE
      Performed by author. In anth.
      SPOA 799

  251 THREE WOMEN AND MR. CLIFFORD
      Performed by author. In anth.
      SPOA 800

Dryden, John
  252 ALL FOR LOVE, OR, THE WORLD
      WELL LOST (exc.)
      Robert Culp. LIST 4007 (pd),
      also 407CX (ac); also MAGICT
      4007

Duberman, Martin B.
  253 IN WHITE AMERICA
      Gloria Foster; James Greene;
      Moses Gunn; Claudette Nevins;
      Michael O'Sullivan; Fred Pin-
      kard. COLUMB KOS 2430

Dumas, Alexandre, fils
  254 DAME AUX CAMELIAS (in English as
      CAMILLE
      CAED TC 1175 (pd), also CDL
      51175 (ac)

Durrell, Lawrence
  255 IRISH FAUSTUS
      Read by the author. LVA 201
      (2 pd)

Dürrenmatt, Friedrich
  256 BESUCH DER ALTEN DAME (exc., in
      orig. German)
      Therese Giehse. In anth.
      DEUTGR 2571-011
  257 HERKULES UND DER STALL DES
      AUGIAS (exc., in orig. German)
      Read by the author. DEUTGR
      LPMS 43013
  258 METEOR (exc., in orig. German)
      Therese Giehse; F. Dürrenmatt.
      In anth. DEUTGR 2571-011 (pd),
      also in anth. 3321-011 (ac)
  259 STRINDBERG
      Marji Bank; D. Nicholas
      Ruddall. In anth. ALLMEDIA
      (ac)

Eliot, T. S.
  260 COCKTAIL PARTY
      Alec Guiness as Harcourt-Rei-
      lly; Cathleen Nesbitt as
      Julia; Robert Flemyng as Ed-
      ward Chamberlayne; Eileen
      Peel as Lavinia Chamberlayne;

Eliot, T. S. cont'd.
    COCKTAIL PARTY, cont'd.
        Ernest Clark as Alexander Mac-
        Colgie Gibbs; Irene Worth as
        Celia Coplestone; Grey Blake as
        Peter Quilpe. DECCA DL 9004/5
        (2 pd), also DXA 100; also
        BRUNSW LAT 8009/10
261 COCKTAIL PARTY (exc., in German
    as DIE COCKTAILPARTY)
        Gustaf Gründgens; Marianne
        Hoppe; Elisabeth Flickenschildt;
        Paula Denk; Günther Lüders; Kurt
        Langanke; Adolf Dell. DEUTGR
        2571 023
262 FAMILY REUNION
        Flora Robson as Agatha; Paul
        Scofield as Harry; Sybil Thorn-
        dike as Amy; Alan Webb as
        Charles Piper; Rosalie Crutchley
        as Ivy; Pauline Jameson as Vio-
        let; Alan Wheatley as Gerald
        Piper. CAED TRS 308 (3 pd),
        also CDL 5308 (3 ac)
263 FAMILY REUNION (exc.)
        Alec Guiness. In anth. ARGO
        PLP 1206/7
264 FAMILY REUNION (exc.)
        In anth. CAED TC 1045 (pd), also
        CDL 51045 (ac)
265 FAMILY REUNION (exc., in German
    as DER FAMILIENTAG)
        Elisabeth Flickenschildt; Ella
        Büchi; Fritz von Friedl. In
        anth. DEUTGR 2570 013
266 MURDER IN THE CATHEDRAL
        Robert Donat as Becket; John
        Warner as First Tempter; Doug-
        las Campbell as Second Tempter;
        Newton Blick as Third Tempter;
        William Squire as Fourth Temp-
        ter; Paul Rogers as First
        Knight; Robin Bailey as Second
        Knight; Daniel Thorndyke as
        Third Knight; John Phillips as
        Fourth Knight; Bruce Sharman as
        Messenger. ANGEL 3505B (2 pd)
267 MURDER IN THE CATHEDRAL
        Richard Pasco as Becket. ARGO
        ZSW 553/4 (2 pd), also SAY 26
268 MURDER IN THE CATHEDRAL
        Paul Scofield as Becket; Pat-
        rick Magee as Tempter;
        Cyril Cusack as Priest;

Wendy Hiller, Cathleen Nesbitt, Glenda Jackson as Women;
Julian Glover; Michael Gwynn;
Alec McCowen; Geoffrey Dunn;
Antony Nicholls; June Jago;
Harry Andrews; Douglas Wilmer;
James Hayter; Michael Aldridge.
CAED TRS 330 (2 pd), also CDL
5330 (2 ac)
269 MURDER IN THE CATHEDRAL
        Vox Poetica Repertory Co. LC
        T 2555 (at)
270 MURDER IN THE CATHEDRAL (exc.)
        Read by the author. In anth.
        CAED TC 1045, also CDL 51045
271 MURDER IN THE CATHEDRAL(exc.)
        Robert Speaight. HMV B8499
272 MURDER IN THE CATHEDRAL (exc.,
    in French as MEURTRE DANS LA
    CATHÉDRALE)
        Jean Vilar. In anth. ADÈS
        TS 30 LA 552
273 SWEENEY AGONISTES
        HMV CLP 1924

Elser, Frank B., jt. auth. with
    Connelly, Marc, q. v.

Enzensberger, Hans Magnus
274 UNTERGANG DER TITANIC (exc., in
    orig. German)
        Read by the author. DEUTGR

Euripides
275 BAKCHAI (exc., in English as THE
    BACCHAE)
        MICHMED 9374 (16mm film, also
        vc)
276 HEKABE (exc., in Modern Greek)
        Katina Paxinou; Alexis Minotis.
        CAED TC 1127
277 HIPPOLYTOS (exc., in French as
    HIPPOLYTE)
        Nerval; Fechter. In anth.
        HACH 320E899
278 ION (exc., in English)
        MICHMED 9372 (16mm film, also
        vc)
279 IPHIGENEIA HE EN AULIDI (exc.,
    in French as IPHIGÉNIE À AULIS)
        Morane; Deschamps. In anth.
        HACH 320E899
280 IPHIGENEIA HE EN TAUROIS (exc.,
    in English as IPHIGENIA IN TAURIS

MICHMED 9373 (16mm film, also vc)

281 MEDEIA (in English as MEDEA)
Judith Anderson as Medea; Anthony Quayle as Jason; Catherine Lacey as Nurse; Arthur Hewlett as Tutor; Alan Webb as Creon; Hugh Manning as Aegeus; Robin Lloyd as Messenger; Kit Williams as Son. CAED TRS 302 (2 pd), also CDL 5302 (2 ac)

282 MEDEIA (in English as MEDEA, adapted by Robinson Jeffers)
Judith Anderson as Medea; Arnold Moss as Jason; Raymond Edward Johnson as Creon; Everett Sloan as Aegeus; Doris Rich as Nurse. DECCA DL 9000

283 MEDEIA (exc., in German as MEDEA)
Maria Wimmer. In anth. DEUTGR 140 011

284 MEDEIA (exc., in English as MEDEA)
MICHMED 9370 (16mm film, also vc)

285 TROIADES (in French as LES TROY-ENNES)
Morane; Fechter. In anth. HACH 320E899

286 Miscellaneous exc.
John F. C. Richards. In anth. FOLKW 9984

Farquhar, George
287 BEAUX' STRATAGEM (exc.)
Edith Evans as Mrs. Sullen; Ralph Truman as Squire Sullen; Pauline Jameson as Dorinda; Miles Malleson as Scrub. In an anth. ANGEL 35213; also in anth. EMI HLM 7108

Ferrero, Leo
288 ANGELICA (in orig. Italian)
Luisa Rossi; Luigi Vannucchi. CETRA CLV 0611/2 (2 pd)

Fitzthum, Horst
289 SPAGATHAPHM (in orig. German)
Fritz Muliar. PREISR SPR 3133

Fletcher, John, jt. auth. with Beaumont, Francis, q. v.

Fletcher, Lucille
290 SORRY, WRONG NUMBER
Agnes Moorehead. DECCA DL 9062; also LIST DL 34806

Francis, John Oswald
291 POACHER
Dewi Williams as Tomos Shon; Rachel Thomas as Marged Shon; Emoys James as Dici Bach Dwl; Emrys Cleaver as Dafydd Hughes. QUAL BMP 2026

Franck, Pierre
292 FAISEUR (exc.)
Charles Dullin. In anth. ADÈS 7003 (2 pd)

Franko, Ivan
293 BUDKA NO. 27 (in orig. Ukrainian)
N. Kolofidin as Panko Seredushchy; V. Dementieva as Olena; E. Kozyreva as Zosla; A. Gribov as Prokop Zavada; L. Kruglov as Gnat Sirotyuk. MK D 02908-9

294 VKRADENE SHCHASTYA (in orig. Ukrainian)
A. Buchma. MK D 06029-34 (3 pd)

Frisch, Max
295 ANDORRA (orig. German)
Ernst Schröder as Lehrer; Peter Brogle as Andri; Heidemarie Hatheyer as Señora; Rolf Henniger as Pater; Willy Birgel as Doktor; Kathrin Schmid as Barblin; Angelica Arndts as Mutter; Kurt Beck as Soldat; Carl Kuhlmann as Wirt; Peter Ehrlich as Tischler; Otto Mächtlinger as Geselle; Gert Westphal as Jemand; Elmar Schultze as Idiot. DEUTGR 2751 001 (2 pd), also 44012/13

Fry, Christopher
296 LADY'S NOT FOR BURNING
John Gielgud as Thomas Mendip; Richard Burton as Richard; Pe-

Fry, Christopher, cont'd.
    LADY'S NOT FOR BURNING, cont'd.
        nelope Munday as Alizon Eliot;
        David Evans as Nicholas Devize;
        Nora Nicholson as Margaret De-
        vize; Richard Leech as Humphrey
        Devize; George Howe as Hebble
        Tyson; Pamela Brown as Jennet
        Jourdemayne; Eliot Makeham as
        Chaplain; Peter Bull as Edward
        Tappercoom; Esme Percy as
        Matthew Skipps. DECCA DL
        9508/9, also DX 110 (2 pd)
    297 LADY'S NOT FOR BURNING
        The Canadian Players. LC T
        3453 (at)

García Lorca, Federico
    298 BODAS DE SANGRE (exc., in orig.
        Spanish)
        María Douglas; Raúl Dantés. In
        anth. CAED TC 1067, also CDL
        51067
    299 BODAS DE SANGRE (exc., in French
        as NOCES DE SANG)
        HACH 320E935
    300 DOÑA ROSITA LA SOLTERA, O, EL
        LENGUAJE DE LAS FLORES (in orig.
        Spanish)
        Aurora Bautista; Alejandro
        Maximino. GMS D 7136/37 (2 pd),
        also REGAL LCX 136-137
    301 YERMA (in orig. Spanish)
        Aurora Bautista as Yerma; En-
        rique A. Diosdado as Juan; Maria
        Gámez as Vieja Pagana; Nuria
        Espert as María; Dolores Gis-
        pert as Muchacha 1; Luisa Es-
        pala as Muchacha 2; Emilio
        Freixas as Nilo; Fernando
        Ulloa as Hombre 1; Ramón Va-
        ccaro as Hombre 2; Maribel Ca-
        sals as Hembra; Juan Luis Su-
        ari as El Macho. GMS D 7138/9
        (2 pd); also REGAL LCX 138-139

Garson, Barbara
    302 MACBIRD!
        Stacy Keach. EVERG 004

Genet, Jean
    303 BALCON (in English as THE BALCONY)
        Pamela Brown; Patrick Magee;
        Cyril Cusack; Eileen Atkins;
        Roland Culver; Colin Blakely;

        Nigel Davenport; Denholm
        Elliott. CAED TRS 316 (3 pd),
        also CDL 5316 (3 ac)
    304 BALCON (exc., in English as THE
        BALCONY)
        Alan Webb as General; Pauline
        Jamieson as Irma; Wendy Craige
        as Girl; Nigel Davenport as
        Executioner. In anth. CAED
        TC 1134, also in CDL 51134
    305 BONNES (exc., in English as THE
        MAIDS)
        Brenda Bruce as Solange; Tran
        Bassett as Claire. In anth.
        CAED TC 1134, also in CDL
        51134
    306 NÈGRES (exc., in English as THE
        BLACKS)
        Barbara Assoon as Felicity;
        Olivier Cole; Jacqueline Le
        Maitre; Booker Bradshaw; John
        Thomas; Roy Stewart. In anth.
        CAED TC 1134, also in CDL
        51134
    307 PARAVENTS (exc., in English as
        THE SCREENS)
        Max Adrian as Madani; Sheila
        Burrell as Mother. In anth.
        CAED TC 1134, also CDL 51134

Géraldy, Paul
    308 GILBERT ET MARCELLIN
        Read by the author. LVA 20

Gide, André
    309 OEDIPE (exc., orig. French)
        Jean Vilar. In anth. ADÈS
        TS 30 LA 552; also SPOA 924
    310 OEDIPE (exc., orig. French)
        In anth. HACH ESH 320.872

Gilfond, Henry
    311 WICK & THE TALLOW
        Irene Dailey; John Aspinall;
        Nancy Howard; Shirley Leinwand;
        Beverly Shimmin; Del Shorter.
        FOLKW 9529 (2 pd)

Gilroy, Frank
    312 SUBJECT WAS ROSES
        Jack Albertson; Irene
        Dailey; Martin Sheen.
        COLUMB ADOS 708 (3 pd), also
        DOL 308 and DOS 687

Giono, Jean
   313 BOUT DE LA ROUTE (exc., orig.
       French)
          Jeanne Moreau as Mina; Alain
          Cuny as Jean. In anth. FEST
          FLDX 150

Giraudoux, Jean
   314 ÉLECTRE (exc., orig. French)
          Simone Valère as Électre;
          Jean Deschamps as Égisthe.
          In anth. HACH 320E875
   315 ENFANTS HUMILIÉS (exc., orig.
       French)
          Louis Jouvet. In anth. ADÈS
          19.015/16
   316 GUERRE DE TROIE N'AURA PAS LIEU
       (orig. French)
          M. Mauban; C. Minazzoli; C.
          Mangey; P. Vaneck; J. Vilar;
          P. Mazzotti; J. F. Rémi.
          In anth. ADÈS TS 25 LA 554
   317 GUERRE DE TROIE N'AURA PAS LIEU
       (exc., orig. French)
          Louis Jouvet as Hector;
          Pierre Renoir as Ulysse. In
          anth. ADÈS 19.015/16, also in
          13.032, also in 7007/8 and in
          HACH ES 320E875
   318 INTERMEZZO (exc., orig. French)
          Louis Jouvet; Tessier. In
          anth. ADÈS 7007/8, also in
          19.015/16 and in 13.032
   319 INTERMEZZO (exc., orig. French)
          Elisabeth Hardy as Isabelle;
          Jean-Paul Moulinot as Inspec-
          teur; Georges Riquier as Maire;
          Jean-Pierre Darras as Le Dro-
          guiste. In HACH 320E875
   320 JUDITH (exc., orig. French)
          Edwige Feuillère as Judith;
          Jean Debucourt as Holopherne.
          In anth. HACH 320E875
   321 ONDINE (exc., orig. French)
          Louis Jouvet; D. Blanchar. In
          anth. ADÈS 19.015/16, also in
          13.032 and in 7007/8
   322 ONDINE (exc., orig. French)
          Jean-Paul Moulinot as Juge;
          Pierre Hatet as Hans; Georges
          Riquier as Roi des Ondins;
          Elisabeth Hardy as Ondine;
          Jean-Pierre Darras as 2nd Juge.
          In anth. HACH 320E875

   323 POUR LUCRÈCE (exc., orig. French)
          E. Feuillère as Paola;
          Simone Valère as Lucile. In
          anth. HACH 320E875
   324 SIEGFRIED (exc., orig. French)
          Jean Deschamps as Siegfried;
          Edwige Feuillère as Gene-
          viève. In anth. HACH 320E875
   325 SODOME ET GOMORRHE (exc., orig.
       French)
          Jean Desailly as Ange; Ed-
          wige Feuillère as Lia. In
          anth. HACH 320E875
   326 Miscellaneous exc., orig. French
          J. Desailly; J. Debucourt;
          L. Jouvet; P. Renoir; E.
          Feuillère; J. Deschamps;
          S. Valère. In anth. HACH
          320E801

Goethe, Johann Wolfgang von
   327 FAUST (orig. German)
          Gustaf Gründgens as Mephis-
          topheles; Paul Hartmann as
          Faust; Käthe Gold; Elisabeth
          Flickenschildt; Will Quadflieg;
          Ullrich Haupt; Max Eckard;
          Maria Becker; Antje Weisgerber.
          DEUTGR 2755 006 (6 pd); also
          HERDER 78 716 and DEUTGR 3392
          007 and 43021/3 (6 ac)
   328 FAUST (in French)
          Comédie Française. PERIOD
          FRL 1551/2 (2 pd)
   329 FAUST I (orig. German)
          Gustaf Gründgens as Mephisto-
          pheles; Paul Hartmann as
          Faust; Käthe Gold as Margarete;
          Max Eckard; Peter Esser; Ull-
          rich Haupt; Hansgeorg Lauben-
          thal; Marthe Schwerdtlein; Eli-
          sabeth Flickenschildt; Rudolf
          Therkatz. DEUTGR 2753 002
          (3 pd)
   330 FAUST I (orig. German)
          Fita Benkhoff; Horst Caspar as
          Faust; Emmy Graetz; Ullrich
          Haupt; Erich Ponto as Mephis-
          topheles; Hermann Schomberg;
          Antje Weisgerber as Margarete.
          EUROD 88 034 XFW (3 pd)
   331 FAUST I (orig. German)
          Rolf Günther. SCHUMM 1276 (ac)

Goethe, Johann Wolfgang von,
      cont'd.
332 FAUST II (orig. German)
      Will Quadflieg; Gustaf Gründ-
      gens; Maria Becker; Antje Weis-
      gerber; Ullrich Haupt; Her-
      mann Schomberg; Sebastian
      Fischer; Volker Brandt. DEUTGR
      2753-003 (3 pd)
333 FAUST (exc., in French)
      Verley; Topart; Jarry. In anth.
      HACH 320E898
334 FAUST I (exc., orig. German)
      Paul Hartmann as Faust; Gustaf
      Gründgens as Mephistopheles;
      Käthe Gold as Margarete; Elisa-
      beth Flickenschildt as Marthe;
      Karl Viebach as Schüler.
      DEUTGR 34 002, also 40 001
335 FAUST II (exc., orig. German)
      G. Gründgens as Mephisto;
      W. Quadflieg as Faust. In
      anth. DEUTGR 140 025
336 FAUST II (exc., orig. German)
      Elisabeth Flickenschildt; Ella
      Büchi; Fritz von Friedl. In
      anth. DEUTGR 2570 013
337 GÖTZ VON BERLICHINGEN (orig.
      German)
      Ewald Balser; Albin Skoda;
      Judith Holzmeister; Raoul Aslan;
      Hilde Mikulicz; Helmut Janatsch;
      Alfons Lipp; Fred Hennings; Ul-
      rich Bettac; Fred Liewehr;
      PERIOD FRL 1553
338 GÖTZ VON BERLICHINGEN (exc., orig.
      German)
      Heinrich George. In anth. TELEF
      6.41003 AS
339 IPHIGENIE AUF TAURIS (orig. German)
      Maria Becker; Ewald Balser; Will
      Quadflieg; Rolf Henniger; Heinz
      Moog. DEUTGR 2760 102 (3 pd)
340 IPHIGENIE AUF TAURIS (exc., orig.
      German)
      Maria Becker. In anth. DEUTGR
      40 008, also in 43002
341 IPHIGENIE AUF TAURIS (exc., orig.
      German)
      Maria Wimmer. In anth. DEUTGR
      140 011
342 STELLA (orig. German)
      Aglaja Schmid; Paula Wessely;
      Will Quadflieg; R. Bernhard;

J. Dahmen; A Grosske; J.
Kaestel; G. Bothur; W. Walter; J. Aust; A. Amrhein.
DEUTGR 2759 002 (2 pd), also
168 076/77
343 STELLA
      INTERNAT 32382 (ac)
344 TORQUATO TASSO (exc., orig.
      German)
      Maria Wimmer. In anth. DEUTGR
      140 011
345 URFAUST (exc., orig. German)
      Walter Reyer; Boy Gobert; Sonja
      Sutter; Susi Nicoletti; Peter
      Weck. FOLKW 9571

Goetz, Curt
346 HERBST (orig. German)
      Valerie von Martens; Herta
      Staal; Curt Goetz; Klaus
      Miedel. In anth. EMI 063-028
      511
347 MÄRCHEN - EINE KITSCHIGE BEGEBEN-
      HEIT (orig. German)
      Curt Goetz; Alfred Huttig; Val-
      erie von Martens; Theodor Grieg;
      Hans Radvanyi. DEUTGR 44024
348 RACHE (orig. German)
      Curt Goetz; Valerie von Martens;
      Klaus Kammer. In anth. EMI 063-
      028 511

Gogol, Nikolai
349 REVIZOR (orig. Russian)
      Maly Theatre, Moscow) MK
      D 010943-50
350 REVIZOR (exc., orig. Russian)
      Yu. Tolubeyev; I. Gorbachov.
      In anth. MK D 10597-8
351 ZHENITBA (orig. Russian)
      MK D 014247-50

Goldsmith, Oliver
352 SHE STOOPS TO CONQUER
      Michael Williams as Charles;
      Judi Dench as Kate; Eliza-
      beth Spriggs; Leslie Sands;
      Wayne Sleep as Lumpkin. BBC
      ECN 072 (2 ac)
353 SHE STOOPS TO CONQUER
      Alastair Sim; Claire Bloom;
      Brenda de Banzie; Alan Howard;
      Tony Tanner; Tarn Bassett;
      Llewellyn Rees; John Moffatt;

Peter Bayliss; Patricia So-
merset; Eric Jones; Norman
Mitchell. CAED TRS 309 (3 pd),
also CDL 5309 (3 ac)
354 SHE STOOPS TO CONQUER
Swan Theatre Players. SPOA
958/9 (2 pd), also 8047/8 (2 ac)
355 SHE STOOPS TO CONQUER
TIMLIF (vc 3/4)
356 SHE STOOPS TO CONQUER (exc.)
Max Adrian; Claire Bloom;
Anthony Quayle. In anth. CAED
TC 4002, also in CDL 54002
357 SHE STOOPS TO CONQUER (exc.)
Robert Culp as Charles, son;
Hiram Peckins as Sir Charles
Marlow; Jack Perdew as Richard
Hardcastle; Scott Hale as George
Hastings; Lawrence Chelsi as
Lumpkin; Elayne Carroll as Mrs.
Hardcastle; Helen McCall as Kate
Hardcastle; Nancy Ponder as
Miss Constance Neville; Claudia
Pinza as Pimple. LIST 4010 (pd),
also 410 CX (ac)

Gordin, J.
358 Miscellaneous exc., in Yiddish
BRUNO BR 50196

Gordon, Ruth
359 YEARS AGO (exc.)
Fredric March; Florence El-
dridge; Alan Hewitt. In anth.
DECCA DL 9002

Gorky, Maxim
360 EGOR BULYCHOV I DRUGIE (orig.
Russian)
Vakhtangov Theatre, Moscow.
MK ND 01033-8 (3 pd)
361 NA DNE (orig. Russian)
Moscow Art Theatre. MK ND
37-44 (4 pd)
362 NA DNE (orig. Russian)
A. Dmokhovskaya; N. Batalov;
S. Blinnikov; V. Ershov; A.
Zhiltsov; G. Konsky; P.
Massalsky. SSSR D 037-044
(4 pd)
363 NA DNE (exc., orig. Russian)
V. Kachalov. In anth. MK
D 7285/6
364 VARVARY (orig. Russian)
Maly Theatre, Moscow. MK D

010553-8 (3 pd)
365 VASSA ZHELEZNOVA (orig. Russian)
Maly Theatre, Moscow. MK
D 07235-8 (2 pd)
366 VRAGI (orig. Russian)
Moscow Art Theatre. MK D
09913-18 (3 pd)

Gozzi, Carlo
367 AUGELLIN BELVERDE (exc., orig.
Italian)
R. Cominetti; C. Antonini.
In anth. EIA DSM 201

Gray, Madeleine, jt. auth. with
Roussin, André, q. v.

Gray, Simon
368 BUTLEY
Alan Bates; Jessica Tandy;
Richard O'Callaghan; Susan Eng-
el; Michael Byrne; Georgina
Hale; Simon Rouse; John Savi-
dent; Oliver Maguire; Colin
Haigh; Darien Angadi; Susan
Woodridge; Lindsay Ingram; Patti
Love; Belinda Low. CAED TRS
362 (3 pd), also CDL 5362 (3 ac)

Green, Paul
369 IN ABRAHAM'S BOSOM (exc.)
Read by the author. In anth.
SPOA 719
370 ROLL SWEET CHARIOT (exc.)
Read by the author. In anth.
SPOA 719

Grillparzer, Franz
371 DES MEERES UND DER LIEBE WELLEN
(orig. German)
Käthe Gold. In anth. DEUTGR
43002
372 KÖNIG OTTOKARS GLÜCK UND ENDE
(orig. German)
Ewald Balser as Ottokar; Li-
selotte Schreiner as Margarete;
Heinz Moog as Benesch; Otto
Schmöle as Milota; Albin Skoda
as Zawisch; Lona Dubois as Ber-
ta; Alfred Neugebauer as Braun;
Franz Höbling as Bela; Judith
Holzmeister as Kunigunde;
Attila Hörbiger as Rudolf; Fred
Liewehr; Eduard Volters; Felix
Steinböck; Albert Rueprecht;

Grillparzer, Franz, cont'd.
  KÖNIG OTTOKARS GLÜCK UND ENDE,
    cont'd.
      Walter Stummvoll; Michael
      Janisch; Hermann Wawra; Raoul
      Aslan; Julius Karsten; Otto
      Tressler; Franz Herterich;
      Otto Kerry; Helmut Krauss;
      Karl Schramel; Maria Jezel;
      Margarethe Dux; Lilly Ka-
      roly; Erika Berghöfer; Karl
      Friedl; Fritz Horn. AMADEO
      AVRS 6130/2 (3 pd)

Guillen de Castro
  373 MOCEDADES DEL CID (exc., orig.
      Spanish)
        In anth. PLEI 32.158

Guitry, Sacha
  374 AMOUR MASQUÉ (exc., orig. French)
        Yvonne Printemps. In anth.
        EMI 2C154-14.344
  375 ECOUTEZ BIEN, MESSIEURS (orig.
      French)
        S. Guitry; J. Fusier-Gir; L.
        Marconi; R. Passeur. DECCA
        173.125/6 (2 pd)
  376 FAISONS UN RÊVE (exc., orig.
      French)
        R. Lamoureux. PHIL B 76.414R
  377 JEAN DE LA FONTAINE (exc., orig.
      French)
        Yvonne Printemps. In anth. EMI
        2C154-14.344
  378 MARIETTE OU COMMENT ON ÉCRIT
      L'HISTOIRE (exc., orig. French)
        Yvonne Printemps. In anth.
        EMI 2C154-14.344
  379 MOT DE CAMBRONNE (exc., orig.
      French)
        J. Fusier-Gir. FON 460.735
        ME (pd45)
  380 MOT DE CAMBRONNE (orig. French)
        M. Moreno; P. Carton; J. Delu-
        bac; S. Guitry. PAT VSM/FKLP
        7.006
  381 MOZART (exc., orig. French)
        Reynaldo Hahn; Yvonne Printemps.
        In anth. EMI 2C154-14.344

Hacks, Peter
  382 GESPRÄCH IM HAUSE STEIN ÜBER DEN
      ABWESENDEN HERRN VON GOETHE
      (orig. German)

Nicole Heesters. DEUTGR
2755 007 (2 pd)

Hafner, Philipp
  383 EVAKATHEL UND SCHNUDI (orig.
      German)
        Fritz Muliar. In anth.
        PREISR PR 3238

Hall, Donald
  384 EVENING'S FROST
        American National Theatre and
        Academy. LC T 4767 (at)

Hansberry, Lorraine
  385 RAISIN IN THE SUN
        Ossie Davis; Ruby Dee; Claudia
        McNeil; Diana Sands; Leo-
        nard Jackson;Zakes Mokae; Sam
        Schacht; Harold Scott. CAED
        TRS 355 (3 pd), also CDL
        5355 (e ac)
  386 TO BE YOUNG, GIFTED AND BLACK
        James Earl Jones; Barbara Baxley;
        Claudia McNeil; Tina Sattin;
        Camille Yarbrough; Garn Stephens;
        John Towey. CAED TRS 342 (3 pd),
        also CDL 5342 (3 ac)
  387 TO BE YOUNG, GIFTED AND BLACK
        Ruby Dee; Al Freeman, Jr;
        Claudia McNeil; Barbara Barrie;
        Lauren Jones; Roy Schneider;
        Blythe Danner. NET ISBN 0-699-
        29668-4 (16mm film)

Hart, Moss
  388 LADY IN THE DARK (exc.)
        Read by the author. In anth.
        SPOA 725, also in 7146
  389 MAN WHO CAME TO DINNER (exc.)
        Read by the author. In anth.
        SPOA 725, also in 7146

Hasek, Jaroslav, and Kohout,
  Pavel
  390 JOSEF SCHWEJK, ODER, SIE HABEN
      UNS ALSO DEN FERDINAND ERSCHLA-
      GEN (orig. German)
        Valter Taub; Walter Ruch;
        Ilse Laux; Fritz Holzer; Karl
        Merkatz; Fritz Grieb; Jörg
        Liebenfels; Karl Meixner; Fritz
        Wagner; Hans Ulrich; Gerhard
        Hirsch; Benno Gellenbech; Hans
        Irle. DEUTGR 2571 036

Hauptmann, Gerhart
  391 BIBERPELZ (exc., orig. German)
      Lucie Mannheim; Theo Lingen;
      Eduard Wandrey; Reinhold Bernt;
      E. Dunskus; Edith Hancke; M.
      Chevalier; R. Bogus; M. Reid;
      E. Thormann; R. Breitag; O.
      Czarski; H. Weissbach. DEUTGR
      44 015
  392 FLORIAN GEYER (exc., orig. German)
      Heinrich George. In anth. TELEF
      6.41003 AS

Hebbel, Friedrich
  393 HERODES UND MARIAMNE (orig.
      German)
          INTERNAT (ac)
  394 HERODES UND MARIAMNE (exc., orig.
      German)
      Maria Wimmer. In anth. DEUTGR
      140 011
  395 MARIA MAGDALENE (exc., orig.
      German)
      Heinrich George; Gustaf
      Gründgens. In anth. TELEF
      6.41003 AS

Hecht, Ben, and MacArthur,
Charles
  396 FRONT PAGE
      Robert Ryan; Peggy Cass; Bert
      Convy; Margaret Hamilton;
      Katharine Houghton; Val Avery;
      Conrad Janis; John McGiver;
      Julia Meade; Don Porter; Arnold
      Stang, Tom Atkins; Will Grego-
      ry; James Flavin; Morison Gam-
      pel; Walter Flanagan; Charles
      White; Geoffrey Garland; Bruce
      Blaine; Patrick Desmond; Ed
      Riley. CAED TRS 351 (3 pd),
      also CDL 5351 (3 ac)

Hellman, Lillian
  397 LITTLE FOXES (exc.)
      Tallulah Bankhead; Kent Smith;
      Eugenia Rawls; Howard Smith;
      Paul Byron. In anth. DECCA DL
      9009

Heywood, John
  398 JOHAN JOHAN
      John Laurie as Johan Johan; Molly
      Rankin as Wife; Francis DeWolff
      as Priest. In anth. DOVER 99715-4

399 PLAY OF THE WETHER
    Allan McClelland as Merry
    Report. In anth. DOVER 99716-2

Hochhut, Rolf
  400 STELLVERTRETER (exc., orig. Ger-
      man)
      Hannes Messemer; Michael Degen.
      DEUTGR 168 078

Hochwälder, Fritz
  401 HEILIGE EXPERIMENT (orig. German)
      Ewald Balser; Albin Skoda; Paul
      Hoffmann; Heinrich Schweiger;
      Hans Thimig; Heinz Woester;
      Heinz Moog; Andreas Wolf; Hel-
      muth Janatsch; Hanns Obonya.
      AMADEO AVRS 6239

Hofmannsthal, Hugo von
  402 JEDERMANN (orig. German)
      Karl Blühm as Gott der Herr;
      Ernst Deutsch as Tod; Ernst
      Ginsberg as Teufel; Will Quad-
      flieg as Jedermann; Adrienne
      Gessner as Mutter; Martha Wall-
      ner as Buhlschaft; Maria Becker
      as Glaube; Erich Auer as Guter
      Gesell; Hanns Ernst Jäger as
      Mammon; Hilde Mikulicz as Gute
      Werke. DEUTGR 43032
  403 TOR UND DER TOD (orig. German)
      Walther Reyer; Albin Skoda;
      Hans Thimig; Alma Seidler;
      Aglaja Schmid; Andreas Wolf.
      AMADEO AVRS 6138

Housman, Laurence
  404 VICTORIA REGINA
      Helen Hayes; Ian Martin. In
      anth. DECCA DL 9002

Howe, Tina
  405 Miscellaneous exc.
      Read by the author. In anth.
      PAC (2 ac)

Hughes, Langston
  406 JERICO-JIM CROW
      Gilbert Price as Boy; Micki
      Grant as Girl; Rosalie King as
      Old Woman; Joseph Attles as
      Old Man; Dorothy Drake as Woman;
      William Cain. FOLKW 9671 (2 pd)

Hugo, Victor
  407 HERNANI (exc., orig. French)
        Samy Frey as Hernani; Des-
        caut; Destoop; Nassiet. BOR SSB
        107; also SPOA SSB 107
  408 HERNANI (exc.)
        GMS D 7013
  409 HERNANI (exc., orig. French)
        In anth. HACH 320.859
  410 HERNANI (exc., orig. French)
        Jean Deschamps as Hernani;
        Marguerite Perrin as Dona Sol.
        In anth. HACH 320E892, also
        320E898
  411 RUY BLAS (orig. French)
        Comédie Française. GMS 7044-
        46 (3 pd)
  412 RUY BLAS (orig. French)
        Bouquet; Deschamps; Dac-
        qmine; Versini; Benoit; Vir-
        lojeux; Marquet; Haudepin.
        HACH 320E859/61 (3 pd)
  413 RUY BLAS (exc., orig. French)
        L. Lemarchant; G. Wilson;
        S. Fainsilber. In anth. ADÈS
        TS 30 LA 522
  414 RUY BLAS (exc., orig. French)
        Gerard Philipe. In anth. ADÈS
        7005/6, also in 19013
  415 RUY BLAS (exc., orig. French)
        Jean Louis Trintignant as Ruy
        Blas; Borgeaut; Gence; Topart;
        Piat. BOR SSB 101, also SPOA
        SSB 101
  416 RUY BLAS (exc., orig. French)
        Deschamps; Bouquet; Dacqmine.
        HACH 190E964, also 320E892, and
        320 914
  417 RUY BLAS (exc., orig. French)
        In anth. HACH 320.859
  418 Miscellaneous exc., orig. French
        In anth. HACH 320.924

Ibsen, Henrik
  419 BYGMESTER SOLNESS (in English as
        MASTER BUILDER)
        Maggie Smith as Hilde; Michael
        Redgrave as Solness; Celia John-
        son as Wife; Max Adrian. CAED
        TRS 307 (2 pd), also CDL 5307
        (2 ac)
  420 BYGMESTER SOLNESS (exc., in Eng-
        lish as THE MASTER BUILDER)
        Robert Culp. LIST 4008R(pd), al-
        so 408 CX (ac)

  421 DUKKEHJEM (in English as A
        DOLL'S HOUSE)
        Claire Bloom as Nora Helmer;
        Donald Madden; Camila Ashland;
        Patricia Elliott, Robert Ger-
        ringer, Roy Shuman, Kate Wilkin-
        son. CAED TRS 343 (3 pd),
        also CDL 5343 (3 ac)
  422 DUKKEHJEM (in English as A DOLL'S
        HOUSE)
        Cara Duff McCormick. In anth.
        MINN 29121.5 (5 pd)
  423 DUKKEHJEM (in English as A DOLL'S
        HOUSE)
        AIMS (16mm film)
  424 DUKKEHJEM (exc., in English as
        A DOLL'S HOUSE)
        Jane Fonda as Nora. LEARNCO
        ISBN 0-699-03714-X (16mm film)
  425 DUKKEHJEM (exc., in English as
        A DOLL'S HOUSE)
        Robert Culp. LIST 4013 (pd),
        also 413 CX (ac)
  426 DUKKEHJEM (exc., in English as
        A DOLL'S HOUSE)
        Alexander Kirkland Acting
        Group. MAGICT CTG 4013
  427 FOLKEFIENDE (in English as AN
        ENEMY OF THE PEOPLE)
        Sydney Walker; James Blendick;
        Barbara Cason; Philip Bosco;
        David Birney; Stephen Elliott;
        Timmy Ousey; Barry Symonds; Don
        Plumley; Tandy Cronyn; Con-
        rad Bain; Macon McCalman, Esth-
        er Benson; Robert Benson; Jo-
        seph Boley; Richard Bowler;
        James Cook; Dan Sullivan; Ro-
        bert Levine; David Little; Mi-
        chael Miller; Susan Sharkey;
        George Van Den Houten. CAED
        TRS 349 (3 pd), also CDL 5349
        (3 ac)
  428 GENGANGERE (in English as GHOSTS)
        Sonja Lanzener; Yuri Rasovs-
        ky; Roslyn Alexander. In anth.
        ALLMEDIA (ac)
  429 GENGANGERE (exc., in English as
        GHOSTS)
        Robert Culp as Alving; Elayne
        Carroll as Mrs. Alving; Law-
        rence Chelsi as Manders; Mary
        Jasperson as Regina. LIST
        4002 (pd), also 402 CX (ac);
        also MAGICT 4002

430 HEDDA GABLER (in English)
    Joan Plowright as Hedda Gabler;
    Anthony Quayle as Judge Brack;
    Cathleen Nesbitt as Juliana Tes-
    man; Patrick Magee as Eilert
    Loevborg; Michael Gwynn as Geor-
    ge Tesman. CAED TRS 322 (3pd),
    also CDL 5322 (3 ac)
431 HEDDA GABLER (in English)
    Eva LeGallienne. MILLER TM
    102/4 (3 pd)
432 HEDDA GABLER (in English)
    Eva LeGallienne as Hedda Gab-
    ler; Richard Waring; Carmen
    Matthews; Andrew Cruikshank;
    Davis Lewis; Marion Evanson;
    Phillippa Bevans. THEAMA
    GRC 861 (3 pd)
433 HEDDA GABLER (in English)
    Janet Suzman. TIMLIF (vc 3/4)
434 HEDDA GABLER (exc., in English)
    Eva Le Gallienne; Philip Bour-
    neuf. In anth. DECCA DL 9002
435 HEDDA GABLER (exc.)
    FFHS (16mm film)
436 HEDDA GABLER (exc.)
    In anth. FOLKW 9841/2
437 PEER GYNT
    The Canadian Players. LC
    T 2498 (at)
438 PEER GYNT (exc.)
    Clara Pontoppidan; Mogens Wieth.
    In anth. TONO X 25033
439 VILDANDEN (in English as WILD
    DUCK)
    TIMLIF (vc 3/4)

Ionesco, Eugène
440 CANTATRICE CHAUVE (orig. French)
    Odette Piquet as Mme. Smith;
    Claude Mansard as M. Smith;
    Jacqueline Staup as Bonne; Ni-
    colas Bataille as M. Martin;
    Thérèse Quentin as Mme. Martin;
    Jacques Legré as Pompier.
    In anth. GMS D 7095/6; also in
    PHIL B 77.999L
441 CANTATRICE CHAUVE (orig. French)
    Trétau de Paris Théâtre Co. In
    LC T 3502 (at)
442 CANTATRICE CHAUVE (orig. French)
    Read by the author. LVA 11
443 CANTATRICE CHAUVE (exc., orig.
    French)

Charron; Gaudeau. In anth. HACH
320.938
444 CHAISES (in English as THE CHAIRS)
    Siobhan McKenna; Cyril Cusack;
    Eugène Ionesco. CAED TRS 323
    (2 pd), also CDL 5323 (2 ac)
445 CHAISES (orig. French)
    Read by the author. LVA 15
446 CHAISES (exc., orig. French)
    Mauclair; Chelton. In anth.
    HACH 320.938
447 JACQUES, OU LA SOUMISSION (exc.,
    orig. French)
    Gence; Noëlle; Alycia; Deiber;
    Aumont. In anth. HACH 320.938
448 JACQUES, OU LA SOUMISSION (exc.,
    in Italian as JACQUES O LA SOTTO-
    MISSIONE)
    V. Moriconi; G. Mauri; A.
    Ninchi; C. Enrici. In anth.
    CETRA LPZ 2064
449 LEÇON (orig. French)
    Jacqueline Staup; Rosette Zucch-
    alli; Marcel Cuvelier. In anth.
    GMS D 7095/6
450 LEÇON (orig. French)
    Read by the author. LVA 5
451 LEÇON (exc., orig. French)
    Ajoret; Marchat. In anth. HACH
    320.938
452 RHINOCÉROS (in English)
    Zero Mostel; Gene Wilder;
    Karen Black; Robert Weil;
    Joe Silver; Marylin Chris; Ro-
    bert Fields; Melody Santangelo;
    Lou Cutell; Don Calfa; Kath-
    ryn Harkin; Lorna Thaver;
    Howard Morton; Percy Rodri-
    gues. CAED TRS 364 (2 pd),
    also CDL 5364 (2 ac)
453 RHINOCÉROS (exc., orig. French)
    Barrault. In anth. HACH 320.938
454 RHINOCÉROS (exc., orig. French)
    Simone Valère as Daisy; J.-L.
    Barrault as Béranger; William
    Sabatier as Jean; J. Parédès as
    Logician; Robert Lombard as
    Vieux Monsieur. VEGA T31SP8003
455 ROI SE MEURT (exc., orig. French)
    Mauclair; Quentin; Dubois;
    Chelton; Depuy; Lemaire. In
    anth. HACH 320.938
456 SHEPHERD'S CHAMELEON
    LC T 3602 (at)

Ionesco, Eugène, cont'd
457 VICTIMES DU DEVOIR (exc., orig.
    French)
        Sissia; Gence; Aumont; Arnaud.
        In anth. HACH 320.938

Irving, Washington
458 RIP VAN WINKLE (exc.)
        Read by Joseph Jefferson.
        In anth. AUDIOR 2465

Jacker, Corinne
459 Miscellaneous exc.
        Read by the author. In anth.
        PAC (2 ac)

James, Henry
460 TURN OF THE SCREW
        Virginia McKenna. CMS (2 pd)

Jeffers, Robinson
461 TOWER BEYOND TRAGEDY
        Vox Poetica Repertory Co. LC
        T 2413 (at)

Jeffers, Robinson, adapter see
    Euripides, MEDEIA, entry 282

Jolly, Alphons, jt. auth. with
    Labiche, Eugène Marin, q. v.

Jonson, Ben
462 VOLPONE
        BBC ISBN 0-699-31233-7 (16mm
        film)
463 VOLPONE
        TIMLIF (vc 3/4)
464 VOLPONE (exc., in French)
        Charles Dullin. In anth.
        ADÈS 7003

Kakhar, Abdullah
465 OGRIK TISHLAR (in orig. Uzbek;
    transl. title: Bad Teeth)
        Khamza Drama Theatre. MK D
        9815-20

Keane, John Brendan
466 SIVE
        NEALON 002

Kelly, George
467 CRAIG'S WIFE
        CENT 010-1946 (ac)

Kemp, William
468 ROWLAND
        Ian Wallace as Robert; A.
        Leigh as Margaret; Dudley
        Jones as Sexton; Denis
        Quilley as Rowland. In anth.
        DOVER 99722-7

Khamza, Khakimzade
469 BAI AND THE FARMHAND (in Uzbek)
        Khamza Drama Theatre. MK
        D 6879/86 (4 pd)

Kilty, Jerome
470 DEAR LIAR (in Russian)
        A. Stepanova as Mrs. Camp-
        bell; A. Ktorov as Shaw.
        MK D 011515-18 (2 pd)

King, Philip
471 ON MONDAY NEXT
        Robert Morley; Margaret
        Rutherford; Olive Sloane; Kay
        Kendall. In anth. LEARNC
        ISBN 0-699-37095-7 (16mm film)

Kingsley, Sidney
472 DETECTIVE STORY
        Wendell Corey. CENT 010-1908
        (ac)

Kipphardt, Heinar
473 IN DER SACHE J. ROBERT OPPENHEI-
    MER (orig. German)
        Münchner Kammerspiele.
        DEUTGR 144 019/20 (2 pd)
474 IN DER SACHE J. ROBERT OPPENHEI-
    MER (in English as IN THE MATTER
    OF J. ROBERT OPPENHEIMER)
        Joseph Wiseman; Harry Townes;
        Eduard Franz; Whitfield Connor;
        Philip Bosco; Robert Phelen;
        Ralph Bell; Cec Linder; Char-
        les Cioffi; Stephen Elliott;
        Herbert Berghof; Stefan Schna-
        bel; Ronald Weyand; Tony Van
        Bridge. CAED TRS 336 (3 pd)

Kleist, Heinrich von
475 AMPHITRYON (exc., orig. German)
        Will Quadflieg; Friede Kuz-
        many; Elisabeth Goebel. In
        anth. DEUTGR 40 006, also in
        43 048

476 KÄTHCHEN VON HEILBRONN (orig.
    German)
    INTERNAT (ac)
477 KÄTHCHEN VON HEILBRONN (exc.,
    orig. German)
    Will Quadflieg. In anth.
    DEUTGR 40 006
478 KÄTHCHEN VON HEILBRONN (exc.,
    orig. German)
    Ingrid Andree; Erich Schel-
    low; Joseph Dahmen. In anth.
    DEUTGR 42 013
479 PENTHESILEA
    INTERNAT (ac)
480 PENTHESILEA (exc., orig. German)
    Maria Becker; Sebastian Fischer.
    In anth. DEUTGR 40 008, also
    in 43 048
481 PRINZ FRIEDRICH VON HOMBURG
    (orig. German)
    Schaubühne am Halleschen Ufer,
    Berlin. DEUTGR DG 2576 009/11
    (3 pd)
482 PRINZ FRIEDRICH VON HOMBURG
    (orig. German)
    Bruno Ganz as Prinz; Peter
    Lühr, Olaf Bison; Peter Fritz;
    Jutta Lampe; Willem Menne; Wolf
    Redl; Werner Rehm; Otto Sander;
    Katharina Türschen; Peter Stein;
    Botho Strauss. DEUTGR 2750 005
    (3 pd)
483 PRINZ FRIEDRICH VON HOMBURG
    (exc., in French as LE PRINCE DE
    HOMBOURG)
    Gerard Philipe. In anth. ADÈS
    19.013
484 PRINZ FRIEDRICH VON HOMBURG (in
    French as LE PRINCE DE HOMBOURG)
    Verley; Le Marchand; Rival. In
    anth. HACH 320E898
485 PRINZ FRIEDRICH VON HOMBURG (exc.,
    orig. German)
    Thomas Holtzmann; Käthe Haack;
    Lieselotte Rau; Matthias Wieman.
    In anth. DEUTGR 42 013
486 PRINZ FRIEDRICH VON HOMBURG (exc.,
    in French as LE PRINCE DE HOMBOURG)
    R. Mollien; M. Chaumette; M.
    Doll; In anth. ADÈS TS 30
    LA 522
487 ZERBROCHENE KRUG (orig German)
    Roma Bahn; Lina Carstens;
    Eva Ingeborg Scholz; Kurt

Ehrhardt; Claus Hofer;
Günther Lüders; Walter Rich-
ter. EUROD 89 140 XDW (2 pd)

Kohout, Pavel, jt. auth with
    Hasek, Jaroslav, q. v.

Korneichuk, Alexander
488 PLATON KRECHET (in Russian)
    Moscow Art Theatre. MK D
    011805-10 (3 pd)

Kraus, Karl
489 LETZTEN TAGE DER MENSCHHEIT
    (exc., orig. German)
    Read by the author. PREISR
    3238, also 3009, 3014, and
    3018

Kroetz, Franz Xaver
490 WEITERE AUSSICHTEN (orig. German)
    Therese Giehse. DEUTGR 2570
    012
Kyd, Thomas
491 SPANISH TRAGEDIE
    Carleton Hobbs as Hieronimo;
    John Gabriel as Lorenzo; John
    Westbrook as Balthazar; De-
    nise Bryer as Bel-imperia. In
    anth. DOVER 99722-1

La Rosa, Renzo
492 COLPI DI TIMONE (orig. Italian)
    Gilberto Govi; Anna Bolens;
    Luigi Dameri; Enrico Ardizzone;
    Sergio Fosco; Andrea Municchi;
    Ariano Praga; Giorgio Bixio;
    Jole Lorena; Pina Camera.
    CETRA LPB 35034 (pd), also
    MC 76 (ac)

Labiche, Eugène, and Jolly, Alphonse
493 GRAMMAIRE (orig. French)
    RODALE RO 1

Labiche, Eugène, and Martin,
Édouard
494 VOYAGE DE M. PERRICHON (orig.
    French)
    Gilbert Robin as Majorin;
    Michel Galabru as Perrichon;
    Corinne Juresco as Henriette;
    Odile Malet as Mme. Perrichon;

John Barton as Malory;
Tony White as Narrator; John
Holmstrom as Urre and Mor-
dred; Harry Andrews as King
Arthur; William Squire as
Launcelot; Tony Church as
Gawaine; Gary Watson as Bors;
Joan Hart as Quenever.
LONDON ZPR 116/8 (3 pd), also
KZPC 116/8 (3 ac), also A4369

Mankowitz, Wolf
  512 BESPOKE OVERCOAT
        David Kossoff. GOLDGUI 0145

Manzoni, Alessandro
  513 ADELCHI (exc., in orig. Italian)
        Mario Leone. In anth. EIA
        DSM 140

Marceau, Félicien
  514 OEUF (orig. French)
        Read by the author. LVA 30

Marivaux, Pierre Carlet de Cham-
   blain de
  515 FAUSSES CONFIDENCES (orig. French)
        J.-L. Barrault; J. Desailly;
        P. Bertin; M. Renaud; S. Valère;
        DECCA 163.157/8 (2 pd); also
        LONDON 91042/3
  516 FAUSSES CONFIDENCES (exc., orig.
        French)
        Jean-Louis Barrault; Madeleine
        Renaud. In anth. SPOA 715 (pd),
        also 48-6 (ac)
  517 HEUREUX STRATAGÈME (exc., orig.
        French)
        G. Page; C. Minazzoli; R.
        Mollien; J. Berthier. VEG
        TNP 12
  518 JEU DE L'AMOUR ET DU HASARD
        (orig. French)
        Comédie Française. GMS DISC
        7047-8 (2 pd)
  519 JEU DE L'AMOUR ET DU HASARD
        (orig. French)
        Lebrun; Sinigalia; Calvé;
        Duby; Guisol; Jemma.
        HACH ESH 320.879/80 (2 pd)
  520 JEU DE L'AMOUR ET DU HASARD
        (orig. French)
        M. Escande; J. Toja; J.
        Bertheau; J. Charon; H. Per-
        drière; M. Boudet. PAT DTX

204/5 (2 pd)
  521 JEU DE L'AMOUR ET DU HASARD
        (exc., orig. French)
        Lebrun; Sinigalia; Calvé.
        HACH ESH 190.999
  522 JEU DE L'AMOUR ET DU HASARD
        (exc., orig. French)
        Maurice Chambreuil as Orgon;
        Julien Bertheau as Dorante;
        Jacques Charon as Pasquin;
        Jacques Clancy as Mario;
        Gisèle Casadeus as Lisette;
        Mondy Dalmès as Silvia. PERIOD
        FRL 1502
  523 JEU DE L'AMOUR ET DU HASARD
        (exc., orig. French)
        M. Chambreuil; J. Berteau;
        J. Charon; J. Clancy; G. Ca-
        sadeus; M. Dalmès. PLEI
        T 523
  524 Miscellaneous exc.
        In anth. HACH 320.924

Marlowe, Christopher
  525 EDWARD II
        Ian McKellen as King Edward;
        Timothy West as Mortimer;
        Diane Fletcher as Queen Isa-
        bella; James Laurenson as
        Gaveston. LONDON ZPR 113/5
        (3 pd), also SAY 82 (3 ac)
  526 EDWARD II
        TIMLIF (vc 3/4)
  527 JEW OF MALTA (exc.)
        In anth. LEX 7650/55
  528 TAMBERLAINE (exc.)
        In anth. LEX 7650/55
  529 TRAGICAL HISTORY OF DR. FAUSTUS
        Richard Burton. ANGEL S
        36378
  530 TRAGICAL HISTORY OF DR. FAUSTUS
        Frank Silvera as Faustus;
        Fredrick Rolf as Mephistophi-
        lis; Julian Berry; Terence Kil-
        burn; David Thayer; Chester
        Stratton; Darren McGavin; Rich-
        ard Farmer; Richard Purdy;
        Stefan Gierasch; Mae Questell;
        Allen Stevenson; John Helde-
        brand; Cavada Humphrey; Frede-
        rick Worlock; John Pavelko.
        CAED TC 1033
  531 TRAGICAL HISTORY OF DR. FAUSTUS
        RCA A 312

Marlowe, Christopher, cont'd.
  532 TRAGICAL HISTORY OF DR. FAUSTUS
      (exc.)
        Richard Burton; Andreas Teuber;
        David Wood; David McIntosh.
        ANGEL 36378
  533 TRAGICAL HISTORY OF DR. FAUSTUS
      (exc.)
        Robert Culp. LIST 4005 (pd),
        also 405 CX (ac)
  534 TRAGICAL HISTORY OF DR. FAUSTUS
      (exc.)
        Derek Godfrey. In anth.
        LONDON SAY 18
  535 TRAGICAL HISTORY OF DR. FAUSTUS
      (exc.)
        In anth. LONGMAN 3
  536 TRAGICAL HISTORY OF DR. FAUSTUS
      (exc.)
        PROTHM (ac)

Martin, Edouard, jt. auth. with
  Labiche, Eugene, q. v.

Martin, Marty
  537 GERTRUDE STEIN GERTRUDE STEIN
      GERTRUDE STEIN
        Par Carroll. CAED TRS 367
        (2 pd), also CP 367 (2 ac)

Mauriac, François
  538 ASMODÉE (exc., orig. French)
        Gisèle Casadesus; Fernand
        Ledoux. In anth. FEST FLDX 74
  539 ASMODÉE (exc., orig. French)
        Fernand Ledoux as Blaise;
        James Sparrow as Harry. In
        anth. HACH ESH 320.878
  540 MAL-AIMÉS (exc., orig. French)
        Claude Dauphin as Virelade;
        Emmanuèle Riva as Elisabeth.
        In anth. HACH 320.878

Mayakovsky, Vladimir
  541 BANYA (exc., in Russian)
        MK D 011691-4 (2 pd)

Medwall, Henry
  542 FULGENS AND LUCRES
        In anth. DOVER 99713-8

Mell, Max
  543 APOSTELSPIEL (orig. German)
        Hans Thimig as Grossvater;
        Johanna Matz as Magdalen;

Helmut Janatsch as Johannes;
        Michael Janisch as Petrus.
        AMADEO AVRS 6101

Merz, Carl, jt. auth. with
  Qualtinger, q. v.

Metastasio, Pietro
  544 ATTILIO REGOLO (exc., orig.
      Italian)
        Gianni Solaro; Maria Leone.
        In anth. EIA DSM 0137

Michaels, Sidney
  545 DYLAN
        Alec Guiness; Kate Reid; James
        Ray; Barbara Berjer; Martin
        Garner; Jenny O'Hara. COLUMB
        DOL 301 (3 pd), also DOS 701

Middleton, Thomas
  546 CHANGELING
        Martin Jarvis; Sharon Duce;
        Barry Foster. BBC ECN 103 (ac)

Mihura, Miguel
  547 MARIBEL Y LA EXTRAÑA FAMILIA
        Read by the author. In anth.
        AGUILAR GPE 11 102

Miller, Arthur
  548 AFTER THE FALL
        Jason Robards as Quentin;
        Barbara Loden as Maggie;
        Crystal Field as Felice;
        Salome Jens as Holga; Pa-
        tricia Roe as Mother; Mi-
        chael Strong as Dan; Paul
        Mann as Father; Faye Duna-
        way as Elsie. CAED TRS 326
        (4 pd), also CDL 5326 (4 ac)
  549 AFTER THE FALL
        Jason Robards as Quentin;
        Barbara Loden as Maggie; Mari-
        clare Costello as Louise; Vir-
        ginia Kaye as Rose; Paul Mann
        as Ike; Michael Strong as Dan;
        Salome Jens as Holga; Zohra
        Lampert as Felice; David J.
        Stewart as Lon. MERC OCS 4-
        6207 (4 pd), also OCM 4-2207
  550 CRUCIBLE
        Jerome Dempsey; Alexandria
        Stoddard; Theresa Merritt;
        Pamela Payton-Wright; Crickett

Coan; Pauline Flanagan;
Ben Hammer; Kathleen Doyle;
Nora Heflin; Robert Foxworth;
Aline MacMahon; Sydney Walker;
Robert Phelan; Martha Henry;
Wendell Phillips; John Newton;
Richard Kline; Robert Symonds;
Stephen Elliott; Doris Rich;
Stuart Pankin. CAED TRS 356 (4
pd), also CDL 5356 (4 ac)

551 CRUCIBLE (exc.)
Read by the author. In anth.
SPOA 704 (pd), also in 8045(ac)

552 CRUCIBLE (exc.)
CA 623 (ac)

553 CRUCIBLE (exc.)
PROTHM 1 EP 1 (ac)

554 DEATH OF A SALESMAN
Lee Cobb as Willy Loman; Mil-
dred Dunnock; Michael Tolan as
Biff; Gene Williams as Happy;
Dustin Hoffman; Camila Ashland;
Ralph Bell; Royal Beal; George
Coe; Francine Beers; Tom Pedi;
Ann Wedgeworth; Joyce Aaron.
CAED TRS 310 (3 pd), also CDL
5310 (3 ac)

555 DEATH OF A SALESMAN
Thomas Mitchell as Willy Loman;
Arthur Kennedy as Biff; Mildred
Dunnock as Linda; Howard Smith
as Charley; Thomas Chalmers as
Uncle Ben; Cameron Mitchell as
Happy; Alan Hewitt as Howard
Wagner; Don Keefer as Bernard;
Winifred Cushing as Woman; Ann
Driscoll as Jenny; Arthur Miller
as Narrator. DECCA DL 9006/7
(2 pd), also DNA/DXA 102

556 DEATH OF A SALESMAN (exc.)
EAV A5F 0906 (ac)

557 DEATH OF A SALESMAN (exc.)
Read by the author. In anth.
SPOA 704, also in 8045

558 INCIDENT AT VICHY
Jack Waltzer as Waiter; Michael
Strong as Lebeau; David J.
Stewart as Monceau; Stanley Beck
as Bayard; Clinton Kimbrough as
Professor; Joseph Wiseman as
Leduc; Hal Holbrook as Major;
David Wayne as Von Berg; Paul
Mann as Marchand; Barry Primus
as Guard; Harold Scott as Gypsy;

Jack Waltzer as Waiter.
CAED TRS 318 (2 pd), also CDL
5318 (2 ac); also MERC OCS2-62
111

559 REASON WHY
Eli Wallach; Robert Ryan. BFA
ISBN 0-699-01719-X (16mm film)

560 VIEW FROM THE BRIDGE
Richard Castellano as Louis;
Carmine Caridi as Mike; Mit-
chell Jason as Alfieri; Robert
Duvall as Eddie; Linda Eske-
nas as Catherine; Jeanne Kaplan
as Beatrice; Ramon Bieri as
Marco. CAED TRS 317 (2 pd),
also CDL 5317 (2 ac); also
MERC OCM2 2212

Miller, Henry
561 JUST WILD ABOUT HARRY
Read by the author. LVA 202/3

Miller, Hugh
562 BARE BOARDS AND A PASSION
LC T 3179 (at)

Milosz, Oscar Vladislas de Lubicz
563 RUBEZAHL, OU, SCÈNES DE DON JUAN
Laurent Terzieff; Pascale de
Boysson; Laudenbach; Aufaure;
Walter; Servant; Perot. ADÈS
11.501

564 RUBEZAHL, OU, SCÈNES DE DON JUAN
(exc.)
In anth. ADÈS 10.034

Milton, John
565 COMUS
Ronald Pickup as Comus; Barbara Jefford as Lady. BBC
ECN 100 (ac)

566 COMUS
William Squire as Attendant
Spirit; Ian Holm as Comus;
Barbara Jefford as Lady; Ro-
bert Tear, Margaret Neville,
Susan Longfield as Singers.
LONDON PLP 1024/5 (2 pd)

567 COMUS (exc.)
Anthony Quayle. In anth. CAED
TC 1259, also in CDL 51259

568 COMUS (exc.)
Jefford; Squire; Watson;
Garland; Holm; Rawlings; Church;

Milton, John, cont'd.
    COMUS, cont'd.
        McCarthy. In anth. LONDON
        RG 544/5
  569 SAMSON AGONISTES
        Michael Redgrave as Samson;
        Max Adrian, Manoa; Faith Brook
        as Dalila; Neil McCarthy as
        Harapha of Gath. CAED TC
        2028 (2 pd), also CDL 52028(2ac)
  570 SAMSON AGONISTES (exc.)
        Barbara Jefford; William Squire;
        Gary Watson; Patrick Garland;
        Ian Holm; Margaret Rawlings;
        Tony Church; Denis McCarthy.
        LONDON PLP 1024/5, also RG 544/5
  571 SAMSON AGONISTES (exc.)
        Anthony Quayle. In anth. CAED
        TC 1259, also in CDL 51259

Molière, Jean-Baptiste Poquelin
  572 AMPHITRYON (exc., orig. French)
        Robert Hirsch; Richard; Meyer;
        Parédès. In anth. ADÈS 13031
  573 AMPHITRYON (exc., orig. French)
        Barrault; Renaud. In anth.
        SPOA 715 (pd), also in 48-6(ac)
  574 AVARE (orig. French)
        Comédie Française. GMS DISC
        7058-60 (3 pd)
  575 AVARE (orig. French)
        Baquet; Desailly; Fabbri; Rau-
        zena; Vaneck; Rosay; Sellers;
        Valère. HACH 320.832/33 (2 pd)
  576 AVARE (orig. French)
        M. Escande; J. Meyer; J. Cha-
        ron; J. Piat; M. Porterat; J.-P.
        Roussillon; A. Feydeau; M. Bou-
        det; D. Gence; M. Grellier.
        PAT DTX 296/8 (3 pd)
  577 AVARE (orig. French)
        Eyser; Camoin; Arrieu; Marco-
        Béhar; Eine; Pralon; Barlier;
        Moreau; Noesen; F. Seigner; C.
        Hiegel. PAT 11.337/39 (3 pd)
  578 AVARE (in English as THE MISER)
        Robert Symonds as Harpagon;
        Lloyd Battista as Valère;
        Blythe Danner as Elise; David
        Birney as Cléante; Roger Ro-
        binson as La Flèche; Ronald
        Weyand as Master Simon; Lili
        Darvas as Frosine; Douglas Hayle
        as Brindavoine; James Cook; Ray

Fry; Priscilla Pointer; Stephen Elliott; Paul Sparer.
CAED TRS 338 (2 pd), also CDL
5338 (2 ac)
  579 AVARE (exc., orig. French)
        Jean Vilar. In anth. ADÈS
        TS 30 LA 552; also in SPOA 924
  580 AVARE (exc., orig. French)
        Charles Dullin. In anth.
        ADÈS 7003/4 (2 pd)
  581 AVARE (exc., orig. French)
        Desbois; Bouquet; Paturel;
        Fertey; Merval; Guiomar.
        BOR SSB 125; also SPOA SSB 125
  582 AVARE (exc., orig. French)
        Ledoux. HACH 190E857
  583 AVARE (exc., orig. French)
        In anth. HACH 320.914
  584 AVARE (exc., orig. French)
        Jean Deschamps. In anth.
        HACH 460E803/5
  585 AVARE (exc., orig. French)
        P. Palau; J. Brochard. LUM
        LD 3.249
  586 AVARE (exc., orig. French)
        PAT EA 10.030
  587 AVARE (exc., orig. French)
        Denis d'Inès as Harpagon;
        Béatrice Bretty as Frosine;
        Jean Debucourt as Valère;
        Louis Seigner as Maître Jac-
        ques; Jacques Charon as La
        Flèche; Jacques Clancy as
        Cléante. PERIOD FRL 1506
  588 AVARE (exc., orig. French)
        Jean-Gabriel Gaussens. In
        anth. SPOA 822
  589 BOURGEOIS GENTILHOMME (orig.
        French)
        Henri Tisot; G. Morel; Pre-
        vost; Gil; Dunan; Jourdan; Li-
        tvac; Galbeau; Renot. BOR
        SSB 111; also SPOA SSB-111
  590 BOURGEOIS GENTILHOMME (orig.
        French)
        B. Blier; F. Périer; J. Hil-
        ling; L. deFunès; J.-M. Ama-
        to; J. Parédès; G. Pierauld;
        J. Topart; Y. Duchateau; R.
        Berthier; M. Mercadier; G. Page;
        A. Poivre; F. Descart. CTP
        MC 20.120/2; also VOG COF 11
        (3 pd)

591 BOURGEOIS GENTILHOMME (orig.
    French)
        Dhéran; Delamare; F. Seigner;
        D. Benoît; Grellier; Chamonin;
        Giraudeau; Mallabrera; J.-C.
        Benoit. GID 2.464 (3 pd)
592 BOURGEOIS GENTILHOMME (orig.
    French)
        Comédie Française. GMS DISC
        7031-33 (3 pd)
593 BOURGEOIS GENTILHOMME (orig.
    French)
        Desmarets; Darléac; Fabbri;
        Mauban; Dacqmine; Les Frères
        Jacques; Philippe; Benoit;
        Poiret et Serrault; Vattier;
        Velle; Virlojeux; Salvador.
        HACH ESH 320.842/44 (3 pd)
594 BOURGEOIS GENTILHOMME (orig.
    French)
        M. Escande; J. Meyer; L. Seig-
        ner; J. Charon; R. Manuel; G.
        Chamarat; J. Piat; J.L. Jemma;
        B. Bretty; M. Boudet; H.
        Perdrère; A. de Chauveron.
        PAT DTX 168/70 (3 pd)
595 BOURGEOIS GENTILHOMME (exc., orig.
    French)
        Fabbri; Vattier; Velle; Salva-
        dor; Arletty; Desmarets. HACH
        190E885
596 BOURGEOIS GENTILHOMME (exc., orig.
    French)
        Les Frères Jacques; D. Benoît;
        J. Fabbri. HACH 190E886
597 BOURGEOIS GENTILHOMME (exc., orig.
    French)
        Raymond Souplex; Lucien Baroux.
        In anth. LUM LD 3.240; also in
        SPOA 794
598 BOURGEOIS GENTILHOMME (exc., orig.
    French)
        Fernand Ledoux as M. Jourdain;
        Pierre Larguey as Maître de Phi-
        losophie; Jacques Gheusi as Dor-
        ante; Jacques Ciron as Covi-
        elle; Pierre Barrat as Cléante;
        Françoise Rosay as Mme. Jour-
        dain; Mathilde Casadeus as Nico-
        le; Christine Vall as Dorimène;
        Claude Chantal as Lucile.
        PERIOD FRL 1512; also PLEI P
        3.102

599 BOURGEOIS GENTILHOMME (exc., orig.
    French)
        D. Gence; C. Samie; B. Dheran;
        G. Cattand; R. Gérôme; O.
        Hussenot. PHIL E1E 9.130 (pd45)
600 BOURGEOIS GENTILHOMME (exc., orig.
    French)
        A. Wartel; F. Priollet; R.
        Party; D. Provence; E. Ker.
        PHIL B 77.905 L
601 DÉPIT AMOUREUX (exc., orig.
    French)
        A. Gaylor; C. Oger; F. Guiot;
        A. Lionel; D. Prévost; F.
        Timmerman. In anth. ADÈS TS 25
        LA 526
602 DON JUAN (orig. French)
        Vilar; Chaumette; Minazzoli;
        Deschamps; Mollien; Wilson.
        HACH 320E041/2 (2 pd)
603 DON JUAN (orig. French)
        Jacques Charon as Sganarelle;
        Georges Descrières as Don Juan;
        J.-P. Roussillon as Pierrot;
        Michel Aumont as Dimanche; Louis
        Eymond; Jean-Louis Jemma; René
        Arrieu; Simon Eine; Michel Ber-
        nardy; Serge Maillat; Jean-Noël
        Sissia; Buron; Samie; Paula
        Noëlle; Alberte Aveline; Lud-
        mila Mikaël. PAT C061-10.648/
        49 (2 pd)
604 DON JUAN (exc., orig. French)
        Jean Vilar. In anth. ADÈS TS30
        LA552
605 DON JUAN (exc., orig. French)
        Jean Vilar; Sorano; Moulinot.
        HACH 190E899
606 DON JUAN (exc., orig. French)
        J. Marchat; L. Baroux. In
        anth. LUM LD 3.248
607 ÉCOLE DES FEMMES (orig. French)
        L. Jouvet; J. Richard; F. René;
        L. Lapara; G. Riquier; P. Re-
        noir; M. Etcheverry; M. Me-
        linand. GMS DISC 7062/4; also
        PAT PCX 5003/6; also VSM C161-
        12.097/9 (3 pd)
608 ÉCOLE DES FEMMES (in English as
    SCHOOL FOR WIVES)
        Brian Bedford as Arnolphe; Joan
        van Ark as Agnes; Paul Ballan-
        tyne as Chrysalde; David Dukes

Molière, Jean-Baptiste Poquelin,
  cont'd.
        SCHOOL FOR WIVES, cont'd.
        as Horace; Gordon Gould as
        Oronte; James Greene as Alain;
        George Pentecost as Notary;
        Peggy Pope as Georgette; Ma-
        rio Siletti as Enrique. CAED
        TRS 344 (3 pd), also CDL 5344
        (3 ac)
609 ÉCOLE DES FEMMES (exc., orig.
    French)
        Jouvet; Blancher. In anth.
        ADÈS 7007/8, also in 19.015
610 ÉCOLE DES FEMMES (exc., orig.
    French)
        Périer; Ogier; Pernet. BOR
        SSB 117
611 ÉCOLE DES FEMMES (exc., orig.
    French)
        C. Desbois; G. Wilson. VEGA
        TNP 3
612 ÉTOURDI (orig. French)
        LUM LD 3.231 (pd16)
613 ÉTOURDI (exc., orig. French)
        J. Echantillon; F. Timmer-
        man; G. Montillier; R. Garri-
        vier. In anth. ADÈS TS 25
        LA 526
614 FEMMES SAVANTES (orig. French)
        Comédie Française. GMS DISC
        7052-53 (2 pd)
615 FEMMES SAVANTES (orig. French)
        Ledoux; Bouquet; Deschamps;
        Vaneck; Mauban; Pierry; Ro-
        say; Sellers; Varte. HACH
        ESH 320.837/8 (2 pd)
616 FEMMES SAVANTES (orig. French)
        Escande; Debucourt; Charon; Mar-
        co-Behar; Rollan; Jemma; Dela-
        mare; Boudet; Perdrière; De
        Chauveron; Girardot, Ancel.
        PAT C061-10.630/31 (2 pd),
        also DTX 214/5
617 FEMMES SAVANTES (orig. French)
        Denis d'Ines as Vadius; Mau-
        rice Chambreuil as Chrysale;
        Jean Debucourt as Clitandre;
        Louis Seigner as Ariste; Jac-
        ques Charon as Trissotin;
        Teddy Bilis as Notaire; Le
        Goff as Julien. PERIOD FRL
        1510-11 (2 pd)
618 FEMMES SAVANTES (exc., orig.
    French)

        Henri Rollan; Denise Gence;
        Lude; Mériko; Maistre. BOR
        SSB 109; also SPOA SSB 109
619 FEMMES SAVANTES (exc., orig.
    French)
        Ledoux; Deschamps; Furet;
        Rosay; Pierry; Varte. HACH
        190E871/2, also 320.914 (2 pd)
620 FEMMES SAVANTES (exc., orig.
    French)
        M. Perrey; P. Lecomte. In anth.
        LUM LD 3.247
621 FEMMES SAVANTES (exc., orig.
    French)
        Y. Gaudeau; M. Barbulée; C. le
        Couey; R. Gérôme; O. Hussenot.
        PHIL E1E9.129 (pd45)
622 FEMMES SAVANTES (exc., orig.
    French)
        Mireille Perrey as Philaminte;
        Pierre Lecomte as Trissotin;
        Jacques Berger as Crysale;
        Marie Laurence as Armande; Lu-
        cette Verdal as Martine; Oli-
        vier Lebeaut as Clitandre; Vi-
        viane Gosset as Bélise; Fran-
        cine Dartois as Henriette. In
        anth. SPOA SA 793
623 FOURBERIES DE SCAPIN (orig.
    French)
        GMS DISC 7068/69 (2 pd)
624 FOURBERIES DE SCAPIN (orig.
    French)
        Roussin; Benoit; Dufilho;
        Mercure; Mollien; Noël; Page;
        Parédès. HACH ESH 320.854
        (2 pd)
625 FOURBERIES DE SCAPIN (orig.
    French)
        Robert Hirsch; Jacques Charon;
        Jean-Louis Jemma; Jacques Toja;
        Sereys; Arnaud; Camoin; Boudet;
        Samie; André. PAT C061-10.623/4
        (2 pd), also DTX 245/6
626 FOURBERIES DE SCAPIN (orig.
    French)
        Périer; Desmarets; Desailly;
        Fabbri; De Funès; Pierauld;
        Rich; Morel; Pelays. CTP MC
        20.132/3 (2 pd), also CTP 25.
        005/30 (pd16); also VOG COF 12
627 FOURBERIES DE SCAPIN (exc., orig.
    French)
        Hirsch; Richard; Meyer; Parédès.
        In anth. ADÈS 13.031

628 FOURBERIES DE SCAPIN (exc., orig.
    French)
        Jean Paul Roussillon as Scapin;
        Bertin; Mirat. BOR SSB 112;
        also SPOA SSB 112
629 FOURBERIES DE SCAPIN (exc., orig.
    French)
        Roussin; Mercure. HACH 190E947
630 FOURBERIES DE SCAPIN (exc., orig.
    French)
        Rocca. In anth. LUM LD 3.241
631 GEORGES DANDIN (orig. French)
        J. Meyer; M. Daems; M. Pierry;
        A.-M. Mailfer; J.-H. Duval; F.
        Timmerman. ADÈS TS25 LA 508
632 JALOUSIE DE BARBOUILLÉ (exc.,
    orig. French)
        Jouvet; René. In anth. ADÈS
        7007/8
633 MALADE IMAGINAIRE (orig. French)
        R. Carlès; M. Mercadier; J.
        Lehmann; M. Marquet; Valle-
        Valdy; R. Souplex; J. Charon;
        G. Vidal; Desay; M. Carpentier;
        Le Person; M. de Rieux. In
        anth. DECCA 99.070/74 (5 pd),
        also 163.507/8
634 MALADE IMAGINAIRE (orig. French)
        Chamarat; Roussillon; Pieplu;
        Maistre; D. Benoit; Coster;
        Berton; Chamonin; Mallabrera.
        GID 2.658/585 (3 pd)
635 MALADE IMAGINAIRE (orig. French)
        GMS DISC 7074-76 (3 pd)
636 MALADE IMAGINAIRE (orig. French)
        Galabru; Bedos; Baroux; Cassan;
        Daumier; Deschamps; Pacôme;
        Pascal; Vattier. HACH 320E
        856-8 (3 pd)
637 MALADE IMAGINAIRE (orig. French)
        Charon; Eyser; Toja; Dautun;
        F. Seigner; C. Hiégel. PAT C161
        -12.132/33 (2 pd)
638 MALADE IMAGINAIRE (orig. French)
        J. Meyer; L. Seigner; R. Manuel;
        G. Chamarat; J. Piat; J.-P.
        Roussillon; H. Rollan; L. Conte;
        M. Boudet; M. Grellier. PAT
        DTX 300/2 (3 pd)
639 MALADE IMAGINAIRE (exc., orig.
    French)
        Gence; Sauvage; Tissier. BOR
        SSB 115

640 MALADE IMAGINAIRE (exc., orig.
    French)
        R. Carlès; M. de Rieux. DECCA
        455.574 (pd45)
641 MALADE IMAGINAIRE (exc., orig.
    French)
        Galabru; Bedos; Baroux; Virlo-
        jeux; Cassan. HACH 190E965
642 MALADE IMAGINAIRE (exc., orig.
    French)
        Galabru as D'Argan. In anth.
        HACH 320.914
643 MALADE IMAGINAIRE (exc., orig.
    French)
        Lucien Baroux; Raymond Sou-
        plex. In anth. LUM LD 3.240;
        also in SPOA 794
644 MALADE IMAGINAIRE (exc., orig.
    French)
        F. Ledoux; P. Larquey; J.
        Parédès; J. Ghensi; J. Cabanis;
        J.-J. Lagarde; R. Saltel;
        P. Laugier; F. Rosay; D. Clair;
        C. Chantal; E. Demay. PLEI
        P 3.113
645 MÉDECIN MALGRÉ LUI (orig. French)
        Fernandel; B. Bretty; Cabanis;
        J. Charon; D. Dheran; M. Perrey;
        G. Chamarat; Seyrac; M. de
        Rieux; Breze; Perrin. In anth.
        DECCA 99.070/74
646 MÉDECIN MALGRÉ LUI (orig. French)
        A. Bellec; G. Bellec; Soubeyran;
        Tourenne; Rosy Varte; Denise Be-
        noit; Frédérique Hébrard; Degex.
        HACH ESH 320.876/7 (2 pd)
647 MÉDECIN MALGRÉ LUI (exc., orig.
    French)
        J. Richard; J. Meyer; P.
        Saint-Georges; C. Courtel;
        J.-H. Duval; F. Timmerman; J.
        Ardouin. ADÈS TS25 LA 514
648 MÉDECIN MALGRÉ LUI (exc., orig.
    French)
        Jouvet; Etiévant; Bertin. In
        anth. ADÈS 7007/8, also in 19.015
649 MÉDECIN MALGRÉ LUI (exc., orig.
    French)
        Hirsch; Richard; Meyer; Parédès.
        In anth. ADÈS 13.031
650 MÉDECIN MALGRÉ LUI (exc., orig.
    French)
        Varte; F. Seigner; Jacques Du
        Filho; Renot; Rambal. BOR

Molière, Jean-Baptiste Poquelin,
  cont'd.
    MÉDECIN MALGRÉ LUI, cont'd.
      SSB 116, also SPOA SSB 116
651 MÉDECIN MALGRÉ LUI (exc., orig.
    French)
      Fernandel; J. Charon; G. Chama-
      rat; Cabanis; M. de Rieux; B.
      Dhéran; B. Bretty; M. Perrey.
      DECCA 163.749
652 MÉDECIN MALGRÉ LUI (exc., orig.
    French)
      G. Bellec; Varte; A. Bellec;
      Hébrard; Benoit; Soubeyran.
      HACH 190E992
653 MÉDECIN MALGRÉ LUI (exc., orig.
    French)
      L. Baroux. In anth. LUM LD
      3.241
654 MÉDECIN MALGRÉ LUI (exc., orig.
    French)
      Jean Meyer; Louis Seigner as
      Géronte; Jacques Charon as
      Lucas; Robert Manuel as Valère;
      Robert Hirsch as M. Robert;
      Jacques Clancy as Léandre;
      Maurice Porterat as Thibaut;
      Jean-Louis Le Goff as Perron;
      Béatrice Bretty; Micheline
      Boudet as Martine; Denise
      Pezzani as Lucinde. PERIOD
      FRL 1508; also PLEI T 525
655 MÉDECIN MALGRÉ LUI (exc., in
    English as THE DOCTOR IN SPITE OF
    HIMSELF)
      Robert Culp. LIST 4009 (pd);
      also 409 CX (ac)
656 MISANTHROPE (orig. French)
      Renaud Mary; Page; Bouquet;
      Castelot. BOR SSB 104; also
      SPOA SSB-104
657 MISANTHROPE (orig. French)
      Barrault; Desailly; Bertin;
      Renaud; Galland; Valère;
      Cattand; Grandval; Jobin;
      Nerval; Juillard. In anth.
      DECCA 99.070/74 (5 pd)
658 MISANTHROPE (orig. French)
      Le Poulain; H. Virlojeux;
      Jean-Louis Jemma; E. Riva;
      M. Mauban. HACH 320E911/12
      (2 pd)
659 MISANTHROPE (orig. French)
      Théâtre du Vieux Colombier. LC
      T 3057 (at)

660 MISANTHROPE (in English)
      Richard Easton as Alceste;
      Sydney Walker as Philinte;
      Alan Brasington as Basque;
      Keene Curtis as Oronte;
      Christine Pickles as Célimène;
      Patricia Conolly as Eliante;
      Betty Miller as Arsinoé; Jo-
      seph Bird as Clitandre; Ellis
      Rabb as Acaste; Michael Durrell;
      Ralph Williams. CAED TRS 337
      (2 pd), also CDL 5337 (2 ac)
661 MISANTHROPE (in English)
      FFHS ISBN 0-699-36997-5
      (16mm film)
662 MISANTHROPE (exc., orig. French)
      J. Meyer; F. Fabian; J. Darcan-
      te; C. Courtel. ADÈS TS 25 LA
      509
663 MISANTHROPE (exc., orig. French)
      DECCA 163.714/5
664 MISANTHROPE (exc., orig. French)
      Gérard Philipe; Maria Casarès.
      In anth. FEST FLD 166; also in
      GMS D 7065
665 MISANTHROPE (exc.)
      In anth. FOLKW 9841/2
666 MISANTHROPE (exc., orig. French)
      J. Bertheau. LUM LD 3.242
667 MISANTHROPE (exc., orig. French)
      Pierre Dux as Alceste; Jean
      Debucourt as Philinte; Jacques
      Charon as Oronte; Pierre Gallon
      as Acaste; Jean-Louis Jemma as
      Clitandre; Mony Dalmès as Céli-
      mène; Louise Conte as Arsinoé;
      Yvonne Gaudian as Eliante.
      PERIOD FRL 1504 (2 pd); also
      PLEI 522
668 MISANTHROPE (exc., orig. French)
      Jean-Louis Barrault; Madeleine
      Renaud. In anth. SPOA 715,
      also in 48-6
669 PRÉCIEUSES RIDICULES (orig.
    French)
      François Périer; Nerval; Doat;
      Mazzotti; Lude. BOR SSB 124;
      also SPOA SSB 124
670 PRÉCIEUSES RIDICULES (orig.
    French)
      Parédès; Piéplu; Harry-Max;
      D. Benoit; Evenou; Leroux;
      Nocher; Istria; Frantz; Llorca.
      HACH ESH 320.890

Montherlant, Henri de, cont'd.
  692 PORT ROYAL (orig. French)
        Comédie Française. GMS DISC
        7037-39 (3 pd)
  693 PORT ROYAL(orig. French)
        J. Debucourt; H. Rollan; R.
        Faure; L. Conte; A. Ducaux;
        M. Boudet; Y. Gaudeau; A. de
        Chauveron; L. Noro; S. Nivette;
        D. Gence; C. Winter; Raoul-
        Henry; Vitray; Eymond; Vibert;
        Le Goff; Drancourt; Rio;
        Duard. PAT DTX 236/8, also
        C 061-10.625/7 (3 pd)
  694 PORT ROYAL (exc., orig. French)
        Annie Ducaux; Renée Faure. In
        FEST FLDX 73
  695 PORT ROYAL (exc., orig. French)
        Nathalie Nerval as Soeur Fran-
        çoise; Yves Furet as Lieute-
        nat; Jean-Paul Moulinot as
        Archevêque; Emmanuèle Riva as
        Soeur Angélique. In anth.
        HACH 320E885
  696 REINE MORTE (orig. French)
        Comédie Française. GMS DISC
        7040-42 (3 pd)
  697 REINE MORTE (orig. French)
        J. Yonnel; M. Escande; J. Ber-
        theau; L. Seigner; J. Eyser;
        R. Faure; M. Dalmès; S. Nivette.
        PAT DTX 256/8 (3 pd)
  698 REINE MORTE (exc., orig. French)
        Jean Yonnel; Mony Dalmès. In
        anth. FEST FLDX 73
  699 REINE MORTE (exc., orig. French)
        Jean Yonnel as Ferrante; Em-
        manuèle Riva as Inès. In anth.
        HACH 320.885
  700 VILLE DONT LE PRINCE EST UN
      ENFANT (orig. French)
        J. Desailly; P. Gothot; J. Simo-
        net; H. Rollan; H. Tisot; P.
        Clair; A. Bourseiller. PAT
        DTX 266/8 (3 pd)
  701 Miscellaneous exc.
        A. Ducaux; R. Faure; J. Debu-
        court; M. Auclair; M. Dalmès;
        J. Yonnel; H. de Montherlant. In
        FEST FLD 73

Moore, Honor
  702 Miscellaneous exc.
        Read by the author. In anth.
        PAC (2 ac)

Moratín, Nicolas Fernandez de
  703 COMEDIA NUEVA (exc., orig.
      Spanish)
        In anth. ADÈS 32.162
  704 SÍ DE LAS NIÑAS (exc., orig.
      Spanish)
        In anth. ADÈS 32.162

Muñiz, Carlos
  705 TINTERO (orig. Spanish)
        Read by the author. In anth.
        AGUILAR GPE 11 102

Musset, Alfred de
  706 CAPRICE (orig. French)
        Comédie Française. GMS DISC
        7054
  707 CAPRICE (orig. French)
        M. Escande; R. Camoin; L.
        Delamare; C. Winter. PAT
        DTX 273
  708 CAPRICE (orig. French)
        H. Doublier; M.-R. Carlie;
        C. Demay; M. Bray. PLEI
        P 3.116
  709 CAPRICES DE MARIANNE (orig.
      French)
        Page; Maistre; Rich; Jor;
        Trintignant. BOR SSB 126
  710 CAPRICES DE MARIANNE (exc.,
      orig. French)
        Gerard Philipe; G. Page; R.
        Mollien. In anth. ADÈS 13030,
        also in 7.005/6, &in TS30LA522
  711 CAPRICES DE MARIANNE (exc., orig.
      French)
        Jean-Louis Barrault; Madeleine
        Renaud. In anth. SPOA 715 (pd),
        also 48-6 (ac)
  712 LORENZACCIO (orig. French)
        Gérard Philipe as Lorenzo;
        J. Vilar as Cibo; J. Deschamps
        as Strozzi; Chaumette; Mina-
        zzoli; Daniel Ivernel as Le
        Duc Alexandre; Wilson. HACH
        320E808/9 & 270E810 (3 pd)
  713 LORENZACCIO (exc., orig. French)
        L. Lemarchand; G. Wilson; S.
        Fainsilber. In anth. ADÈS TS30
        LA 522
  714 LORENZACCIO (exc., orig. French)
        Gerard Philipe. In anth. ADÈS
        7005/6
  715 LORENZACCIO (exc., orig. French)
        Pierre Vaneck as Lorenzo;

Henri Rollan as Strossi;
Georges Aminel as Le Duc; René
Farabel as Recitant; Jean-
Jacques Aslanian; Pierre Con-
stant; Sylvia Favre; Pierre
Olivier; Robert Party. BOR
SSB 102; also SPOA SSB 102

716 LORENZACCIO (exc., orig. French)
Philipe; Vilar; Deschamps.
HACH 190E856

717 LORENZACCIO (exc., orig. French)
Pierre Vaneck. In anth. HACH
320E058

718 ON NE BADINE PAS AVEC L'AMOUR
(orig. French)
J.-P. Aumont; P. Bertin; P.
Larquey; R. Suplex; R. Vattier;
M. Delavaivre; J. Morane; P.
Carton. DECCA 163.555/6 (2 pd)

719 ON NE BADINE PAS AVEC L'AMOUR
(orig. French)
Vattier; Parédès; Moulinot;
Bertin; Etcheverry; Sapritch;
Vimes. HACH ESH 320.959 (3 pd)

720 ON NE BADINE PAS AVEC L'AMOUR
(exc., orig. French)
S. Flon; C. Lasquin. In anth.
ADÈS TS 30 LA 522

721 ON NE BADINE PAS AVEC L'AMOUR
(exc., orig. French)
Gerard Philipe; Suzanne Flon;
Christane Lasquin. In anth.
ADÈS 13 030, also in 7.005/6

722 ON NE BADINE PAS AVEC L'AMOUR
(exc., orig. French)
J.-P. Aumont; J. Morane. DECCA
455.568 (pd45)

723 ON NE BADINE PAS AVEC L'AMOUR
(exc., orig. French)
Pierre Vaneck. In anth. HACH
320E058, also in 320E898

724 ON NE BADINE PAS AVEC L'AMOUR
(exc., orig. French)
M. Delavaivre; B. Dhéran. LUM
LD 1.277 (pd45)

725 ON NE SAURAIT PENSER À TOUT
(orig. French)
Escande; Charon; Manuel;
Gaudeau; Winter. PAT C061-
10.629; also DTX 216

Namiki Gohei
726 KANJINCHO (in English as THE
SUBSCRIPTION LIST)

Institute for Advanced Studies
in the Theatre Arts. LC T 5270
(at)

Nestroy, Johann
727 LUMPAZI VAGABUNDUS (orig. German)
Erich Auer; Heinz Conrads; Fritz
Muliar; Alma Seidler; Käthe
Gold; Christine Hörbiger; Fred
Liewehr; Hans Thimig; Leo-
pold Rudolf; Louise Martini;
Marianne Schönauer; Karl Far-
kas. AMADEO AVRS 1021/22 (2 pd)

728 SCHLIMMEN BUBEN IN DER SCHULE
(orig. German)
Richard Eybner; Hermann Thimig;
Heinz Conrads; Egon von Jordan;
Fritz Muliar; Lotte Ledl; Dag-
ny Servaes. AMADEO AVRS 1004

Nicolaj, Aldo
729 SALZ UND TABAK (orig. German)
Therese Giehse. In anth.
DEUTGR 140 012

Norton, Thomas. jt. auth. with
Sackville, Thomas, q. v.

Oboler, Arch
730 DROP DEAD
CAPITOL ST 1763

O'Casey, Sean
731 JUNO AND THE PAYCOCK
Seamus Kavanagh as Jack Boyle;
Siobhan McKenna as Juno Boyle;
Leo Leydon as Johnny Boyle;
Maureen Cusack as Mary Boyle;
Cyril Cusack as Daly; Maire
Kean as Marsie Madigan. ANGEL
3540 (2 pd); also CAED TRS 358
(2 pd) and CDL 5358 (2 ac);
also SERAPH IB 6014

732 JUNO AND THE PAYCOCK (exc.)
Read by the author. In anth.
CAED TC 1012, also in CDL 51012

733 PICTURES IN THE HALLWAY (exc.)
Staats Cotsworth; Muriel Kirk-
land; Rae Allen; Alvin Epstein;
Paul Shyre; Robert Geiringer.
RIVERS RLP 7006/7 (2 pd)

734 TIME TO GO
American National Theatre and
Academy. In anth. LC T 3071

O'Casey, Sean, cont'd.
  735 Miscellaneous exc.
          Read by the author. In anth.
          CAED TC 1198, also in CDL 51198

Olmo, Lauro
  736 CAMISA (orig. Spanish)
          Read by the author. In anth.
          AGUILAR GPE 11 102

O'Neill, Eugene
  737 AH, WILDERNESS
          Tony Schwab as Richard Miller;
          Frank Coleman IV as Tommy;
          Lucy Saroyan as Mildred; Alex
          Wipf as Arthur Miller; Ger-
          aldine Fitzgerald as Essie Mil-
          ler; Laurinda Barrett as Lily;
          Stefan Gierasch as Sid; Larry
          Gates; Hansford Rowe; Camilla
          Ritchey; William Dolive; Peggy
          Pope; Robert Legionaire; Henry
          Calvert; Brenda Currin. CAED
          TRS 340 (3 pd), also CDL 5340
          (3 ac)
  738 AH, WILDERNESS (exc.)
          Garry Walberg as Boy; Dana Kraus
          as Girl. In anth. AUDIODR 3085
  739 ANNA CHRISTIE (exc.)
          Patricia Barry as Anna; Garry
          Walberg as Matt. In anth. AUDI-
          DR 3085
  740 BEYOND THE HORIZON (exc.)
          Bill Forrest as Rob; Dana Kraus
          as Ruth. In anth. AUDIODR 3085
  741 EMPEROR JONES
          James Earl Jones as Brutus Jones;
          Stefan Gierasch as Henry Smith-
          ers; Osceola Archer as Old Nati-
          ve Woman; Zakes Mokae as Lem.
          CAED TRS 341 (2 pd), also CDL
          5341 (2 ac)
  742 HAIRY APE (exc.)
          Jason Robards, Jr. In anth.
          COLUMB A OL 5900
  743 HUGHIE
          Jason Robards. COLUMB OS 2760,
          also OL 6360
  744 ICEMAN COMETH
          Lee Marvin as Hickey; Fredric
          March as Harry Hope; Robert
          Ryan as Larry Slade; Jeff Brid-
          ges as Don Parritt; Bradford
          Dillman as Willie Oban; Sorrell

Booke; Hildy Brooks; Nancy Juno
Dawson; Evans Evans; Martyn
Green; Moses Gunn; Clifton James; John McLiam; Stephen Pearlman; Tom Pedi; George Voskovec;
Bart Burns; Don McGovern. CAED
TRS 359 (4 pd), also CDL 5359
(4 ac)
  745 ICEMAN COMETH (exc.)
          Jason Robards, Jr. In anth.
          COLUMB AOL 5900
  746 LONG DAY'S JOURNEY INTO NIGHT
          Geraldine Fitzgerald as Mary
          Tyrone; Robert Ryan as James Ty-
          rone; Stacy Keach as James Tyro-
          ne Jr., James Naughton as Ed-
          mund Tyrone; Paddy Croft as
          Cathleen. CAED TRS 350 (4 pd),
          also CDL 5350 (4 ac)
  747 LONG DAY'S JOURNEY INTO NIGHT
  (exc.)
          Jason Robards. In anth. COLUMB
          A OL 5900
  748 MOON FOR THE MISBEGOTTEN
          Salome Jens as Josie Hogan;
          Jack Kehoe as Mike Hogan; W. B.
          Brydon as Phil Hogan; Micha-
          el Ryan as James Tyrone; Gar-
          ry Mitchell as Harder. CAED
          TRS 333 (3 pd), also CDL 5333
          (3 ac)
  749 MOON FOR THE MISBEGOTTEN (exc.)
          Jason Robards, Jr. In anth.
          COLUMB A OL 5900
  750 MORE STATELY MANSIONS (exc.)
          Ingrid Bergman as Deborah:
          Arthur Hill as Simon; Col-
          leen Dewhurst as Simon's Wife;
          Vincent Dowling; Helen Craig;
          Robert Earl Jones; Fred Stewart;
          Lawrence Linville; Richard
          Bowler. CAED TRS 331 (3 pd),
          also CDL 5331 (3 ac)
  751 MOURNING BECOMES ELECTRA
          Jane Alexander as Lavinia;
          Lee Richardson as Ezra Mannon;
          Peter Thompson as Orin; Sada
          Thompson as Christine; Roy
          Cooper; Robert Stattel; Mau-
          reen Anderman; Manry Cooper;
          Matt Conley; Martha Miller;
          Janice Fuller; Robert Blumen-
          feld; Gene Nye; Tom Tarpey;
          Edwin McDonough. CAED TRS 345

(4 pd), also CDL 5345 (4 ac)
752 MOURNING BECOMES ELECTRA (exc.)
      Bill Forrest as Orin; Dana
      Kraus as Lavinia. In anth.
      AUDIODR 3085
753 STRANGE INTERLUDE
      William Prince as Charles Mars-
      den; Franchart Tone as Henry
      Leeds; Geraldine Page as Nina
      Leeds; Ben Gazzara as Darrell;
      Pat Hingle as Sam Evans; Betty
      Field as Amos Evans; Richard
      Thomas as Gordon Evans; Jane
      Fonda as Madeline Arnold;
      Geoffrey Horne as Gordon Evans.
      COLUMB DOS 688, also DOL 288
      (5 pd)
754 STRANGE INTERLUDE (exc.)
      Patricia Barry as Nina; Garry
      Walberg as Sam; Bill Forrest as
      Ned. In anth. AUDIODR 3085

Orczy, Emmuska
755 SCARLET PIMPERNEL (exc.)
      Ian Richardson. CAED CDL 51647
      (ac)

Orengo, Luigi
756 SOTTO A CHI TOCCA (orig. Italian)
      Gilberto Govi; Enrico Ardizzone;
      Luigi Dameri; Sergio Fosco; Anna
      Bolens; Mercedes Brognoli; Ari-
      ano Praga; Anna Caroli. CETRA
      LPB 35046 (pd), also MC 164 (ac)

Orlovitz, Gil
757 GRAY (exc.)
      Read by the author. LC T 2898
      (at)

Osborne, John
758 LOOK BACK IN ANGER (exc.)
      PROTHM 1EP 5 (ac)
759 LUTHER
      Stacy Keach; Alan Badel; Judi
      Dench; Hugh Griffith; Patrick
      Magee; Robert Stephens; Leo-
      nard Rossiter; Peter Cellier;
      Thomas Heathcote; Julian Glo-
      ver; Matthew Guiness; Maurice
      Denham; Bruce Carstairs; Mal-
      colm Stoddard. CAED TRS 363
      (2 pd), also CDL 5363 (2 ac)

Ostrovsky, Alexander
760 BEDNOST' NE POROK (orig. Russian)
      Maly Theatre, Moscow. MK D
      013259-62 (2 pd)
761 BESHANYE DEN'GI (orig. Russian)
      Maly Theatre, Moscow. MK D
      013069-76 (4 pd)
762 GORACHEE SERDTSE (orig. Russian)
      Moscow Arts Theatre. MK D
      011163-70 (4 pd)
763 GROZA (orig. Russian)
      Maly Theatre, Moscow. MK D
      010559-64 (3 pd)
764 POSLEDNYAYA ZHERTVA (exc., orig.
      Russian)
      Moscow Art Theatre. MK D
      013111-16 (3 pd)
765 POSLEDNYAYA ZHERTVA (orig.
      Russian)
      SSSR D 097/104 (4 pd)
766 SHUTNIKI (exc., orig. Russian)
      Yu. Tolubeyev; L. Shelentsova.
      In anth. MK D 10597-8

Ostuzhev, Aleksandr Alekseevich
767 Miscellaneous exc.
      In anth. MELOD 12133-4

Ottolenghi, Giuseppe
768 IN PRETURA (orig, Italian)
      Gilberto Govi; Anna Caroli;
      Luigi Dameri; Bruno Smith;
      Enza Turco; Sandro Merli;
      Armando Bandini; Vittorio Duse.
      CETRA LPB 35047 (pd), also MC
      168 (ac)

Pagnol, Marcel
769 CÉSAR (orig. French)
      Raimu as César. PAT CTX 40.321
770 FANNY (orig. French)
      COLUMB FH 502
771 FANNY (orig. French)
      Catherine Rouvel as Fanny.
      In anth. HACH 320E920
772 MARIUS (orig. French)
      COLUMB CCTX 240.322 D
773 MARIUS (orig. French)
      Jean Sagols as Marius.
      In anth. HACH 320E920
774 SCHPOUNTZ (orig. French)
      Henri Tisot as Irénée; Catherine
      Rouvel as Françoise. In anth.
      HACH 320E920

Pagnol, Marcel, cont'd.
   775 TOPAZE (orig. French)
         Fernand Gravey as Topaze;
         Marie Daems as Susy Courtois;
         Henri Vilbert as Régis; René
         Clermont as Tamise; Duvaleix;
         Genevieve Badin; Germaine Grain-
         val; Robert Le Flon; Dominique
         Varennes. FEST FLD 171 (3 pd)

Palmerini, Ugo
   776 ARTICOLO V (orig. Italian)
         Gilberto Govi; Pina Camera;
         Anna Caroli; Mercedes Brog-
         noli; Claudio D'Amelio; Enrico
         Ardizzone; Jole Lorena; Nella
         Meroni. CETRA LPB 35041/42
         (2 pd)

Peretz, I. L.
   777 BONTCHE SCHWEIG
         TIKVA
   778 TALE OF CHELM
         TIKVA

Perl, Arnold
   779 TEVYA AND HIS DAUGHTERS
         Mike Kellin; Anna Berger;
         Paul E. Richards; Carroll Con-
         roy; Conrad Bromberg; Joan Har-
         vey; Howard Da Silva. COLUMB
         OL 5225

Pick, Rudolf
   780 NELKENBURG; EIN RITTERLICH SPIEL
         (orig. German)
         Fritz Muliar. In anth. PREISR
         PR 3238

Pinero, Arthur
   781 TRELAWNY
         TIMLIF (vc 3/4)

Pinter, Harold
   782 HOMECOMING
         Cyril Cusack as Sam; Ian Holm
         as Lenny; Michael Jayston as
         Teddy; Vivien Merchant as Ruth;
         Terence Rigby as Joey; Paul
         Rogers as Max. CAED TRS 361
         (2 pd), also CDL 5361 (2 ac)
   783 NO MAN'S LAND
         John Gielgud as Spooner; Ralph
         Richardson as Hirst; Terence

Rigby as Briggs. CAED TRS
369 (2 pd), also CDL 5369 (2 ac)

Pirandello, Luigi
   784 COSÌ È SE VI PARE (exc., orig.
       Italian)
         Irma and Emma Gramatica. In
         anth. CETRA CLC 0856
   785 ENRICO IV (orig. Italian)
         Ruggero Ruggeri as Enrico;
         Germana Paolieri as Matilda
         Spina; Giovanna Caverzaghi as
         Frida; Gualtiero Rizzi as Nelli;
         Gino Sabbatini as Belcredi;
         Guido Verniani as Genoni.
         CETRA CLC 0909/10 (2 pd)
   786 ENRICO IV (in French as HENRI IV)
         J. Vilar; R. Ciggio. VEGA TNP 6
   787 ENRICO IV (exc., in French as
       HENRI IV)
         Jean Vilar; Y. Gasc; R. Coggio;
         M. Cousonneau. In anth. ADÈS
         TS 30 LA 552; also in SPOA 924
   788 PIACERE DELL' ONESTÀ (exc., in
       French as LA VOLUPTÉ DE L'
       HONNEUR)
         Charles Dullin. In anth.
         ADÈS 7003
   789 SEI PERSONAGGI IN CERCA D'AUTORE
       (exc., in English as SIX CHARAC-
       TERS IN SEARCH OF AN AUTHOR)
         FFHS (16mm film)
   790 SEI PERSONAGGI IN CERCA D'AUTORE
       (in English as SIX CHARACTERS IN
       SEARCH OF AN AUTHOR)
         MANT ISBN 0-699-39100-8 (16mm
         film)
   791 UOMO DAL FIORE IN BOCCA (orig.
       Italian)
         V. Gassmann; E. Aldini; C.
         Montagna; A. Cucari. In anth.
         CETRA CLC 0824
   792 Miscellaneous exc., in French
         Balachova; Bretty; Faure;
         C. Pitoeff; Blin; Debucourt;
         Ledoux; Meyer; Paturel;
         Vilar; Vitold. In anth. HACH
         ESH 320.937

Plautus
   793 AMPHITRYON (in French)
         Parédès.   In anth. HACH
         320E909

794 AULULARIA (in French as LA
      MARMITE)
        Parédès. In anth. HACH
        320E909
795 POENULUS (in French as LES
      CARTHAGINOIS)
        Maurin; Rochefort; Virlo-
        jeux. In anth. HACH 320E909

Pogodin, Nikolai
  796 KREMLEVSKIE KURANTY (in orig.
      Russian)
        Moscow Art Theatre. MK ND
        03834-41 (4 pd)

Puget, Claude André
  797 GRAND POUCET (orig. French)
        Read by the author. LVA 32
  798 JOURS HEUREUX (orig. French)
        Read by the author. LVA 29

Pushkin, Alexander Sergeyevich
  799 KAMENNYY GOST' (exc., orig.
      Russian)
        A. Tarasova; V. Kachalov. In
        anth. MK D 9385-6
  800 MOZART I SALIERI (exc., orig.
      Russian)
        Y. Yakhontov. In anth. MK D
        04578-9
  801 PIR VO VREMYA CHUMY (exc.,
      orig. Russian)
        V. Kachalov. In anth. MK
        D 9385-6
  802 RUSALKA (exc., orig. Russian)
        O. Malysheva; Ye. Turchaninova.
        In anth. MK D 9385-6
  803 SKUPOY RYKAR (exc., orig. Russian)
        A. Ostozhev. In anth. MK D
        9385-6

Qualtinger, Helmut, and Merz,
  Carl
  804 HINRICHTUNG (exc., orig. German)
        Helmut Qualtinger. PREISR SPR
        3134

Racine, Jean
  805 ALEXANDRE (exc., orig. French)
        In anth. HACH 320E836
  806 ANDROMAQUE (orig. French)
        Catherine Sellers as Andromaque;
        Nita Klein as Hermione; Lau-
        rent Terzieff as Oreste; George

Descrières as Pyrrhus; Jean
        Negroni as Recitant; Annie Mon-
        nier; Sabine Ravel. BOR SSB
        103; also SPOA SSB 103
807 ANDROMAQUE (orig. French)
        Jean Deschamps; Pierre Vaneck;
        Jean-Pierre Aumont; Fernand
        Ledoux; Eléonore Hirt; Maria
        Mauban; Natalie Nerval. HACH
        320E834/35 (2 pd)
808 ANDROMAQUE (exc., orig. French)
        J. Chevrier; M. Tristani; M.
        Bell; M. Marquet; M. Hermant.
        DECCA 163.131
809 ANDROMAQUE (exc., orig. French)
        In anth. GMS D 7013
810 ANDROMAQUE (exc., orig. French)
        M. Mauban. HACH 190E854/5 (2 pd)
811 ANDROMAQUE (exc., orig. French)
        In anth. HACH 320E836
812 ANDROMAQUE (exc., orig. French)
        Jean Yonnel as Oreste; Mau-
        rice Escande as Pyrrhus; Louis
        Eymond as Pylade; Véra Ko-
        rène as Hermione; Annia Du-
        caux as Andromaque. PERIOD
        FRL 1492; also PLEI T 541
813 ANDROMAQUE (exc., orig. French)
        R. Faure; C. Nollier; B. Cremer;
        C. Carpentier; S. Delannoy;
        R. Miller. PHIL E1 E9.145
        (pd45)
814 ATHALIE (orig. French)
        Maria Meriko; Jean Deschamps;
        Michel Bouquet; Bernard Noël;
        Maria Mauban; Didier Haudepin.
        HACH 320E862/64 (3 pd)
815 ATHALIE (orig. French)
        Antoine Balpétré as Joad;
        G. Dalton; P. Barrat; Louis
        Brézé as Abner; Jean Cabanis as
        Ismaël; Pierre Salas as Aza-
        rias; Fanny Robiane as Athalie;
        Madeleine Roland as Josabeth;
        Simone Rouyer as Joas; A. Ber-
        toli. PLEI P 3.097
816 ATHALIE (exc., orig. French)
        Deschamps; Meriko. HACH 190E
        967
817 ATHALIE (exc., orig. French)
        In anth. HACH 320E812
818 ATHALIE (exc., orig. French)
        In anth. HACH 320E836
819 ATHALIE (exc., orig. French)
        In anth. HACH 320.914

Racine, Jean, cont'd.
  820 BAJAZET (exc., orig. French)
        In anth. HACH 320E836
  821 BÉRÉNICE (orig. French)
        M. Escande; P.-E. Deiber;
        J. Marchat; L. Eymond; J.
        Deschamps; A. Ducaux; J.
        Morane. PAT DTX 240/41 (2 pd)
  822 BÉRÉNICE (exc., orig. French)
        Descant; Aminel; Leuvrais;
        Rousselet. BOR SSB 118
  823 BÉRÉNICE (exc., orig. French)
        Gérard Philipe; Maria Casarès.
        In anth. FEST FLD 166
  824 BÉRÉNICE (exc., orig. French)
        Comédie Française. GMS D
        7050/51 (2 pd)
  825 BÉRÉNICE (exc., orig. French)
        GMS D7065
  826 BÉRÉNICE (exc., orig. French)
        In HACH 320E836
  827 BÉRÉNICE (exc., orig. French)
        André Haber as Titus; Pierre
        Barrat as Antiochus; Louis
        Brézé as Paulin; Fanny Robiane
        as Bérénice; Jeanne Hardeyn as
        Phénice. PERIOD FRL 1514;
        also PLEI P 3.101
  828 BRITANNICUS (orig. French)
        Michel Bouquet; Casarès; Topart;
        Guiomar. BOR SSB 110; also
        SPOA SSB 110
  829 BRITANNICUS (orig. French)
        P. Vaneck; Libolt; J. Deschamps;
        J. Topart; M. Casarès; Versini;
        Fechter. HACH 320E881-3 (3 pd)
  830 BRITANNICUS (orig. French)
        Hirsch; Deiber; Bernardy;
        Chaumette; Ducaux; Ajoret;
        Gence. PAT C061-10633-35 (3 pd)
  831 BRITANNICUS (exc., orig. French)
        Versini; Vaneck; Topart.
        HACH 190E107
  832 BRITANNICUS (exc., orig. French)
        Casarès; Vaneck; Topart. HACH
        190E108
  833 BRITANNICUS (exc., orig. French)
        In anth. HACH 320E836
  834 BRITANNICUS (exc., orig. French)
        Antoine Balpétré as Burrhus;
        Gérald Dalton as Néron; Pierre
        Barrat as Britannicus; Louis
        Brézé as Narcisse; Fanny Robi-
        ane as Agrippine; Anne Bertoli

        as Junie. PLEI P 3.096
  835 ESTHER (orig. French)
        Catherine Sellers; Eléonore
        Hirt; Jean Deschamps; Pierre
        Blanchar; Michel Bouquet;
        Noël; Nerval. HACH 320E839/
        40 (2 pd)
  836 ESTHER (exc., orig. French)
        Sellers. HACH 190E890
  837 ESTHER (exc., orig. French)
        In anth. HACH 320E836
  838 ESTHER (exc., orig. French)
        A. Balpétré; G. Dalton;
        L. Breze; J. Cabanis; P.
        Barrat; F. Robiane; M. Ro-
        land; J. Hardeyn; A. Bertoli.
        PLEI P 3.098
  839 IPHIGÉNIE (orig. French)
        Deschamps; Monfort; Topart;
        Cingal; Paulin; Nerval.
        HACH ESH 320.950 (3 pd)
  840 IPHIGÉNIE (exc., orig. French)
        Borgeaud; Casile; Negroni;
        Topart. BOR SSB 122
  841 IPHIGÉNIE (exc., orig. French)
        In anth. HACH 320E836
  842 IPHIGÉNIE (exc., orig. French)
        Antoine Balpétré as Agamemnon;
        André Haber as Achille; Louis
        Brézé as Ulysse; Fanny Robiane
        as Clytemnestra; Claude Chantal
        as Iphigénie; P. Salas; A.
        Bertoli. PERIOD FRL 1515; also
        PLEI P 3-103
  843 MITHRIDATE (exc., orig. French)
        In anth. HACH 320E836
  844 PHÈDRE (orig. French)
        Marie Bell as Phèdre; Henriette
        Barreau as Oenone; Raymond Ge-
        ronne as Théramène; Claude Gi-
        raud as Hippolyte; Robert Le-
        gran as Panope. GMS D 7120/22
        (3 pd)
  845 PHÈDRE (orig. French)
        Riva; Conte; Versini; Deiber;
        Maistre; Paulin. HACH ESH
        320.928 (3 pd)
  846 PHÈDRE (orig. French)
        M. Escande; A. Falcon; J.
        Chevrier; M. Bell; M. Dal-
        mes; L. Conte. PLEI T 512
        (2 pd)
  847 PHÈDRE (exc., orig. French)
        Maria Casarès as Phèdre;

Germaine Kerjean as Oenone;
Pierre Ollivier as Thésée;
Jean Negroni as Récitant;
Michel Ruhl as Hippolyte. BOR
SSB 106; also SPOA SSB 106
848 PHÈDRE (exc., orig. French)
In anth. GMS D 7013
849 PHÈDRE (exc., orig. French)
In anth. HACH 320E812
850 PHÈDRE (exc., orig. French)
In anth. HACH 320E836
851 PHÈDRE (exc., orig. French)
Maurice Escande as Thésée; Jean
Chevrier as Théramène; André
Falcon as Hippolyte; Maria Bell
as Phèdre; Mony Dalmès as Ari-
cie; Louise Conte as Oenone.
PERIOD FRL 1505
852 PHÈDRE (exc., orig French and
English)
Edwige Feuillere as Phèdre
(in French); M. Seldes as
Phèdre (in English). FOLK
9909
853 PHÈDRE (exc., in English)
Institute for Advanced Studies
in the Theatre Arts. LC T 4731
(at)
854 PHÈDRE (exc., in German as
PHAEDRA)
Maria Wimmer. In anth.
DEUTGR 140 011
855 PLAIDEURS (orig. French)
Denise Grey; Simone Valère;
Lucien Baroux; J. Desailly;
F. Ledoux; J. Parédès; H.
Virlojeux. HACH 329E841
856 PLAIDEURS (orig. French)
Jean Schmitt as Dandin; Jean-
Claude Balard as Léandre;
Jacques Gheusi as Chicanneau;
Pierre Pernet as Petit-Jean;
Guy Parigot as l'Intimé;
Françoise Valois as Isabelle;
Jeanette Granval as Comtesse.
857 PLAIDEURS (exc., orig. French)
Georges Chamarat as Dandin.
Olivier Hussenot as Chicanneau;
Jeanne Fusier-Gir as La Com-
tesse; Danielle Ajoret as Isabe-
lle; Alain Feydeau as Léandre.
BOR SSB 108; also SPOA SSB 108
858 PLAIDEURS (exc., orig. French)
Baroux; Desailly; Parédès;

Virlojeux. HACH 190E909
859 PLAIDEURS (exc., orig. French)
Parédès. In anth. HACH 320.914
860 Miscellaneous exc., orig. French
G. Descrières; J.-L. Jemma;
J. Deschamps; M. Mauban; Y.
Furet; J. Negroni; J. Maurane;
N. Nerval; P. Blanchar; D.
Ajoret; C. Sellers. In anth.
HACH 320E836
861 Miscellaneous exc., orig. French
In anth. HACH 320E924

Radványi, Netty
862 SIEBTE KREUZ (orig. German)
Willi A. Kleinau; Harry Hin-
demith. LITERA 860134-35 (2pd)

Raimund, Ferdinand
863 VERSCHWENDER (orig. German)
Marianne Schönauer as Fee Che-
ristane; Walter Berg as Azur;
Fred Liewehr as Julius; Heinz
Moog as Wolf; Josef Meinrad as
Valentin; Inge Konradi as Rosa;
Albin Skoda; Andreas Wolf; Gün-
ther Bauer; Alma Seidler; Hans
Thimig; Lona Dubois; Carl Bosse;
Adolf Böhmer; Peter Gerhard;
Guido Wieland; Hanns Obonya;
Erna Frost; Friedl Jary; Claus
Logau; Josef Wichart; Wolfgang
Gasser. AMADEO AVRS 6200/01
(2 pd)

Rakhmanov, Leonid
864 BURNYI SKLON ZHIZNI (orig.
Russian)
Moscow Art Theatre. MK D
010053-6

Rattigan, Terence
865 BROWNING VERSION
Lee Richardson; Sheila Allen;
Keith Reddin; Edmond Genest;
Dalton Dearborn; Josh Clark;
Joyce Fideo. CAED TRS 370
(2 pd); also CDL 5370 (2 ac)
866 CAUSE CELÈBRE
Diana Dors. In anth. MINN
29126-31 (3 pd)

Renard, Jules
  867 PAIN DE MÉNAGE (orig. French)
        Simone Valère; Jean Desailly.
        In anth. ADÈS 7016/17 (2 pd)
  868 PAIN DE MÉNAGE (orig. French)
        In anth. RODALE RO 3
  869 PLAISIR DE ROMPRE (orig. French)
        Madelaine Renaud; Bernard Noël.
        In anth. ADÈS 7016/17
  870 POIL DE CAROTTE (original French)
        Madeleine Renaud; Georges Wil-
        son; Gérard Lartigan; Denise
        Benoit. In anth. ADÈS 7016/17
  871 POIL DE CAROTTE (orig. French)
        Seigner; Roussillon; Bovy;
        De Chauveron. PAT C061-10.628,
        also DTX 253

Richards, Ivor Armstrong
  872 TOMORROW MORNING, FAUSTUS!
        Read by the author. LC T 3345
        (at)

Ridley, Arnold
  873 GHOST TRAIN
        LONDON LLP 414

Rinuccini, Ottavio
  874 DAFNE (exc., orig. Italian)
        C. Antonini. In anth. EIA
        DSM 200

Rivemale, Alexandre
  875 AZOUK (orig. French)
        Read by the author.

Robinson, Edwin Arlington
  876 TRISTRAM
        Arnold Moss. LC T 3174 (at)

Robinson, Lennox
  877 FAR-OFF HILLS (exc.)
        Read by the author. In anth.
        HARVOC D 1018/9
  878 WHITEHEADED BOY (exc.)
        Read by the author. In anth.
        HARVOC D 1018/9

Roblès, Emmanuel
  879 MONTSERRAT (orig. French)
        Denis Manuel; François Chau-
        mette; Michel Etcheverry.
        ADÈS 16.033

Romains, Jules
  880 KNOCK (orig. French)
        L. Jouvet; I. Reyner; R. Bou-
        quet. In anth. COLUMB
        ESJF 1
  881 KNOCK (orig. French)
        Read by the author. LVA 22
  882 KNOCK (orig. French)
        Bernard Blier; Jean Brochard;
        Jane Marken. PERIOD FRL
        1536
  883 KNOCK (exc., orig. French)
        Louis Jouvet; Brochard. In
        anth. ADÈS 7007/8, also in
        19.015
  884 MONSIEUR LE TROUHADEC SAISI PAR
      LA DÉBAUCHE (orig. French)
        Read by the author. LVA 26

Rostand, Edmond
  885 AIGLON (orig. French)
        Pierre Vaneck as Duc de Reich-
        stadt; Jacques Dumesnil as
        Flambeau; François Maistre as
        Prince de Metternich; Henri
        Nassiet as Empereur Franz;
        Raymond Pelissier as Marmont;
        Serge Sauvion as Prokesch;
        Gaëton Jor; Jacques Bouvier;
        Michel Duplaix; Marius Babinot;
        Anne Carrère; Gisèle Touret as
        Comtesse Camerata; Hénia Suchar
        as Thérèse de Lorget; Marie
        Laurence as Archiduchesse.
        DEUTGR 168 900/901 (2 pd), also
        2761.001, also 720-1 IY
  886 AIGLON (exc., orig. French)
        Sarah Bernhardt. In anth.
        AUDIOR 2465
  887 AIGLON (exc., orig. French)
        Maurin; Vibert; Moulinot.
        In anth. HACH 320E969
  888 AIGLON (exc., orig. French)
        J. Martinelli; M. Mélinand.
        In anth. LUM LD 1.212
  889 AIGLON (exc., orig. French)
        P. Lecomte; P. Stephen. In
        anth. LUM LD 1.273
  890 CHANTECLER (exc., orig. French)
        J. Martinelli; M. Mélinand.
        In anth. LUM LD 1.212
  891 CYRANO DE BERGERAC (orig. French)
        Comédie Française. GMS DISC
        7034-36 (3 pd)

892 CYRANO DE BERGERAC (orig. French)
    Jean-Paul Coquelin as Cyrano;
    Jacques Clancy as Christian de
    Neuvillette; Etienne Bierry as
    Ragueneau; Jeanne Boitel as Ro-
    xane; René Delbon as Le Bret;
    Renaud-Mary as Conte de Guiche;
    Paul Bonifas as Carbon. PAT
    DTX 161/63 (3 pd)
893 CYRANO DE BERGERAC (orig. French)
    D. Sorano; F. Christophe; Marken;
    J. Deschamps; H. Noël; M. Galab-
    ru; B. Noël; Beauchamp. VEGA
    8.040/42 (3 pd), also VAL 25
894 CYRANO DE BERGERAC (in English)
    Ralph Richardson as Cyrano;
    Anna Massey as Roxanne; Peter
    Wyngarde as DeGuiche; John
    Fraser as Christian; Michael
    Gwynn as Le Bret; Ronald Fraser
    as Ragueneau; Peter Bayliss as
    Carbon; John Saunders; Emrys
    James; Ronnie Ibbs; Aubrey Woods;
    Gerald James; Daniel Thorndike;
    James Culliford; Eric Jones;
    John Rogers; Edgar Wreford; Ar-
    thur Hewlett; Gerald Rowlands;
    Norman Mitchell; Gillian Lind;
    Eileen Atkins; Sarah Long; Elvi
    Hale. CAED TRS 306 (3 pd), also
    CDL 5306 (3 ac)
895 CYRANO DE BERGERAC (exc., orig.
    French)
    Piat. In anth. HACH 320.914
896 CYRANO DE BERGERAC (exc., orig.
    French)
    Deschamps; Moulinot; Maurin;
    Vilbert; Jemma; Vattier;
    Casadesus. In anth. HACH
    320E969
897 CYRANO DE BERGERAC (exc., orig.
    French)
    J. Martinelli; M. Mélinand.
    LUM LD 1.211 (pd45)
898 CYRANO DE BERGERAC (exc., orig.
    French)
    Jeanne Provost. In anth. SPOA
    985
899 CYRANO DE BERGERAC (exc., orig.
    French)
    D. Sorano. VEGA V45P2221
    (pd45), also 5.628
900 CYRANO DE BERGERAC (exc., in
    English)
    José Ferrer as Cyrano; Edmund

Trcinski as Narrator; Pa-
    tricia Wheel as Roxanne; Robert
    Carroll as Le Bret; Fran Lett-
    on as Meddler; Vincent Dona-
    hue as Valvert; Ralph Clanton
    as De Guiche. CAPITOL W 283
901 CYRANO DE BERGERAC (exc., in
    English)
    Walter Hampden. LF ISBN 0-
    699-06764-2 (16mm film)
902 CYRANO DE BERGERAC (exc., in
    English)
    Herbert Roland as Cyrano.
    PERIOD FRL 1526
903 Miscallaneous exc.
    In anth. HACH 320.924

Rosten, Norman
904 COME SLOWLY, EDEN
    Kim Hunter. LC T 4941 (at)

Roussin, André
905 GLORIEUSES (orig. French)
    Read by the author. LVA 3
906 MAIN DE CÉSAR (orig. French)
    Read by the author. LVA 17
907 OEUFS DE L'AUTRUCHE (orig.
    French)
    Read by the author. LVA 14
908 PETITE HUTTE (orig. French)
    SONOPR THÉATRE 3
909 RUPTURE (orig. French)
    Read by the author. In anth.
    LVA 12
910 TOMBEAU D'ACHILLE (orig. French)
    Read by the author. In anth.
    LVA 12

Roussin, André, and Gray,
Madeleine
911 HÉLÈNE; OU, LA JOIE DE VIVRE
    (orig. French)
    LVA 7

Rueda, Lope de
912 ACEITUNAS (orig. Spanish)
    Manuel Durán as Toruvio;
    Eva Llorens as Agueda; Ma-
    ria Teresa Navarro as Menci-
    guela; Alberto Castilla as
    Aloja. In anth. SPOA 863
913 CARÁTULA (orig. Spanish)
    Manuel Durán as Alameda;
    Alberto Castilla as Salcedo.
    In anth. SPOA 864

933 HUIS-CLOS (exc., Orig. French)
      Simone Vannier as Estelle;
      Michel Vitold as Garcia;
      Françoise Fechter as Inès.
      In anth. HACH 320E869
934 MOUCHES (exc., orig. French)
      Nathalie Nerval as Électre;
      Sami Frey as Oreste. In anth.
      HACH 320E869
935 SÉQUESTRÉS D'ALTONA (exc., orig.
    French)
      Fernand Ledoux as Le Père;
      Michel Duchaussoy as Frantz.
      In anth. HACH 320E869

Sastre, Alfonso
936 GUILLERMO TELL TIENE LOS OJOS
    TRISTES (orig. Spanish)
      Read by the author. In anth.
      AGUILAR GPE 11 102

Schiller, Friedrich
937 BRAUT VON MESSINA (exc., orig.
    German)
      W. Wittsack. In anth. INSPRACH
      TOW 1027/36
938 DON CARLOS (orig. German)
      Schiller-Theater, Berlin.
      TELEF SMA 25072-T (3 pd)
939 DON CARLOS (exc., orig. German)
      Ernst Deutsch. In anth. DEUTGR
      140 013
940 DON CARLOS (exc., orig. German)
      Maria Becker; Ernst Deutsch;
      Ernst Ginsberg; Joana Maria
      Gorvin; Rolf Henniger; Hermine
      Körner; Werner Kraus. In anth.
      DEUTGR 3321 107
941 DON CARLOS (exc., orig. German)
      W. Wittsack. In anth. INSPRACH
      TOW 1027/36
942 JUNGFRAU VON ORLEANS (exc., orig.
    German)
      Walter Wittsack. In anth.
      INSPRACH TOW 1027/36
943 KABALE UND LIEBE (orig. German)
      Will Quadflieg; Walter Franck;
      Leopold Rudolf; Heidemarie Hath-
      eyer; Maria Schell; Nicole
      Heesters; Ewald Balser; B. Hüb-
      ner; A. Gessner; E. Ponto.
      DEUTGR 2759 003 (2 pd)
944 KABALE UND LIEBE (exc., orig. Ger-
    man)
      DEUTGR 40 004

945 KABALE UND LIEBE (exc., orig.
    German)
      Erich Ponto. In anth. DEUTGR
      140 025
946 KABALE UND LIEBE (exc., orig.
    German)
      Ewald Balser; Bruno Hübner;
      Walter Franck; Heidemarie
      Hatheyer; Nicole Heesters;
      Will Quadflieg; Maria Schell.
      DEUTGR 2571 121, also 3321 121
      (ac)
947 KABALE UND LIEBE (exc., orig.
    German)
      In anth. GMS 7125
948 KABALE UND LIEBE (exc., orig.
    German)
      Walter Süssenguth as Von
      Walter; Horst Kaspar as Fer-
      dinand; Gerda Maria Terno as
      Luise; Heinrich George as
      Miller. In anth. TELEF 6.41003
949 MARIA STUART (orig. German)
      Judith Holzmeister; Liselotte
      Schreiner; Vera Balser-Eberle;
      Fred Liewehr; Albin Skoda;
      Walter Reyer; Heinz Moog.
      PERIOD FRL 1554; also AMADEO
      FRL 1554
950 MARIA STUART (exc., orig. Ger-
    man)
      Maria Becker. In anth. DEUTGR
      40 008
951 MARIA STUART (exc., orig. German)
      Maria Becker as Elisabeth; Jo-
      ana Maria Gorvin as Maria Stu-
      art; Karl Blühm as Leicester;
      Hans Thimig as Shrewsbury. In
      anth. DEUTGR 42 004
952 MARIA STUART (exc., orig. German)
      Maria Wimmer. In anth. DEUTGR
      140 011
953 MARIA STUART (exc., in Italian as
    MARIA STUARDA)
      Irma and Emma Gramatica. In
      anth. CETRA CLC 0856
954 RÄUBER (orig. German)
      Peter Lühr; Helmut Griem;
      Martin Benrath; Gisela Stein;
      Nikolaus Paryla. DEUTGR 43 559
      (3 pd), also 2760 101
955 RÄUBER (exc., orig. German)
      Gerd Brüdern as Moser; Rolf
      Henniger as Moor; Ernst Gins-
      berg as Franz Moor. DEUTGR 44005

980 VACH-LACH LAKIS (orig. Yiddish)
    Read by the author. In anth.
    BANNER BAS 1008

Seami
  981 HAGOROMO (orig. Japanese)
      Tatsuo Sakurama. In anth-
      CAED TC 2019
  982 KANTAN (orig. Japanese)
      Hisao Kanze. In anth. CAED
      TC 2019

Shaffer, Peter Levin
  983 ROYAL HUNT OF THE SUN (exc.)
      PROTHM 1EP 2 (ac)

Shakespeare, William
  984 ALL'S WELL THAT ENDS WELL
      Morag Hood as Helena; Anton
      Lesser as Rossillion; Robert
      Stephens as Parolles. BBC
      ECN 192 (2 ac)
  985 ALL'S WELL THAT ENDS WELL
      Claire Bloom; Flora Robson;
      John Stride; Eric Portman.
      CAED SRS 212 (3 pd), also
      CDL 5212 (3 ac)
  986 ALL'S WELL THAT ENDS WELL
      Michael Hordern as King of
      France; James Taylor Whitehead
      as Duke of Florence; Peter Orr
      as Bertram; Max Adrian as Lafeu;
      Patrick Wymark as Parolles;
      John Barton as Rinaldo;
      Gordon Gardner and John Tracy-
      Phillips as Gentlemen; Roy
      Dotrice as Lavache; Philip
      Strick as Soldier; Margaretta
      Scott as Countess of Rousillon;
      Prunella Scales as Helena;
      Esme Church as Widow; Janette
      Richer as Diana; Joan Hart as
      Mariana. LONDON M 4370 (3 pd),
      also ARGO ZPR 229/31, RG 354/6,
      and ZRG 5354/6
  987 ALL'S WELL THAT ENDS WELL
      Ian Charleson as Bertram; An-
      gela Down as Helena; Celia
      Johnson as Countess Rosillion-
      TIMLIF V 6012C (3 vc 3/4)
  988 ALL'S WELL THAT ENDS WELL (exc.)
      Edith Evans as Countess Rousill-
      ion; Vanessa Redgrave as Helena.
      LIVSHA SWW 17A-18A

989 ANTONY AND CLEOPATRA
    Pamela Brown as Cleopatra;
    Anthony Quayle as Antony; Paul
    Daneman as Octavius Caesar;
    James Hayter; David Dodimead as
    M. Aemilius Lepidus; J. Gwill-
    lim; M. Davenport; M. Meacham;
    E. Wreford; J. Hepple; C. John.
    CAED SRS 235 (3 pd), also
    CDL 5235 (3 ac)
990 ANTONY AND CLEOPATRA
    Anthony Quayle; Pamela Brown.
    EAV B1RR083 (3 pd)
991 ANTONY AND CLEOPATRA
    Richard Johnson as Antony;
    Robert Eddison as Octavius
    Caesar; Miles Malleson as Lepi-
    dus; Peter Orr as Sextus Pom-
    peius; Patrick Wymark as Domi-
    tius Enobarbus; John Tracy-
    Philips as Ventidius; Ian Holm
    as Eros; Terrence Hardiman
    as Scarus; James Taylor White-
    head as Maecenas; John Tydeman
    as Agrippa; Gary Watson as Do-
    labella; Ian Lang as Proculeius;
    Anthony Arlidge as Menas; Juli-
    an Curry as Menecrates; George
    Rylands as Varrius; George Ry-
    lands as Taurus; Roger Croucher
    as Canidius; David Jones as
    Silius; Philip Strick as Ale-
    xas; Ian McKellen as Mardian;
    Michael Bates as Seleucus;
    Giles Slaughter as Diomedes;
    Philip Strick as Soothsayer;
    Michael Bates as Clown; Irene
    Worth as Cleopatra; Diana Rigg
    as Octavia; Prunella Scales as
    Charmian; Jill Balcon as Iras.
    LONDON M 4427 (4 pd), also
    ARGO RG 307/10, also ZRG 5307/
    10, also ZPR 221/4; also ARGO
    KZPC 221/4 and SAY 63 (4 ac)
992 ANTONY AND CLEOPATRA
    Colin Blakely as Antony; Jane
    Lapotaire as Cleopatra. TIMLIF
    V 6013 C (3 vc 3/4)
993 ANTONY AND CLEOPATRA (exc.)
    Irene Worth. In anth. ARGO NF4
994 ANTONY AND CLEOPATRA (exc.)
    Barbara Leigh-Hunt; Tony Church;
    Pippa Guard. In anth. ARGO
    SAY 41

Shakespeare, cont'd.
  995 ANTONY AND CLEOPATRA (exc.)
        BERLET ISBN 0-8354-1582-1
        (16mm film)
  996 ANTONY AND CLEOPATRA (exc.)
        Anthony Quayle; Pamela Brown;
        Paul Daneman; David Dodimead;
        James Hayter; Jack Gwillim;
        Nigel Davenport; Michael Mea-
        cham; Edgar Wreford; John Saun-
        ders; James Cairncross; Chris-
        topher Guinee; Ronald Ibbs;
        Peter Bayliss; Thomas Kem-
        pinski; Ronnie Stevens; Nor-
        man Rossington; Newton Blick;
        Jeanna Hepple; Caroline John;
        Sarah Long. CAED TC 1183 (pd),
        also CDL 51183 (ac)
  997 ANTONY AND CLEOPATRA (exc.)
        CONTF ISBN 0-699-01362-3
        (16mm film)
  998 ANTONY AND CLEOPATRA (exc.)
        Peter Finch as Antony; Vivien
        Leigh as Cleopatra. LIVSHA
        SAC 9A-10A
  999 ANTONY AND CLEOPATRA (exc.)
        In anth. MICHMED 9706 (16mm
        film, also vc)
 1000 ANTONY AND CLEOPATRA (exc.)
        MICHMED 9709 (16mm film, also
        vc)
 1001 ANTONY AND CLEOPATRA (exc.)
        PROTHM 1ES 11 (ac)
 1002 ANTONY AND CLEOPATRA (exc.)
        E. Martin Browne; Henzie Rae-
        burn. In anth. SPOA 901
 1003 ANTONY AND CLEOPATRA (exc.)
        UNIVED ISBN 0-699-01363-1
        (16mm film)
 1004 ANTONY AND CLEOPATRA (exc., in
        Russian)
        A. Kohonen; G. Yanikovsky;
        D. Sumarokov; T. Arkhangelskaya.
        In anth. MK D 013603-4
 1005 AS YOU LIKE IT
        David King; Clifford Rose; Ian
        Partridge; Roy Dotrice; Frank
        Duncan; Peter Orr; John Shrap-
        nell; Gordon Gardner; John
        Stride; Carleton Hobbs; George
        Rylands; Max Adrian; Norman
        Mitchell; Tony Church; Richard
        Marquand; Denis McCarthy;
        Janet Suzman; Ann Morrish;

        Yvonne Bonnamy; Freda Dowie;
        Peter Moneur; Francis Corke;
        Geoffrey Shaw; Robert Spencer;
        David Munrow; David Pugsley;
        Richard Lee; Philip Picket.
        ARGO SAY 22 and ZPR 180/2
        (3 pd), also K46K32 and KZPC
        180/2 (3 ac)
 1006 AS YOU LIKE IT
        Laurence Olivier; Elisabeth
        Bergner; Sophie Stewart; Hen-
        ry Ainley. BLACKH ISBN 0-
        699-36719-0 (16mm film, also
        vc)
 1007 AS YOU LIKE IT
        Vanessa Redgrave; Keith Michell;
        Max Adrian; Stanley Holloway; De-
        rek Godfrey; Peter Woodthorpe;
        Richard Easton; Eric Chitty;
        John Nettleton; Brian Murray;
        Tony Robertson; Nigel Stock;
        John Gardiner; Norman Ros-
        sington; Terence Scully;
        William Marlowe; John
        Church; Darien Angadi; John
        Shirley Quirke; David Pinto;
        Judith Stott, Zena Walker, Wen-
        dy Craig. CAED SRS 210 (3 pd),
        CDL 5210 (3 ac)
 1008 AS YOU LIKE IT
        Vanessa Redgrave; Stanley Holl-
        oway. EAV B3RR475 (3 pd)
 1009 AS YOU LIKE IT
        L. Olivier. FI (16mm film)
 1010 AS YOU LIKE IT
        The Canadian Players. LC
        T 2729 (at)
 1011 AS YOU LIKE IT
        Hilton Edwards; Michael Mac-
        Liammoir. LIST SKP 1008 (3 pd),
        also CX 108(2 ac)
 1012 AS YOU LIKE IT
        John Barton as Banished Duke;
        Tony Church as Frederick; Pe-
        ter Bingham as Amiens; Anthony
        Jacobs as Jaques; John Arnott
        as Le Beau; David Buck as
        Charles; Tony White as Oliver;
        David Gibson as Orlando; Denys
        Robertson as Adam; John Wilders
        as Touchstone; Gary Watson as
        Corin; Julian Pettifer as Silv-
        ius; John Bird as William;
        George Rylands as Hymen;

Christine Baker as Rosalind;
Wendy Gifford as Celia; Irene
Worth as Phebe; Mary Fenton as
Audrey. LONDON L 4336 (3 pd),
also RG 125/7

1013 AS YOU LIKE IT
Michael MacLiammoir. SPOWRD
123/5 (3 pd), also SW-A4

1014 AS YOU LIKE IT
Helen Mirren; Richard Pasco;
Brian Stirner; James Bolan;
Angharad Rees. TIMLIF V 6001A
(3 vc 3/4)

1015 AS YOU LIKE IT
Elissa Landi; Dennis King; Frank
Morgan; Gail Patrick. YESTER
15291 (at)

1016 AS YOU LIKE IT (exc.)
Edith Evans as Rosalind; Mi-
chael Redgrave as Orlando; Ur-
sula Jeans as Celia; Peter
Coke as Duke Frederick; Jessie
Evans as Phebe. ANGEL 35220

1017 AS YOU LIKE IT (exc.)
Max Adrian; Vanessa Redgrave.
In anth. ARGO SAY 41

1018 AS YOU LIKE IT (exc.)
Eithne Dunne; Eve Watkinson.
AUDIVS 8012 SC (ac)

1019 AS YOU LIKE IT (exc.)
BFA ISBN 0-699-01776-9
(16mm film, also vc 3/3)

1020 AS YOU LIKE IT (exc.)
M. Redgrave. CAED TC 1170

1021 AS YOU LIKE IT (exc.)
Maurice Evans. In anth.
GOLDEN AA 58

1022 AS YOU LIKE IT (exc.)
John Neville as Orlando; Mag-
gie Smith as Rosalind.
LIVSHA SY 13A-14A

1023 AS YOU LIKE IT (exc.)
In anth. MICHMED 9701 (16mm
film, also vc)

1024 AS YOU LIKE IT (exc.)
In anth. SPOA 767

1025 AS YOU LIKE IT (exc.)
Eithne Dunne; Eve Watkinson;
Christopher Casson. SPOA 880
(pd), also SAC 7010 (ac)

1026 AS YOU LIKE IT (exc.)
E. Martin Browne; Henzie Rae-
burn. In anth. SPOA 901

1027 AS YOU LIKE IT (exc., in Italian
as COME VI PARE)

V. Gassman. In anth. CETRA
CLC 0826 (pd), also MC 80 (ac)

1028 COMEDY OF ERRORS
Denis McCarthy as Solinus; Mi-
chael Hordern as Aegeon; George
Rylands as Antipholus; Mich-
ael Bates as Dromio; Peter Orr
as Balthazar; Clive Swift as
Angelo; Terrence Hardiman as
Merchant; Dudley Jones as
Doctor Pinch; Lally Bowers as
Aemilia; Joan Hart as Adriana;
Janet Richer as Luciana and
Luce or Nell; Prunella Scales
as Courtesan. ARGO RG 311-12
(2 pd), also ZRG 5311-2; also
ZPR 124/5 (2 pd), also KZPC
124/5 (2 ac)

1029 COMEDY OF ERRORS
Alec McCowen; Anna Massey; Har-
ry H. Corbett; Finlay Currie;
Graham Crowden; John Moffat;
Bernard Bresslaw; Wallas Eaton;
David Dodimead; Aubrey Richards;
John Saunders; Rosalind Atkin-
son; Mary Miller; Susan Engel;
James Mellor. CAED SRS 205 (2
pd), also CDL 5205 (2 ac)

1030 COMEDY OF ERRORS
LONDON A 4524 (2 pd), also
OSA 1252

1031 COMEDY OF ERRORS
Cyril Cusack; Charles Gray;
Michael Kitchen; Marsha Fitz-
alan; Roger Daltrey; Wendy Hil-
ler; Joanne Pierce; Suzanne
Bertish. TIMLIF V6031F (vc 1/2)

1032 COMEDY OF ERRORS (exc.)
John Neville as Antipholus;
Michael Flanders as Dromio.
LIVSHA SCE 45A-46A

1033 COMEDY OF ERRORS (exc.)
Folio Theatre Players. SPOA
888 (pd), also 7113 (ac)

1034 CORIOLANUS
Richard Pasco as Coriolanus;
Fabia Drake as Volumnia. BBC
ECN 194 (3 ac)

1035 CORIOLANUS
Richard Burton as Coriolanus;
Jessica Tandy as Volumnia; Ken-
neth Haigh as Aufidius; Michael
Hordern as Menenius; Robert
Stephens; Michael Gwynn; Mar-
tin Benson; Douglas Wilmer;

Shakespeare, cont'd.
    CORIOLANUS, cont'd.
        Dafydd Havard; Llewellyn
        Rees; John Gayford; Neil Robin-
        son; Eric Corrie; John Magnus;
        Roland Bartrop; Robert Seagrave;
        Alan Browning; Kenneth Brom-
        field; Robert St. Clair; W. F.
        McCormick; Colin Watson; Tarn
        Bassett; Audrey Fairfax; Lynn
        Gordon.   CAED SRS 226 (3 pd),
        also CDL 5226 (3 ac)
    1036 CORIOLANUS
        Anthony White as Coriolanus;
        John Arnott as Titus Lartius;
        Donald Beves as Cominius; Tony
        Church as Menenius Agrippa;
        Anthony Jacobs as Sicinius Ve-
        lutus; John Wilders as Brutus;
        John Barton as Tullus Aufidius;
        Peter Woodthorpe as Lieuten-
        ant; Irene Worth as Volumnia;
        Dorothy Mulcahy as Virgilia;
        Christine Baker as Gentle woman.
        LONDON 4415 (4 pd), also ARGO
        RG 135/8, also ZPR 225/8
    1037 CORIOLANUS
        Anew McMaster as Coriolanus;
        Robert Andrews as Cominius;
        Christopher Casson as Menenius;
        William Styles as Sicinius;
        Leo Leyden as Brutus; Nancy
        Manningham as Volumnia; James
        Caffrey as Citizen. SPOWRD
        SW 154-157 (4 pd), also
        A17
    1038 CORIOLANUS
        Anthony Pedley; Foss Ackland;
        Irene Worth; Teddy Kempner;
        Alan Howard; Peter Sands.
        TIMLIF V 6025 E (2 vc 1/2)
    1039 CORIOLANUS (in Italian as CORIO-
    LANO)
        Tino Carraro; Wanda Capodaglio;
        Antonio Battistella; Ottavo Fan-
        fani; Franco Graziosi; Cesare
        Polacco; Enzo Tarascio. CETRA
        CLC 0801/2 (2 pd)
    1040 CORIOLANUS (exc.)
        Tony White; Irene Worth. In
        anth. ARGO ZPR 236/9
    1041 CORIOLANUS (exc.)
        John Stride as Coriolanus; Sy-
        bil Thorndike as Volumnia.
        LIVSHA SCL 49/50A

1042 CORIOLANUS (exc.)
        SPOA SA 888 (pd), also 7113(ac)
1043 CYMBELINE
        Boris Karloff as Cymbeline;
        Paul Daneman as Cloten; John
        Fraser as Posthumus Leonatus;
        Walter Hudd as Belarius; John
        Dane as Guiderius; Robin Palmer
        as Arviragus; Pamela Brown as
        Queen; Claire Bloom as Imogen;
        Alan Dobie; Wallas Eaton; James
        Cairncross, Stephen Moore;
        Harold Lang; Eric House; Eric
        Jones; Douglas Muir; Richard
        Dare; Derek Godfrey, Judith
        South. CAED SRS 236 (3 pd),
        also CDL 5236 (3 ac)
1044 CYMBELINE
        Denis McCarthy as Cymbeline;
        David Rowe-Beddoe as Cloten;
        Ian Lang as Leonatus; Terrence
        Hardiman as Belarius; Andrew
        Parkes as Guiderius; John Shar-
        pe as Arviragus; Roger Hammond
        as Philario; Tony White as Ja-
        chimo; Peter Orr as Caius Lu-
        cius; David Coombs as Pisanio;
        Philip Strick as Cornelius and
        Gaoler; Tom Bussman as Cap-
        tain and Gentleman; John Tracy-
        Phillips as Captain; Trevor
        Nunn as Gentleman; Michael Bur-
        rell as Gaoler; Gillian Webb as
        Queen; Margaret Drabble as Im-
        ogen; Micheline Samuels as Hel-
        en. LONDON 4425 (4 pd), also
        S 1416, also ARGO RG 265/8, al-
        so ZRG 5265/8, also ZPR 240/3
1045 CYMBELINE
        Richard Johnson; Hugh Thomas;
        Claire Bloom; Helen Mirren;
        Michael Pennington; John Kane;
        Nicholas Young; Paul Fesson.
        TIMLIF V 6026 E (4 vc 3/4)
1046 CYMBELINE (exc.)
        Peter Pears; Desmond Dupre;
        John Stride; Alan Bates. In
        anth. ARGO NF4, also SAY 18
1047 CYMBELINE (exc.)
        Read by Robert Donat. In anth.
        ARGO SAY 33, also PLP 1064
1048 CYMBELINE (exc.)
        In anth. ARGO PLP 1072
1049 CYMBELINE (exc.)
        John Gielgud. In anth. COLUMB

OL 5550

1050 CYMBELINE (exc.)
    Folio Theatre Players. SPOA
    889

1051 CYMBELINE (exc.)
    In anth. THEATCL (ac)

1052 HAMLET
    Gielgud; Paul Rogers; Carol
    Brown; Yvonne Mitchell.
    ALP 1482-4 (3 pd)

1053 HAMLET
    Keith Michell; Donald Hous-
    ton; Ron Moody; Helen Cherry;
    Carolyn Seymour. ARGO ZSW
    516-8 (3 pd)

1054 HAMLET
    Michael Redgrave as Hamlet;
    Margaret Rawlings as Queen;
    Barbara Jefford as Ophelia;
    Valentin Dyall as Ghost.
    AUDIBK T-LS-1 (at)

1055 HAMLET
    Ronald Pickup as Hamlet; Ro-
    bert Lang as Claudius; Ange-
    la Pleasence as Ophelia; Max-
    ine Audley as Gertrude; Martin
    Jarvis as Horatio. BBC ECN
    085 (4 ac)

1056 HAMLET
    Paul Scofield as Hamlet; Wil-
    frid Lawson; Diana Wynyard;
    Zena Walker; Roland Culver;
    Charles Heslop; Edward De Sou-
    za; Donald Houston; Richard Dare;
    Eric Jones; Peter Bayliss;
    John Warner; Christopher Guinee;
    Robert Eddison; Aubrey Woods;
    Esmond Knight; Barry Ingham;
    Charles Gray. CAED SRS 232
    (4 pd), also CDL 5232 (4 ac)

1057 HAMLET
    Richard Burton as Hamlet;
    Hume Cronyn; Alfred Drake; Ei-
    leen Herlie; William Redfield;
    George Rose; George Voskovec.
    COLUMB DOL 302, also DOS 702
    (4 pd)

1058 HAMLET
    Maximilian Schell. FI (16mm
    film)

1059 HAMLET
    Nicol Williamson. LEARNC
    (16mm film)

1060 HAMLET
    Patrick Wymark as Claudius;

Anthony White as Hamlet; Miles
Malleson as Polonius; Ian Lang
as Horatio; Peter Orr as Laer-
tes; David Rowe-Beddoe as Val-
temand; Philip Strick as Cor-
nelius; John Tracy-Phillips
as Rosencrantz; Giles Slaughter
as Guildenstern; George Rylands
as Osric; Trevor Nunn as Gentle-
man; Michael Burrell as Doctor
of Divinity; Julian Curry as
Marcellus; David Coombes as
Bernardo; Tom Bussman as Fran-
cisco; Hugh Walters as Reynal-
do; Gary Watson as Fortinbras;
Ronald Allen as Captain; Roger Hammond as Ambassador; Margaretta Scott as Gertrude;
Jeannette Sterke as Ophelia;
William Devlin as Ghost. LONDON
X 5624-8 (5 pd), also OS 25251/
5, also 4507, also OSA 1503

1061 HAMLET
    John Gielgud. RCA LM 6404 (4
    pd), also LFP 7021 (ac)

1062 HAMLET
    Laurence Olivier; Jean Simmons;
    Stanley Holloway; Eileen Her-
    lie; RCAVID (vd)

1063 HAMLET
    Derek Jacobi; Claire Bloom;
    Eric Porter; Patrick Stewart;
    Patrick Allen; Emrys James.
    TIMLIF V 6006 B (4 vc 3/4)

1064 HAMLET (in German)
    Maximilian Schell; Marianne Hop-
    pe; Ellà Büchi; Eduard Marks;
    Werner Hinz; Joseph Offenbach.
    DEUTGR 2760 103 (3 pd)

1065 HAMLET (in Russian as GAMLET)
    Vladimir Retsepter. MELOD
    19841-44 (2 pd)

1066 HAMLET (exc.)
    R. Donat. In anth. ARGO SAY 33

1067 HAMLET (exc.)
    Ian Bannen. In anth. ARGO SAY
    41

1068 HAMLET (exc.)
    Robert Donat. In anth. ARGO
    PLP 1064

1069 HAMLET (exc.)
    In anth. ARGO PLP 1121, also
    DA 4

1070 HAMLET (exc.)
    Read by John Barrymore. In

Shakespeare, cont'd.
    HAMLET, cont'd.
        AUDIOR 2465, also 2280, also
        2201
1071 HAMLET (exc.)
        Michael MacLiammoir; Hilton
        Edwards. AUDIVS 8007 SC
1072 HAMLET (exc.)
        BFA (16mm film, also vc 3/4)
1073 HAMLET (exc.)
        M. Redgrave; R. Richardson.
        In anth. CAED TC 1170
1074 HAMLET (exc.)
        Read by Maurice Evans.
        COLUMB M-340 (2 pd), also MM
        651 (3 pd78)
1075 HAMLET (exc.)
        Richard Burton; Hume Cronyn;
        Alfred Drake; Eileen Herlie;
        George Rose; George Voskovec.
        COLUMB OS 2620
1076 HAMLET (exc.)
        Maurice Evans; Emmett Rogers.
        COLUMB ENTRÉ RL 3107
1077 HAMLET (exc.)
        Richard Burton; John Gielgud.
        COLUMB OL 8020(pd), also PT
        11768 (ac), also 16 12 0048
        (ac)
1078 HAMLET (exc.)
        CRAF (16mm film)
1079 HAMLET (exc.)
        John Gielgud as Hamlet. In
        anth. DECCA DL 9504
1080 HAMLET (exc.)
        Alexander Scourby; R. E. John-
        son; Arnold Moss; Jay Jostyn;
        John Gielgud. In anth. DECCA
        DL 38026
1081 HAMLET (exc.)
        Herbert Beerbohm Tree; Ellen
        Terry. In anth. DELTA DEL
        12020, also in IRCC 3
1082 HAMLET (exc.)
        John Barrymore as Hamlet.
        FAMREC (pd?)
1083 HAMLET (exc.)
        Maurice Evans. In anth. GOLDEN
        AA 58
1084 HAMLET (exc.)
        In anth. IER W3RG94500 (4 pd),
        also W3KG94500 (4 ac)
1085 HAMLET (exc.)
        IFB (16mm film, also vc 3/4)

1086 HAMLET (exc.)
        L. Olivier. LEARNC (16mm film)
1087 HAMLET (exc.)
        Michael Redgrave as Hamlet;
        Margaret Rawlings as Queen;
        Barbara Jefford as Ophelia;
        Valentine Dyall as Ghost.
        LIVSHA SH 5A-6A, also LS
        804-8833
1088 HAMLET (exc.)
        Robert Vaughn; Diana Maddox;
        Joel Michaels. MGM E 4488
1089 HAMLET (exc.)
        MICHMED 9702/3 (16mm film,
        also 2 vc)
1090 HAMLET (exc.)
        NGS (16mm film, also vc 3/4)
1091 HAMLET (exc.)
        Performed by puppets. NIT
        Prog. 3 (vc)
1092 HAMLET (exc.)
        PROTHM 1ES10 (ac)
1093 HAMLET (exc.)
        Richard Chamberlain as Hamlet;
        Michael Redgrave as Polonius;
        Margaret Leighton as Queen;
        Rich. Johnson as King; John
        Gielgud as Ghost; Ciaran Madden
        as Ophelia. In anth. RCA VDM
        119
1094 HAMLET (exc.)
        Laurence Olivier; Harcourt
        Williams; Basil Sydney;
        Stanley Holloway. In anth. RCA
        LM 1924, also LSB 4104, also
        LCT 5
1095 HAMLET (exc.)
        John Gielgud as Hamlet; Do-
        rothy McGuire as Ophelia; Pa-
        mela Brown as Gertrude; Berry
        Kroeger as Claudius; Esme Percy
        as Ghost; George Howe as Poloni-
        us; John Merivale as Horatio;
        Richard Leech as Laertes; Hazel
        Terry as Player Queen; Esme Per-
        cy as Player King; Peter Bull
        as Bernardo; Elliott Makeham
        as Gravedigger; Norman Bird as
        Priest; David Evans as Osric.
        RCA LM 6007 (2 pd)
1096 HAMLET (exc.)
        In anth. SPOA 767
1097 HAMLET (exc.)
        Michael MacLiammoir; Hilton

Edwards. SPOA 781 (pd), also
8007 (ac)

1098 HAMLET (exc.)
Micheal MacLiammhoir; Hilton
Edwards. In anth. SPOA 836/7,
also in 7005

1099 HAMLET (exc.)
Read by Alexander Scourby. In
anth. TRINIT

1100 HAMLET (exc., in German)
Alexander Moissi. In anth.
DELTA DEL 12020

1101 HAMLET (exc., in German)
Will Quadflieg. In anth.
DEUTGR 43 002

1102 HAMLET (exc., in German)
DEUTGR 140 005

1103 HAMLET (exc., in German)
G. Gründgens. EMI 049-
030240M

1104 HAMLET (exc., in Italian as
AMLETO)
V. Gassmann. In anth. CETRA
CLC 0826

1105 HAMLET (exc., in Italian as
AMLETO)
V. Gassman. In anth. CETRA
CLC 0855

1106 HAMLET (exc., in Russian)
V. Kachalov. In anth. MK
D 013603-4

1107 JULIUS CAESAR
Tony Church; Richard Johnson;
William Squire; Ian Holm; Bar-
bara Leigh-Hunt; Roger Croucher;
David King; Gary Watson; George
Rylands; Peter Orr; Yvonne Bon-
namy. ARGO ZPR 218/20 (3 pd);
KZPC 218/20 (3 ac); also DECCA
218/20; also K32K32 and SAY 40
(3 ac)

1108 JULIUS CAESAR
Orson Welles; Martin Gabel.
ARIEL SHO 9

1109 JULIUS CAESAR
Peter Finch as Marcus Antonius;
Patrick Wymark as Brutus.
AUDIBK T-LS-13 (at)

1110 JULIUS CAESAR
Nigel Stock as Julius Caesar;
Anthony Bate as Brutus; Julian
Glover as Mark Antony. BBC ECN
102 (3 ac)

1111 JULIUS CAESAR
Ralph Richardson; Anthony Quayle;

John Mills; Alan Bates; Michael
Gwynn; Christopher Guinee; Llew-
ellyn Rees; Tony Roye; Trevor
Martin; Nigel Davenport; Paul
Hardwick; Douglas Muir; Robin
Lloyd; Graham Crowden; Emrys
James; Aubrey Woods; Peter Bayl-
iss; Gerald James; Eileen Atkins;
Heather Chasen; Stephen Moore.
CAED SRS 230 (3 pd), also CDL
5230 (3 ac)

1112 JULIUS CAESAR
Orson Welles; George Coulouris;
Martin Gabel; Joseph Holland;
Hiram Sherman; John Hoysradt;
John A. Willard; Evelyn Allen;
Muriel Brassler. COLUMB EL 52
(2 pd)

1113 JULIUS CAESAR
Ralph Richardson; Anthony Quayle; John Mills. EAV B3RR094
(3 pd)

1114 JULIUS CAESAR
Orson Welles; Edgar Barrier;
George Coulouris; Everett Sloane.
EAV LE 7570, 7575 (2 pd)

1115 JULIUS CAESAR
FOLKW 9614 (2 pd)

1116 JULIUS CAESAR
LC T 3196 (at)

1117 JULIUS CAESAR
Hilton Edwards; Michael Mac-
Liammoir. LIST SKP 1001 (3 pd),
also CX 101 (2 ac)

1118 JULIUS CAESAR
John Wilders as Caesar; George
Rylands as Octavius; Anthony
White as Marcus Antonius;
Clive Swift as Aemilius Lepidus;
John Dover Wilson as Cicero;
Donald Beves as Publius; John
Barton as Marcus Brutus; Anthony
Jacobs as Cassius; Tony Church
as Casca; Roger Prior as Trebo-
nius; Denys Robertson as Ligari-
us; Michael Jaffe as Decius
Brutus; Gary Watson as Cimber, Me-
ssala; Roderick Cook as Cinna;
John Arnott as Flavius, Arte-
midorus, and Varro; David Buck
as Marullus, Lucilius; Noel An-
nan as Soothsayer; Julian Petti-
fer as Young Cata; John Bird as
Volumnius; Chris Renard as Clit-
us, Strato; Mark Griffiths as

Shakespeare, cont'd.
    JULIUS CAESAR, cont'd.
      Dardanius; Clive Swift as Pin-
      darus; Wendy Gifford as Cal-
      phurnia; Dorothy Mulcahy as
      Portia. LONDON 4334 (3 pd),
      also ARGO RG 132/4, also KZPC
      132/4 (3 ac)
1119 JULIUS CAESAR
      MacLiammoir; Edwards; Casson.
      SPOWRD A 15 (3 pd)
1120 JULIUS CAESAR
      Richard Pasco; Keith Mitchell;
      Charles Gray. TIMLIF V 6000 A
      (2 vc 3/4)
1121 JULIUS CAESAR
      Claude Rains; Thomas Mitchell;
      Walter Abel; Reginald Denny;
      Morris Ankrum. YESTER 15288
      (at), also LIVSHA 898667 (5 pd)
1122 JULIUS CAESAR (exc.)
      Marlowe Dramatic Soc. In anth.
      ARGO PLP 1120, also in DA1
1123 JULIUS CAESAR (exc.)
      Michael MacLiammoir; Hilton Ed-
      wards. AUDIVS 8009 SC
1124 JULIUS CAESAR (exc.)
      BERG ATTS 003
1125 JULIUS CAESAR (exc.)
      BFA (vc 3/4)
1126 JULIUS CAESAR (exc.)
      Orson Welles as Brutus; George
      Coulouris as Marcus Antonius;
      Martin Gabel as Cassius; Jo-
      seph Holland as Caesar; Hiram
      Sherman as Casca; John Hoysradt
      as Decius Brutus; John A.
      Willard as Trebonius and Volum-
      nius. COLUMB MM 325 (5 pd 78)
1127 JULIUS CAESAR (exc.)
      John Gielgud as Antony. In
      anth. COLUMB OL 5550
1128 JULIUS CAESAR (exc.)
      Herbert Beerbohm Tree. In anth.
      DELTA 12020
1129 JULIUS CAESAR (exc.)
      EAV A9R0928
1130 JULIUS CAESAR (exc.)
      Maurice Evans. In anth.
      GOLDEN AA 58
1131 JULIUS CAESAR (exc.)
      IFB (vc 3/4)
1132 JULIUS CAESAR (exc.)
      Peter Finch as Marcus Antonius;
      Patrick Wymark as Brutus;

      LIVSHA SJC 25A-26A
1133 JULIUS CAESAR (exc.)
      Griffith Jones; Ralph Truman;
      Ralph Michael; Arthur Hewlett.
      LONDON LL415
1134 JULIUS CAESAR (exc.)
      Marlon Brando; James Mason;
      John Gielgud; Louis Calhern;
      Edmond O'Brien; Greer Garson;
      Deborah Kerr. MGM E 3033
1135 JULIUS CAESAR (exc.)
      W. J. Holloway. ODEON A 66024/5
      (pd 78)
1136 JULIUS CAESAR (exc.)
      PH KHC 753 (6 pd or ac)
1137 JULIUS CAESAR (exc.)
      PROTHM 1ES5 (ac)
1138 JULIUS CAESAR (exc.)
      In anth. SPOA 767
1139 JULIUS CAESAR (exc.)
      MacLiammoir; Edwards; Casson.
      SPOA 809 (pd), also SAC 7007
      (ac), also SAC 8009 (ac)
1140 JULIUS CAESAR (exc.)
      M. MacLiammoir; Hilton Edwards.
      In anth. SPOA 836/7
1141 JULIUS CAESAR (exc.)
      E. Martin Browne; Henzie Rae-
      burn. In anth. SPOA 901
1142 JULIUS CAESAR (exc.)
      Anew McMaster. In anth. SPOA
      6048 (ac)
1143 JULIUS CAESAR (exc., in German)
      E. Deutsch. In anth. TELEF
      6.48073
1144 JULIUS CAESAR (exc., in Italian as
      GIULIO CESARE)
      V. Gassmann. In anth. CETRA CLC
      0826
1145 JULIUS CAESAR (exc., in Russian)
      V. Kachalov. In anth. MK D
      7285/6, also 013603/4
1146 KING HENRY IV, PART 1
      Donald Sinden. In anth. ARGO
      SAY 60
1147 KING HENRY IV, PART 1
      Harry Andrews as King Henry;
      Richard Johnson as Prince of
      Wales; Charles Thomas as John of
      Lancaster; Edward Atienza as
      Earl of Westmoreland; Basil Hos-
      kins as Blunt; Michael Redgrave
      as Hotspur; Anthony Quayle as
      Falstaff; Pamela Brown as Lady
      Percy; Ann Beach as Lady Mortim-

er; Edith Evans as Mistress
Quickly; Ronald Lewis as Owen
Glendower; Paul Rogers as
Thomas Percy; Mark Dignam; Dav-
id Andrews; Cyril Luckham;
Gordon Jackson; James Grout,
Paul Greenhalgh; William Squire;
Peter Woodthorpe; Gareth Mor-
gan; Geoffrey Bayldon; William
Marlowe; Terry Wale; Frank Wood;
Robert Arnold; Roland Curram;
Henry Knowles. CAED SRS 217
(3 pd), also CDL 5217 (3 ac)

1148 KING HENRY IV, PART 1
Michael Redgrave; Anthony Quayle; Edith Evans. EAV B3RR477
(3 pd)

1149 KING HENRY IV, PART 1
The Canadian Players. LC T
4161 (at)

1150 KING HENRY IV, PART 1
Anthony Jacobs as King Henry;
Gary Watson as Prince of Wales;
Corin Redgrave as Lancaster;
Ian Lang as Westmoreland; John
Tracy-Phillips as Blunt; Frank
Duncan as Worcester; John Bart-
on as Northumberland; Paul Sco-
field as Hotspur; John Wood as
Mortimer; Denis McCarthy as
Scroop; John Arnott as Archi-
bald; William Squire as Glen-
dower; Richard Marquand as
Vernon; Peter Foster as Sir
Michael; Philip Strick as Poins;
Donald Beves as Falstaff; Da-
vid Jones as Gadshill; Simon
Relph as Peto; Anthony Arlidge
as Bardolph; Dilys Hamlett as
Lady Percy; Vivienne Chatterton
as Hostess Quickly; Eirian
James as Lady Mortimer. LONDON
M 4421 (4 pd), also OSA 1409;
also ARGO RG 208/11, also ZRG
5208/11, also ZPR 149/52; also
KZPC 149/52 (4 ac) and SAY 88
(4 ac)

1151 KING HENRY IV, PART 1
Anthony Quayle; Jon Finch;
David Gwillim; Tim Pigott-Smith;
Brenda Bruce; Michele Dotrice;
TIMLIF V 6007 B (3 vc 3/4)

1152 KING HENRY IV, PART 1 (exc.)
Ann Todd. In anth. AMBER 7101

1153 KING HENRY IV, PART 1 (exc.)
Marlowe Soc. In anth. ARGO
PLP 1123, also in DA3

1154 KING HENRY IV, PART 1 (exc.)
BFA (16mm film, also vc 3/4)

1155 KING HENRY IV, PART 1 (exc.)
Herbert Beerbohm Tree. In
anth. DELTA DEL 12020

1156 KING HENRY IV, PART 1 (exc.)
Donald Wolfit as Falstaff;
Richard Gale as Prince of
Wales; Ernest Milton as Henry.
LIVSHA SHE I 27A-28A

1157 KING HENRY IV, PART 1 (exc.)
MICHMED 9700 (16mm film, also
vc)

1158 KING HENRY IV, PART 1 (exc.)
PROTHM 1ES7 (ac)

1159 KING HENRY IV, PART 1 (exc.)
Murray Gilmore as Henry; Char-
les Gill as Lancaster; Colin
Jeavons as Prince of Wales;
John Joseph as Henry Percy;
Alan Edwards as Hotspur;
John Blatchley as Falstaff;
Barry Justice as Thomas Percy;
Jonas Forti as Owen Glendower;
Timothy Cumberbatch as Mortimer;
Peter Bourne as Poins; Mariott
Longman as Lady Percy. SPOA
815 (pd), also 7115 (ac)

1160 KING HENRY IV, PART 2
Max Adrian as Shallow; Felix
Aylmer as Chief Justice; Edith
Evans as Hostess Quickly; Miles
Malleson as Silence; Harry An-
drews as King Henry; Pamela
Brown as Lady Percy; Richard
Johnson as Prince Henry; Antho-
ny Quayle as Falstaff; Joyce
Redman as Doll Tearsheet; Char-
les Thomas; Terry Wale; Paul
Greenhalgh; Mark Dignam; Cyril
Luckham; Robert Arnold; Basil
Hoskins; Jack May; Laurence Har-
dy; James Grout; Gareth Morgan;
Edward Atienza; Roy Marsden;
William Squire; Geoffrey Bayldon;
Darien Angadi; Ronnie Barker;
Henry Knowles; Roland Curram;
Frank Wood; Barry Ashton; Cherry
Morris. CAED SRS 218 (4 pd),
also CDL 5218 (4 ac)

Shakespeare, cont'd.
 1161 KING HENRY IV, PART 2
        Walter Huston; Brian Aherne;
        Walter Connolly; Humphrey Bo-
        garth. In anth. LIVSHA 898667
 1162 KING HENRY IV, PART 2
        Denis McCarthy as Rumor & Scroop;
        Anthony Jacobs as King Henry;
        Gary Watson as Prince Henry; Co-
        rin Redgrave as Lancaster; Ian
        McKellen as Gloucester & Davy;
        Richard Kaye as Clarence; Ter-
        rence Hardiman as Warwick; Ian
        Lang as Westmoreland; Anthony
        Arlidge as Gower; Derek Jacobi
        as Harcourt; John Tracy-Phil-
        lips as Blunt; John Wilders as
        Chief Justice; John Barton as
        Northumberland; Toby Robert-
        son as Mowbray & Silence;
        Clive Swift as Hastings; John
        Tydeman as Bardolph; Rich-
        ard Marquand as John Colevile;
        Frank Duncan as Travers; Da-
        vid Jones as Morton; David
        Coombes as Poins; Donald Beves
        as Falstaff; Philip Strick as
        Bardolph; Tony Church as Pistol;
        Paul Draper as Page; William
        Squire as Shallow; Peter Foster
        as Fang; John Wood as Mouldy;
        Roger Hammond as Shadow & Wart;
        Richard Cotterell as Feeble;
        Simon Relph as Bullcalf; Camille
        Prior as Lady Northumberland;
        Vivienne Chatterton as Hostess
        Quickly; Diana Chatwick as
        Doll Tearsheet. LONDON 4422 (4
        pd), also OSA 1410; also ARGO
        212/15, also ZRG 5212/15, also
        ZPR 153/6; also KZPC 153/6 and
        SAY 89 (4 ac)
 1163 KING HENRY IV, PART 2
        SPOA 816 (pd), also 7116 (ac)
 1164 KING HENRY IV, PART 2 (exc.)
        Marlowe Soc. In anth. ARGO
        PLP 1123, also in DA3
 1165 KING HENRY IV, PART 2 (exc.)
        BFA (16mm film, also vc 3/4)
 1166 KING HENRY IV, PART 2 (exc.)
        M. Redgrave. CAED TC 1170
 1167 KING HENRY IV, PART 2 (exc.)
        IFB (16mm film)
 1168 KING HENRY IV, PART 2 (exc.)
        Donald Wolfit as Falstaff;

        Rich. Gale as Prince of Wales;
        Ernest Milton as King Henry.
        LIVSHA SHE II 29A-30A
 1169 KING HENRY IV, PART 2 (exc.)
        Read by Paul Rogers. In anth.
        SPOA 723
 1170 KING HENRY IV, PART 2 (exc.)
        Jon Finch; Anthony Quayle;
        David Gwillim. TIMLIF V 6008 B
        (vc 3/4)
 1171 KING HENRY V
        John Gielgud; John Rowe as King
        Henry; Alec McCowen; Timothy
        West; Martin Jarvis. BBC ECN
        089 (3 ac)
 1172 KING HENRY V
        Ian Holm; Charles Gray; Ian
        McKellen; Janet Suzman; Ber-
        nard Bresslaw; John Laurie;
        John Gielgud; Frank Wylie;
        Harvey Ashby; Paul Curran;
        Keith Pyott ; Richard Hamp-
        ton; Kenneth MacIntosh; Geoff-
        rey Dunn; George Howe; Aubrey
        Woods; Jack Gwillim; Gerald Jam-
        es; Barry Keegan; John Warner;
        Trevor Martin; Ronnie Stevens;
        Charles Gray; George Benson;
        Christopher Guinee; Edward de
        Souza; Donald Eccles; Harvey
        Ashby; John Moffat; Eithne
        Dunne; Patience Collier; Pau-
        line Jameson. CAED SRS 219 (4
        pd), also CDL 5219 (4 ac)
 1173 KING HENRY V
        L. Olivier. LEARNC (16mm film)
 1174 KING HENRY V
        William Squire as Chorus; Gary
        Watson as King Henry; Julian
        Curry as Humphrey; Ian McKellen
        as Lancaster and Jamy; Denis
        McCarthy as Exeter; John Tracy-
        Phillips as York and Duke of
        Orleans; Peter Orr as Salisbury
        and Court; Donald Beves as West-
        moreland; John Barton as Arch-
        bishop of Canterbury; John Perc-
        eval as Bishop of Ely; John Sha-
        rpe as Boy; Terrence Hardi-
        man as Charles VI; Anthony White
        as Dauphin; George Rylands as
        Duke of Burgundy; Derek Jacobi
        as Duke of Britaine & Ambassador;
        Corin Redgrave as Duke of Bour-
        bon, Rambures, & Grandpré; Frank

Duncan as Constable; Peter
Foster as Earl of Cambridge;
Giles Slaughter as Scroop; Da-
vid Rowe-Beddoe as Grey; Phil-
ip Strick as Erpingham; Trevor
Nunn as Gower; Dudley Jones as
Fluellen; Andrew Parkes as Mac-
morris; Michael Burrell as Bates;
Tony Church as Pistol; Roger
Hammond as Governor of Harfleur;
Suzanne Fuller as Isabel;
Micheline Samuels as Katharine;
Prunella Scales as Alice; Vivi-
enne Chatterton as Hostess.
LONDON 4424 (4 pd), also OSA
1415; also ARGO RG 261/4, also
ZRG 526/4, also ZPR 157/60;
also KZPC 157/60 (4 ac)

1175 KING HENRY V
L. Olivier; Robert Newton; Leslie Banks; Leo Genn. RCAVID (vc)

1176 KING HENRY V
Colin Jeavons as King Henry;
Murray Gilmore as Exeter; John
Joseph as Charles VI; Barry
Justice as Lewis; Jonas Forti as
Constable & Bardolph; Peter
Bourne as Montjoy; Timothy Cumb-
erbatch as Duke of Orleans;
Catherine Clouzot as Princess
Katherine; Mariott Longman as
Alice; John Blatchley as Pistol;
Charles Gill as Nym. SPOA 817
(pd), also 8015 (ac)

1177 KING HENRY V
David Gwillim; Alec McCowen;
Trevor Baxter; Anna Quayle; Rob
Edwards; Brenda Bruce; Bryan
Pringle; Derek Hollis; Jocelyne
Boisseau; Martin Neil. TIMLIF
V 6009 B (3 vc 3/4)

1178 KING HENRY V (exc.)
Richard Pasco. In anth. ARGO
SAY 60

1179 KING HENRY V (exc.)
Marlowe Soc. In anth. ARGO PLP
1123, also in DA3

1180 KING HENRY V (exc.)
AUDIVS 8015 SC

1181 KING HENRY V (exc.)
BERG ATTS 004

1182 KING HENRY V (exc.)
M. Redgrave. CAED TC 1170

1183 KING HENRY V (exc.)
John Gielgud. In anth.

COLUMB OL 5550

1184 KING HENRY V (exc.)
John Gielgud. CONTF ISBN 0-
699-00460-8 (16mm film)

1185 KING HENRY V (exc.)
Walter Hampden. DAGGETT
(pd78)

1186 KING HENRY V (exc.)
Lewis Waller. In anth.
DELTA DEL 12020

1187 KING HENRY V (exc.)
Richard Burton as Henry;
Anna Massey as Katharine.
LIVSHA SHV 41A-42A

1188 KING HENRY V (exc.)
In anth. LONGMAN 3

1189 KING HENRY V (exc.)
Performed by puppets. NIT
PROGR. 1 (vc)

1190 KING HENRY V (exc.)
Barb. Jefford; J. Gielgud;
William Squire; Trevor Martin;
David March. PROTHM 1 ES 1
(ac)

1191 KING HENRY V (exc.)
Laurence Olivier; Harcourt
Williams; Basil Sydney; Stan-
ley Holloway. In anth. RCA
LM 1924, also in LSB 4104

1192 KING HENRY V (exc.)
Foch; Addy; Fleurus. In anth.
THEAMA GRC 2431

1193 KING HENRY VI, PART 1
Richard Marquand as King Henry;
David King as Gloucester;
Carleton Hobbs as Bedford;
Terrence Hardiman as Beaufort;
Denis McCarthy as Henry Beau-
fort; Roger Croucher as John Be-
aufort; Peter Orr as York;
Frank Duncan as Warwick; John
Tydeman as Salisbury; Gary Wat-
son as Suffolk; William Devlin
as Lord Talbot; Gordon Gardner
as John Talbot; Cyril Luckham as
Mortimer; John Nettleton as
Falstaff; John Shrapnel as Lucy;
Raymond Clarke as Glansdale;
Brian Batchelor as Mayor of Lon-
don; David Rowe-Beddoe as Ver-
non; Anthony Arlidge as Basset;
Bob Jones as Lawyer; Patrick
Garland as Charles; V. C. Clin-
ton Baddeley as Reignier; John
Hopkins as Duke of Burgundy;

Shakespeare, cont'd.

KING HENRY VI, PART 1, cont'd.
John Tracy-Phillips as Duke
of Alencon; David Buck as
Bastard of Orleans; John Burton
as General; Ronald Grey as Shep-
herd; Mary Norris as Margaret;
Yvonne Bonnamy as Countess of
Auvergne; Freda Dowie as Joan.
LONDON 4374 (3 pd), also S
1374; also ARGO RG 386/88, also
ZRG 5386/8, also ZPR 161/3

1194 KING HENRY VI, PART 1
Peter Benson; Trevor Peacock.
TIMLIF V 6021 D (2 vc 3/4)

1195 KING HENRY VI (exc.)
M. Redgrave CAED TC 1170

1196 KING HENRY VI, PART 2
Richard Marquand as King Henry;
David King as Cardinal Beaufort;
Peter Orr as York; Richard Words-
worth as Edward; Patrick Wymark
as Richard; Roger Croucher as
Somerset; Gary Watson as Suffolk;
David Jones as Buckingham;
Tony Church as Clifford; John
Shrapnel as Young Clifford; John
Tydeman as Salisbury; Frank Dun-
can as Warwick; Robin Ellis as
Scales; Miles Malleson as Say;
Guy Slater as Stafford; Michael
Turnbull as William Stafford;
Bob Jones as Stanley; David Buck
as Lieutenant; Terrence Hardiman
and Raymond Clarke as Gentlemen;
Dudley Jones as John Hum; Bob
Jones as Southwell; Peter Wood-
thorpe as Bolingbroke; Terrence
Hardiman as a Spirit and Sheriff;
David Burke as Horner and Holla-
nd; Philip Strick as Peter; Mi-
chael Bates as Simpcox; Trevor
Nunn as Iden; Norman Rossington
as Cade; Stephen Thorne as Bevis;
Mary Morris as Margaret; Yvonne
Bonnamy as Eleanor; George Ry-
lands as Margery Jourdain; Patsy
Byrne as Wife of Simpcox.
LONDON 4428 (4 pd), also 1428;
also ARGO RG 389/92, also ZRG
5389/92, also ZPR 164/7

1197 KING HENRY VI, PART 2
Peter Benson; Julia Foster.
TIMLIF V 6022 D (2 vc 3/4)

1198 KING HENRY VI, PART 3
Richard Marquand as King Henry;
Gordon Gardner as Prince of
Wales; Toby Robertson as Louis
XI; David Rowe-Beddoe as Somerset; Trevor Bowen as Exeter;
Bob Jones as Oxford; David Burke
Northumberland; Anthony Arlidge
as Westmoreland; John Shrapnel
as Clifford & Richmond; Peter
Orr as York; Richard Wordsworth
as Edward; Malcolm Page as Rut-
land and Father; Patrick Garland as Clarence; Patrick Wymark
as Gloucester; George Rylands as
Norfolk; Frank Duncan as Warwick;
James Taylor Whitehead as Mon-
tague; Denis McCarthy as Hastings; John Hopkins as Rivers; Dudley Jones as Montgomery; Martin Spencer as Son; Mary Morris
as Queen Margaret; Margaretta
Scott as Lady Grey; Carol Macre-
ady as Bona. LONDON 4429 (4 pd),
also 1429; also ARGO RG 393/6,
also ZRG 5393/6, also ZPR 168/71

1199 KING HENRY VI, PART 3
Peter Benson as King Henry;
Ron Cook as Richard; Julia Fost-
er as Margaret; Bernard Hill as
York; Brian Protheroe as Edward
IV; Mark Wing-Davey as Warwick.
TIMLIF V 6023 D (4 vc 3/4)

1200 KING HENRY VIII
Frank Duncan as King Henry;
Robert Speaight as Wolsey; Ri-
chard Dare as Campeius; Donald
Layne Smith as Cranmer; Denis Mc-
Carthy as Norfolk; Ian Lang as
Buckingham; Peter Orr as Suffolk;
Gary Watson as Surrey; Terrence
Hardiman as Chamberlain; Michael
Bates as Sands; Trevor Nunn as
Cromwell; John Barton as Griffith;
Margaretta Scott as Queen Katha-
rine; Prunella Scales as Anne
Bullen; Vivienne Chatterton as
Old Lady. LONDON M 4226 (4 pd),
also OSA 1426; also ARGO RG 303/
6, also ZRG 5303/6

1201 KING HENRY VIII
John Stride; Timothy West; Ronald Pickup; Julian Glover; Jeremy Kemp; Claire Bloom.

TIMLIF V 6004 A (3 vc 3/4)

1202 KING HENRY VIII (exc.)
Ann Todd. In anth. AMBER 7101

1203 KING HENRY VIII (exc.)
Ralph Richardson. In anth.
ARGO NF 4

1204 KING HENRY VIII (exc.)
R. Donat. In anth. SAY 33,
also in PLP 1059

1205 KING HENRY VIII (exc.)
Michael MacLiammoir; Hilton Edwards. AUDIVS 8009 SC

1206 KING HENRY VIII (exc.)
M. Redgrave. In anth. CAED TC
1170

1207 KING HENRY VIII (exc.)
Sybil Thorndike; Lewis Casson;
Ralph Truman. LONDON LL 578

1208 KING HENRY VIII (exc.)
Edith Evans. In anth. RCA
LRL 1-5037

1209 KING HENRY VIII (exc.)
Sybil Thorndike; Lewis Casson.
SPOA 881

1210 KING JOHN
Donald Wolfit; Kenneth Haigh;
Rosemary Harris; John Rogers;
Gerald Rowlands; Charles Gray;
Richard Hampton; Stephen Dart-
nell; Trevor Martin; David Do-
dimead; Basil Sydney; Michael
Meacham; Michael Aldridge; Er-
nest Milton; Sheila Burrell;
Georgina Ward; Rosalind At-
kinson; Newton Blick. CAED SRS
215 (3 pd)also CDL 5215 (3 ac)

1211 KING JOHN
Michael Hordern as King John;
Anthony Jacobs as Prince Henry
& Pandulph; David Jones as
Bigot; Tony Church as De Burgh;
Roderick Cook as Faulcon-
bridge; David Buck as Philip the
Bastard; John Kimber as Gurney;
George Rylands as Pomfret; Toby
Robertson as King Philip of
France; Richard Marquand as
Dauphin; Roger Prior as Melun;
Gary Watson as Chatillon;
Donald Beves as Citizen; Olive
Gregg as Queen Elinor; Mar-
garetta Scott as Constance;
Christine Baker as Blanch; Freda
Dowie as Lady Faulconbridge.

LONDON 4418 (4 pd), also
OSA 1413; also ARGO RG 168/71,
also ZRG 5168/71, also ZPR 142/5

1212 KING JOHN
SPOWRD A9 (4 pd)

1213 KING JOHN
Leonard Rossiter; Mary Morris;
John Thaw; George Costigan;
William Whymper; Richard Words-
worth; Claire Bloom. TIMLIF
V 6032 F (2 vc 1/2)

1214 KING JOHN (exc.)
Marlowe Soc. In anth. ARGO PLP
1123, also in DA 3

1215 KING JOHN (exc.)
M. Redgrave. In anth. CAED TC
1170

1216 KING JOHN (exc.)
SPOA 784

1217 KING LEAR
Orson Welles; Agnes Moorehead.
AFRTV RU 50-4 3B

1218 KING LEAR
Donald Wolfit as Lear; Rosalina
Iden as Cordelia; Barb. Jefford
as Regan; Coral Browne as
Goneril. AUDIBK T-LS-3 (at)

1219 KING LEAR
Paul Scofield; Rachel Roberts;
Pamela Brown; Cyril Cusack;
Robert Stephens; John Stride;
Wallas Eaton; John Rigers; Tre-
vor Martin; Michael Aldridge;
Andrew Keir; Arthur Hewlett; Wi-
lloughby Goddard; Ronald Ibbs;
Ann Bell. CAED SRS 233 (4 pd),
also CDL 5233 (4 ac); also EAV
B4RR660 (4 pd)

1220 KING LEAR
Arnold Moss. LC T 3082 (at)

1221 KING LEAR
Michael MacLiammoir; Hilton
Edwards. LIST SKP 1004 (4 pd),
also CX 104 (3 ac)

1222 KING LEAR
William Devlin as Lear; Ian Lang
as King of France; John Tracy-
Phillips as Burgundy; Patrick
Creean as Cornwall; Gary Watson
as Albany; William Squire as
Kent; Donald Beves as Gloucester;
Frank Duncan as Edgar; Peter Orr
as Edmund; Michael Burrell as
Curan; Peter Foster as Oswald;

Shakespeare, cont'd.
    KING LEAR, cont'd.
        Terrence Hardiman as Old
        Man; Roger Hammond as Doctor;
        Michael Bakewell as Fool;
        Jill Balcon as Goneril; Pru-
        nella Scales as Cordelia;
        Margaret Rawlings as Regan.
        LONDON 4423 (4 pd), also OSA
        1414; also ARGO RG 280/3, also
        ZRG 5280/3, also ZPR 197/200;
        also KZPC 197/200 and SAY 67
        (4 ac)
1223 KING LEAR
        PH KHC 752 (6 pd & ac)
1224 KING LEAR
        Dublin Gate Theatre. SPOWRD
        SW 134-6 (4 pd)
1225 KING LEAR
        Michael Hordern; Brenda Blethyn;
        John Shrapnel; John Bird;
        Gillian Barge; Penelope Wilton.
        TIMLIF V 6027 E (4 vc 3/4)
1226 KING LEAR
        Thomas Mitchell; Mady Christians;
        Elizabeth Risdon. YESTER 15290
        (at)
1227 KING LEAR (exc.)
        Peggy Ashcroft; Paul Scofield.
        In anth. ARGO NF 4
1228 KING LEAR (exc.)
        Michael Redgrave. In anth.
        ARGO SAY 18
1229 KING LEAR (exc.)
        In anth. ARGO SAY 41
1230 KING LEAR (exc.)
        Marlowe Soc. In anth. ARGO
        PLP 1121, also in DA 4
1231 KING LEAR (exc.)
        Michael MacLiammoir; Hilton Ed-
        wards. AUDIVS 8008 SC
1232 KING LEAR (exc.)
        BERG ATTS 001
1233 KING LEAR (exc.)
        BFA (vc 3/4)
1234 KING LEAR (exc.)
        Read by Dylan Thomas. In anth.
        CAED TC 1158
1235 KING LEAR (exc.)
        Read by James Agee. In anth.
        CAED SWC 2042
1236 KING LEAR (exc.)
        DEANE ISBN 0-699-32754-7 (16mm
        film)

1237 KING LEAR (exc.)
        Donald Wolfit as Lear; Rosa-
        lind Iden as Cordelia; Barbara
        Jefford as Regan; Coral Browne
        as Goneril. LIVSHA SKL 3A-4A
1238 KING LEAR (exc.)
        In anth. MICHMED 9701 (16mm
        film, also vc)
1239 KING LEAR (exc.)
        In anth. MICHMED 9706 (16mm
        film, also vc)
1240 KING LEAR (exc.)
        In anth. MICHMED 9708 (16mm
        film, also vc)
1241 KING LEAR (exc.)
        John Gielgud; I. Worth. RCA
        SB 6740
1242 KING LEAR (exc.)
        In anth. SPOA 767
1243 KING LEAR (exc.)
        Hilton Edwards. SPOA 784 (pd),
        also 7110 (ac)
1244 KING LEAR (exc.)
        M. MacLiammoir; Hilton Edwards.
        In anth. SPOA 836-7; also in
        7005 and 8006
1245 KING RICHARD II
        Richard Pasco; Timothy West;
        Barbara Leigh-Hunt; Yvonne Bon-
        namy; W. Devlin; C. Luckham;
        G. Rylands; G. Watson; P. Orr;
        F. Duncan. ARGO K35K32 (3 ac),
        also SAY 66
1246 KING RICHARD II
        John Gielgud; Keith Mitchell;
        Leo McKern; Michael Hordern;
        Richard Easton; Jeremy Brett;
        Edward Hardwicke; Michael Dea-
        con; Christopher Burgess; Ha-
        rold Lang; Bryan Stanyon; Leslie
        French; John Nettleton; Geoff-
        rey Bayldon; Rachel Gurney;
        Hazel Hughes; Ethel Griffies;
        Amanda Walker; John Church.
        CAED SRS 216 (3 pd), also CDL
        5216 (3 ac)
1247 KING RICHARD II
        George Rylands as King Richard;
        Tony Church as Gaunt & Berkeley;
        John Wilders as Edmund; Anthony
        Jacobs as Bolingbroke; Gary Wat-
        son as Aumerle; Anthony White as
        Mowbray; Donald Beves as Salisb-
        ury; David Buck as Bushy & Fitz-

water; Roger Prior as Bagot;
John Bird as Green; John Barton
as Northumberland & Lord
Marshal; David Gibson as Henry
Percy; Chris Renard as Lord
Willoughby; John Arnott as
Bishop of Carlisle; Denys Robert-
son as Abbot of Westminster;
James Taylor Whitehead as Exton;
David Jones as Captain; Wendy
Gifford as Queen; Irene Worth
as Duchess of Gloucester;
Mary Fenton as Duchess of York.
LONDON 4335 (3 pd), also ARGO
RG 139/41, also ZPR 146/8, also
KZPC 146/8 (3 ac)

1248 KING RICHARD II
Derek Jacobi; John Gielgud; Jon
Finch; Wendy Hiller; Charles
Gray; Mary Morris. TIMLIF
V 6002 A (3 vc 3/4)

1249 KING RICHARD II (in French as LA
TRAGÉDIE DU ROI RICHARD II)
G. Philipe; J. Deschamps; Chaum-
ette; Minazzoli; Mollien; Sora-
no; Wilson. HACH ES 320E039/40
& 270E040 (3 pd)

1250 KING RICHARD II (exc.)
Robert Harris as King Richard;
John Ruddock as Gaunt; Douglas
Seale as York; William Avenelle
as Northumberland; Donald Sinden
as Aumerle; Antony Groser as
Groom. ALLEGRO ALD 8001

1251 KING RICHARD II (exc.)
Richard Pasco. In anth. ARGO
SAY 60

1252 KING RICHARD II (exc.)
Marlowe Soc. In anth. ARGO
PLP 1123, also in DA 3

1253 KING RICHARD II (exc.)
Michael Redgrave. In anth.
CAED TC 1170

1254 KING RICHARD II (exc.)
Maurice Evans. COLUMB RL 3107

1255 KING RICHARD II (exc.)
John Gielgud as Richard. In
anth. COLUMB OL 5550

1256 KING RICHARD II (exc.)
John Gielgud. In anth. DECCA
9002

1257 KING RICHARD II (exc.)
Herbert Beerbohm Tree. In anth.
DEL 12020

1258 KING RICHARD II (exc.)
IFB (vc 3/4)

1259 KING RICHARD II (exc.)
Michael Redgrave as King Richard.
LIVSHA SRII 39A-40A

1260 KING RICHARD II (exc.)
MICHMED 9699 (16mm film, also vc)

1261 KING RICHARD II (exc.)
PROTHM 1ES8 (ac)

1262 KING RICHARD II (exc.)
Paul Rogers. In anth. SPOA 723

1263 KING RICHARD II (exc.)
Folio Theatre Players. SPOA
890 (pd, also ac)

1264 KING RICHARD II (exc.)
Claude Rains; Addy; Rolf;
Cotsworth; Moss; MacGrath.
THEAMA GRC 2431

1265 KING RICHARD II (in French, exc.)
Jean Vilar. In anth. ADÉS
TS 30 LA 552

1266 KING RICHARD II (exc., in German
as KÖNIG RICHARD II)
Ernst Deutsch. In anth. TELEF
6.48073

1267 KING RICHARD II (exc., in Italian
as RICCARDO II)
V. Gassmann. In anth. CETRA
CLC 0855

1268 KING RICHARD III
Robert Stephens as King Richard;
Peggy Ashcroft; Cyril Cusack;
Ian Holm; Jeremy Brett; Glenda
Jackson; Nigel Davenport; Paul
Curran; Gerald James; Richard
O'Callaghan; Keith Pyott;
Arthur Hewlett; John Saunders;
Michael York; Edward De Souza;
Stephen Moore; June Jago; Rich-
ard Hampton; George Benson;
Julian Glover; Willoughby God-
dard; Rosalind Atkinson; Emrys
James; Trevor Martin; Stephen
Dartnell; Wallas Eaton; John
Dane; Derek Seaton; Gerald Row-
lands; Sarah Milton. CAED SRS
223 (4 pd), also CDL 5223 (4 ac),
also EAV B2RR149 (4 pd)

1269 KING RICHARD III
Richard Wordsworth as King Edward IV; David Dickinson as Prince
of Wales; Patrick Garland as
Clarence; Patrick Wymark as
Gloucester; John Shrapnel as Richmond; David Rowe-Beddoe as

Shakespeare, cont'd.
    KING RICHARD III, cont'd.
        Bourchier; John Tracy-Phil-
        lips as Rotherham; William Squi-
        re as Buckingham; John Hopkins
        as Rivers; Corin Redgrave as
        Dorset; Denis McCarthy as Has-
        tings; Terrence Hardiman as
        Stanley; George Rylands as
        Lovel; John Shearer as Vaughan;
        Roger Croucher as Ratcliff;
        Peter Orr as Gatesby; David Buck
        as Tyrrel; David King as Blount;
        John Tydeman as Brakenbury; Mar-
        garetta Scott as Elizabeth; Mary
        Morris as Margaret; Beatrix Leh-
        man as Duchess of York; Prunella
        Scales as Lady Anne; Freda Dow-
        ie as Margaret Plantagenet.
        LONDON 4430 (3 pd), also S 1430;
        also ARGO RG 407/10, also ZRG
        5407/10, also ZPR 172/5; also
        KZPC 172/5 (4 ac)
1270 KING RICHARD III
        Laurence Olivier as Richard;
        John Gielgud as Clarence; Alec
        Clunes as Hastings; Stanley
        Baker as Richmond; Mary Kerrid-
        ge as Queen Elizabeth; John Lau-
        rie as Lovel; Claire Bloom as
        Lady Anne; Ralph Richardson as
        Buckingham; Laurence Naismith as
        Stanley; Pamela Brown as Jane
        Shore; Cedrick Hardwicke as
        Edward IV; Norman Wooland as Ca-
        tesby; Helen Haye as Duchess of
        York; Esmond Knight as Ratcliffe.
        RCA LM 6126 (3 pd)
1271 KING RICHARD III
        Ron Cook as Richard; Michael
        Byrne as Buckingham; Rowena Coo-
        per as Queen Elizabeth; Ju-
        lia Foster as Queen Margaret;
        Zoe Wanamaker as Lady Anne;
        Brian Protheroe as Edward IV;
        Annette Crosbie as Duchess of
        York. TIMLIF V 6020 D (4 vc 3/4)
1272 KING RICHARD III (exc.)
        Edith Evans; Elizabeth Sellars;
        Esme Church. In anth. ARGO
        SAY 41
1273 KING RICHARD III (exc.)
        Richard Burton. In anth. ARGO
        SAY 47

1274 KING RICHARD III (exc.)
        John Barrymore. In anth.
        AUDIOR 2203
1275 KING RICHARD III (exc.)
        John Barrymore. In anth.
        AUDIOR LPA 2281
1276 KING RICHARD III (exc.)
        M. Redgrave. In anth. CAED
        TC 1170
1277 KING RICHARD III (exc.)
        Jay Robinson as Richard;
        Martin Donegan as Richmand.
        FOLKW FL 9874
1278 KING RICHARD III (exc.)
        IFB (vc 3/4)
1279 KING RICHARD III (exc.)
        Peter Finch as Richard.
        LIVSHA SR III 35A-36A
1280 KING RICHARD III (exc.)
        Performed by puppets.
        NIT Prog. 4 (vc)
1281 KING RICHARD III (exc.)
        Laurence Olivier; John Gielgud;
        RCA LM 1940
1282 KING RICHARD III (exc.)
        Folio Theatre. SPOA 891 (pd),
        also 7117 (ac)
1283 KING RICHARD III (exc.)
        E. Martin Browne; Henzie
        Raeburn. In anth. SPOA 901
1284 KING RICHARD III (exc., in French)
        Charles Dullin. In anth. ADÉS
        7003 (2 pd)
1285 LOVE'S LABOR'S LOST
        R. Donat. In anth. ARGO PLP
        1064
1286 LOVE'S LABOR'S LOST
        Anna Massey as Princess of
        France; Eileen Atkins as Ro-
        saline; Michael Kitchen as
        King Ferdinand; John McEnery as
        Berowne; Paul Scofield as
        Don Adriano. BBC ECN 141 (3 ac)
1287 LOVE'S LABOR'S LOST
        Geraldine McEwan; Jeremy Brett;
        Ian Holm; Ian Richardson; Derek
        Jacobi; Clifford Rose; Richard
        Kay; William Squire, Mark Dig-
        nam; James Mellor; Ken Wynne;
        Jane Carr; Don Hawkins; Judy Par-
        fitt; Helen Bourne; Felicity
        Kendal; Sheila Reid. CAED SRS
        207 (3 pd), also CDL 5207 (3 ac)

1288 LOVE'S LABOR'S LOST
     Arnold Moss. LC T 2830 (at)
1289 LOVE'S LABOR'S LOST
     Gary Watson as Berowne;
     Derek Godfrey as Ferdinand; Pet-
     er Orr as Longaville; Ian Lang
     as Dumaine; Robert Eddison as
     Boyet; George Rylands as Mer-
     cade; Max Adrian as Armado;
     Toby Robertson as Nathaniel;
     Tony Church as Holofernes;
     Peter Woodthorpe as Dull; Mi-
     chael Bates as Costard; Freda
     Dowie as Moth; Janette Richer
     as Princess of France; Pru-
     nella Scales as Rosaline;
     Diana Rigg as Katharine; Susan
     Maryott as Maria; Patsy Byrne
     as Jaquenetta. LONDON M4363
     (3 pd, also ac), also OSA 1363;
     also ARGO RG 313/5, also ZRG
     5313/5, also ZPR 129/31
1290 LOVE'S LABOR'S LOST
     TIMLIF V 6028 E (vc 4/4)
1291 LOVE'S LABOR'S LOST (exc.)
     R. Donat. In anth. ARGO SAY 33
1292 LOVE'S LABOR'S LOST (exc.)
     John Gielgud as Berowne. In
     anth. COLUMB OL 5550
1293 LOVE'S LABOR'S LOST (exc.)
     Peter Finch as Berowne; Van-
     essa Redgrave as Rosaline.
     LIVSHA 43A-44A
1294 MACBETH
     Robert Hardy as Duncan; Ian
     Holm as Malcolm; Anthony Quayle
     as Macbeth; Anthony Nichols as
     Banquo; Jack Gwillim as MacDuff;
     Gwen Ffrangcon Davies as Lady
     Macbeth; Jill Balcon as Lady Mac-
     duff; Rachel Roberts, Rosalind
     Atkinson, and Jill Balcon as
     Witches; Stanley Holloway as
     Porter. CAED SRS 231 (3 pd),
     also CDL 5231 (3 ac)
1295 MACBETH
     Marlowe Soc. EAV B3RR467 (3
     pd), also B1KK2821 (2 ac)
1296 MACBETH
     Philip Anglim; Maureen Anderman.
     FFHS (2 vc 3/4)
1297 MACBETH
     The Canadian Players. LC T
     2389 (at)

1298 MACBETH
     Arnold Moss. LC T 3654 (at)
1299 MACBETH
     Alec Guiness; Pamela Brown. LFP
     TC LFP 7053
1300 MACBETH
     Toby Robertson as Duncan; Roger
     Prior as Malcolm; Tony Church as
     Macbeth; John Barton as Banquo;
     Gerald Mosbach as Macduff; Gary
     Watson as Lennox; Derek Jacobi
     as Ross; David Jones as Menteith;
     Chris Renard as Angus; Terrence
     Hardiman as Caithness & Old Man;
     Donald Beves as Siward; Richard
     Marquand as Young Siward; John
     Tracy-Phillips as Seton; Michael
     Bates as Porter; George Rylands
     as English Doctor; John Arnott
     as Scotch Doctor; Clive Swift,
     John Bird, & John Kimber as
     Murderers; Irene Worth as Lady
     Macbeth; Freda Dowie as Lady
     Macduff; Mrs. Shire as Gentle-
     woman; Willa Muir, Freda Dowie,
     & Janette Richer as Weird Siste-
     rs.   LONDON 4343 (3 pd), also
     OSA 1316; also ARGO RG 175/7, al-
     so ZRG 5175/7, also ZPR 201/3,
     also KZPC 201/3 (3 ac), also
     K14K32
1301 MACBETH
     Alec Guiness as Macbeth; Pamela
     Brown as Lady Macbeth; Anthony
     Service as Malcolm; Andrew
     Cruickshank as Banquo; Robin Bai-
     ley as Macduff; Rachel Gurney as
     Lady Macduff; John Bushelle as
     Duncan; Mary O'Farrell, Marga-
     ret Vines, & Jill Nyasa as Wit-
     ches; George Rose as Porter.
     RCA LM 6010 (2 pd), also LFP
     7053 (2 ac)
1302 MACBETH
     Tony Doyle; Jane Lapotaire;
     Mark Dignam; Nicol Williamson;
     James Hazeldine. TIMLIF V 6033
     F (2 vc 1/2)
1303 MACBETH
     Eric Porter; Janet Suzman.
     TIMLIF (2 vc)
1304 MACBETH (exc.)
     Michael Redgrave. In anth.
     ARGO NF 4

Shakespeare, cont'd.
  1305 MACBETH (exc.)
          Tony Church; Paul Whitworth;
          Barbara Leigh-Hunt; Pippa
          Guard; Richard Pasco. In anth.
          ARGO SAY 60
  1306 MACBETH (exc.)
          Marlowe Soc. In anth. ARGO
          PLP 1120, also in DA 1
  1307 MACBETH (exc.)
          Michael Redgrave as Macbeth;
          Barbara Jefford as Lady Macbeth.
          AUDIBK TLS 2 (at)
  1308 MACBETH (exc.)
          John Barrymore. AUDIOR 2202
  1309 MACBETH (exc.)
          BFA (vc 3/4, also 16mm film)
  1310 MACBETH (exc.)
          Anthony Quayle as Macbeth;
          Gwen Ffrangcon-Davies as Lady
          Macbeth; Stanley Holloway as
          Porter. CAED TC 1167
  1311 MACBETH (exc.)
          M. Redgrave. In anth. CAED
          TC 1170
  1312 MACBETH (exc.)
          John Gielgud as Macbeth.
          In anth. COLUMB OL 5550
  1313 MACBETH (exc.)
          John Gielgud. CONTF ISBN o-
          699-00460-8 (16mm film)
  1314 MACBETH (exc.)
          Arthur Bourchier. In anth.
          DELTA 12020
  1315 MACBETH (exc.)
          Blanche Yurka. In anth.
          FOLKW 9841/2
  1316 MACBETH (exc.)
          Flora Robson as Lady Macbeth;
          Philip Huston. HARVOC HFS
          1906/7 (pd 78)
  1317 MACBETH (exc.)
          Michael Redgrave as Macbeth;
          Barbara Jefford as Lady Macbeth.
          LIVSHA SM 1A-2A
  1318 MACBETH (exc.)
          MICHMED 9696 (16mm film, also
          vc)
  1319 MACBETH (exc.)
          NGS (vc 3/4, also 16mm film)
  1320 MACBETH (exc.)
          Barbara Jefford; John Gielgud;
          William Squire; Trevor Martin;
          David March. PROTHM 1ES4 (ac)

  1321 MACBETH (exc.)
          J. Gielgud; I. Worth. In anth.
          RCA SB 6740
  1322 MACBETH (exc.)
          Paul Rogers. In anth. SPOA 723
  1323 MACBETH (exc.)
          In anth. SPOA 767
  1324 MACBETH (exc.)
          Hilton Edwards; Michael Mac-
          Liammoir. SPOA 782 (pd), also
          7006 and 8008 (ac)
  1325 MACBETH (exc.)
          M. MacLiammoir; Hilton Edwards.
          In anth. SPOA 836/7 (2 pd)
  1326 MACBETH (exc.)
          Anew McMaster. In anth. SPOA
          6048 (ac)
  1327 MACBETH (exc.)
          Cotsworth; Le Gallienne; Allen;
          Rolf; Webster. THEAMA GRC 2431
  1328 MACBETH (exc.)
          TIMLIF (vc 3/4)
  1329 MACBETH (exc.)
          Maria Wimmer. In anth. DEUTGR
          140011
  1330 MACBETH (exc., in Italian as
       MACHBETH)
          V. Gassmann. In anth. CETRA
          CLC 0826
  1331 MACBETH (exc.)
          Maurice Evans as Macbeth;
          Judith Anderson as Lady
          Macbeth. FI (16mm film)
  1332 MACBETH (exc.)
          IFB (16mm film)
  1333 MEASURE FOR MEASURE
          John Gielgud as Angelo; Ralph
          Richardson as Duke; Margaret
          Leighton as Isabella; Mark
          Dignam; Tony White; Alec McCowen;
          William Marlowe; Alexis Kanner;
          Christopher Burgess; Brian Mur-
          ray; Paul Vieyra; Ronald Barker;
          Lee Montague; Elric Hooper;
          Renee Asherson; Miranda Con-
          nell; Hazel Hughes. CAED SRS
          204 (3 pd), also CDL 5204 (3 ac);
          also EAV B2 RR 186 (3 pd)
  1334 MEASURE FOR MEASURE
          Arnold Moss. LC T 2609 (at)
  1335 MEASURE FOR MEASURE
          Toby Robertson as Vincentio;
          George Rylands as Angelo & Mis-
          tress Overdone; John Bird as

Escalus; Richard Marquand as
Claudio; Anthony Jacobs as Lucio;
Derek Jacobi and Chris Renard
as Gentlemen; Terrence Hardiman
as Provost; Roger Prior as Peter;
David Brierley as Elbow; Donald
Beves as Pompey; John Kimber as
Abhorson; Clive Swift as Barnar-
dine; Janette Richer as Isabella;
Dorothy Mulcahy as Mariana; Pen-
elope Balchin as Juliet; Camille Prior as Francisca. LONDON
4417 (4 pd), also OSA 1411;
also ARGO RG 164/7 and ZRG 5164/
7 and ZPR 232/5 (4 pd); also CP
232/5 (4 ac)

1336 MEASURE FOR MEASURE
    SPOWRD 176/8 (3 pd)

1337 MEASURE FOR MEASURE
    Kate Nelligan; Tim Pigott-Smith;
    Kenneth Colley. TIMLIF V 6005 A
    (3 vc 3/4)

1338 MEASURE FOR MEASURE (exc.)
    Darien Angadi; Desmond Dupre.
    In anth. ARGO NF 4

1339 MEASURE FOR MEASURE (exc.)
    Eric Portman as Angelo. LIVSHA
    SMM 37A-38A

1340 MEASURE FOR MEASURE (exc.)
    In anth. LONGMAN 3

1341 MERCHANT OF VENICE
    Peggy Ashcroft as Portia; Eric
    Portman as Shylock. AUDIBK
    TLS 15 (at)

1342 MERCHANT OF VENICE
    Hugh Griffith as Shylock; Do-
    rothy Tutin as Portia; Harry An-
    drews as Antonio; Laurence Har-
    dy as Duke of Venice; Jere-
    my Brett as Bassanio; Ronnie
    Barker as Launcelot Gobbo; Zena
    Walker as Jessica; Judith Stott;
    Roy Marsden; Frank Wood; Roy
    Dotrice; Ken Wynne; Ian Holm;
    Derek Godfrey; Robin Philips;
    Stephen Moore; Basil Moskins;
    Mark Dignam. CAED SRS 209
    (3 pd), also CDL 5209 (3 ac)

1343 MERCHANT OF VENICE
    Orson Welles. COLUMB MC 6
    (12 pd 78)

1344 MERCHANT OF VENICE
    Donald Beves as Duke of Venice;
    John Barton as Prince of Moroc-

co; Toby Robertson as Prince of
Arragon; George Rylands as Antonio; Gary Watson as Bassanio;
Anthony Jacobs as Gratiano;
Gerald Mosback as Solanio; Derek Jacobi as Salerio; Richard
Marquand as Lorenzo; Tony Church
as Shylock; Clive Swift as Tu-
bal; Michael Bates as Lance-
lot Gobbo; Terrence Hardiman as
Old Gobbo; Christopher Renard as
Balthazar; John Tracy-Phillips
as Stephano; Margaretta Scott
as Portia; Christine Baker as
Nerissa; Janette Richer as
Jessica. LONDON 4416 (4 pd),
also OSA 1412; also ARGO RG 160
/3, also ZRG 5160/3, also ZPR
138/41; also KZPC 138/41 and
SAY 83 (4 ac); also EAV B3 RR
101 (4 pd), also B1KK2822 (2
ac)

1345 MERCHANT OF VENICE
    M. MacLiammoir; Hilton Edwards.
    In anth. SPOA 836/7 (2 pd)

1346 MERCHANT OF VENICE
    Warren Mitchell; Gemma Jones;
    John Franklyn-Robbins. TIMLIF
    V 6014 C (2 vc 3/4)

1347 MERCHANT OF VENICE (in French as
    LE MARCHAND DE VENISE)
    S. Valère; D. Sorano; J. De-
    sailly; G. Cattaud. ADÉS TS 25
    LA 533, also 13.034

1348 MERCHANT OF VENICE (exc.)
    Dorothy Tutin. In anth. ARGO
    SAY 41

1349 MERCHANT OF VENICE (exc.)
    Marlowe Soc. In anth. ARGO
    PLP 1122, also in DA 2

1350 MERCHANT OF VENICE (exc.)
    Ellen Terry. In anth. AUDIOR
    2465

1351 MERCHANT OF VENICE (exc.)
    Michael MacLiammoir; Hilton Ed-
    wards. AUDIVS 8011SC

1352 MERCHANT OF VENICE (exc.)
    BERG ATTS 008

1353 MERCHANT OF VENICE (exc.)
    BFA (vc 3/4)

1354 MERCHANT OF VENICE (exc.)
    Michael Redgrave. CAED TC
    2013 (2 pd)

Shakespeare, cont'd.
  1355 MERCHANT OF VENICE (exc.)
          Tyrone Power; Ellen Terry.
          In anth. DELTA 12020
  1356 MERCHANT OF VENICE (exc.)
          Paul Sparer; Nancy Marchand;
          John Randolph. LEX 7540;
          also EAV A9R0929
  1357 MERCHANT OF VENICE (exc.)
          Peggy Ashcroft as Portia;
          Eric Portman as Shaylock.
          LIVSHA SMV 31A-32A
  1358 MERCHANT OF VENICE (exc.)
          MICHMED 9697 (16mm film,
          also vc)
  1359 MERCHANT OF VENICE (exc.)
          John Westbrook. In anth.
          PEARL SHE 539
  1360 MERCHANT OF VENICE (exc.)
          PROTHM 1ES6 (ac)
  1361 MERCHANT OF VENICE (exc.)
          J. Gielgud; I. Worth.
          In anth. RCA SB 6740
  1362 MERCHANT OF VENICE (exc.)
          Ellen Terry. In RCA
          64194
  1363 MERCHANT OF VENICE (exc.)
          In anth. SPOA 766
  1364 MERCHANT OF VENICE (exc.)
          Hilton Edwards; M. MacLiammoir.
          SPOA 810 (pd), also 7009 and
          8011 (ac)
  1365 MERCHANT OF VENCIE (exc.)
          Emerson; Webster; Allen.
          In anth. THEAMA
  1366 MERCHANT OF VENICE (exc., in
          German as KAUFMANN VON VENEDIG)
          E. Deutsch. In DEUTGR 140013
  1367 MERRY WIVES OF WINDSOR
          Anthony Quayle as Falstaff;
          Micheal MacLiammoir; Joyce
          Redman; Murray Melvin; Alec
          McCowen; John Laurie; Ernest
          Milton; Ronnie Stevens; Michael
          Hordern; Anthony Nicholls;
          Michael Howe; Aubrey Richards;
          Trevor Martin; Peter Bayliss;
          Gerald Rowlands; Eric Jones;
          June Jago; Judith Stott;
          Hazel Hughes. CAED SRS 203
          (3 pd), also CDL 5203 (3 ac)
  1368 MERRY WIVES OF WINDSOR
          Patrick Wymark as Falstaff;
          Peter Orr as Fenton; Terrence
          Hardiman as Shallow; Gordon

Gardner as Slender; Frank Dun-
can as Ford; Anthony Arlidge as
William Page; Dudley Jones as
Evans; Roy Dotrice as Doctor
Caius; David Buck as Host; An-
thony Handy as Bardolph; Tony
Church as Pistol; Philip Strick
as Nym; Dowie, Freda as Robin;
Norman Mitchell as Simple;
Raymond Clarke as Rugby; Geral-
dine McEwan as Mistress Ford;
Angela Baddeley as Mistress Page;
Susan Maryott as Anna Page;
Beatrix Lehmann as Mistress
Quickly. LONDON 4372 (3 pd),
also S 1372; also ARGO RG 351/3,
also ZRG 5351/3, also ZPR 189/91
  1369 MERRY WIVES OF WINDSOR
          Alan Bennett; Richard O'Callagh-
          an; Tenniel Evans; Bryan Mar-
          shall; Richard Griffiths; Gordon
          Gostelow; Nigel Terry; Michael
          Robbins; Miranda Foster. TIMLIF
          V 6029 E (2 vc 1/2)
  1370 MERRY WIVES OF WINDSOR (in French
          as LES JOYEUSES COMMÈRES DE
          WINDSOR)
          Compagnie Fabbri. ADÈS TS 25
          LA 518
  1371 MERRY WIVES OF WINDSOR (exc.)
          M. Redgrave. In anth. CAED TC
          1170
  1372 MERRY WIVES OF WINDSOR (exc.)
          Paul Rogers. In anth. SPOA 723
  1373 MIDSUMMER NIGHT'S DREAM
          Sarah Churchill as Helena;
          Stanley Holloway as Bottom.
          AUDIBK TLS 12 (at)
  1374 MIDSUMMER NIGHT'S DREAM
          Paul Scofield; Joy Parker;
          Barbara Jefford; John Stride;
          Jack Gwillim; Miles Malleson;
          Edward De Souza, John Warner;
          Gerald James; Ronald Fraser;
          Murray Melvin; Newton Blick;
          Jerry Verno; Michael Faulkes;
          Patricia Routledge; Caroline
          John; Kit Williams; Janet Aust;
          Sarah Acket. CAED SRS 208 (3
          pd), also CDL 5208 (3 ac); also
          EAV B1RR279
  1375 MIDSUMMER NIGHT'S DREAM
          Diana Rigg; David Warner. FI
          (16mm film)

1376 MIDSUMMER NIGHT'S DREAM
     FOLKW 9872
1377 MIDSUMMER NIGHT'S DREAM
     KING (2 vc)
1378 MIDSUMMER NIGHT'S DREAM
     Robert Helpman as Oberon;
     Moira Shearer as Titania;
     Stanley Holloway as Bottom;
     Anthony Nicholls; Margaret Cour-
     tenay; Anna Walford; Patrick
     Macnee; Terence Longdon; John
     Warner; Norman Rossington.
     LFP TC 7062; also RCA LM 6115
     and LVT 3002 (3 pd)
1379 MIDSUMMER NIGHT'S DREAM
     Frank Duncan as Theseus; Joan
     Hart as Hippolyta; Julian Curry
     as Egeus; John Tracy-Phillips
     as Demetrius; Ian McKellen as
     Lysander; Terrence Hardiman as
     Philostrate; Jeannette Sterke
     as Hermia; Prunella Scales as
     Helena; Miles Malleson as
     Quince; Peter Woodthorpe as
     Bottom; John Sharp as Flute &
     Moth; John Wood as Snout;
     Trevor Nunn as Starveling;
     Christopher Kelly as Snug; An-
     thony White as Oberon; Jill
     Balcon as Titania; Richard Gool-
     den as Puck; Elizabeth Proud as
     Peaseblossom; George Rylands as
     Cobweb; Richard Kay as Mustard
     seed. LONDON 4349 (3 pd), also
     OSA 4344; also ARGO RG 250/2,
     also ZRG 5250/2, also ZPR 132/4;
     also KZPC 132/4 (3 ac), also
     K52K32 and SAY 38
1380 MIDSUMMER NIGHT'S DREAM
     J. Gielgud; I. Worth. In anth.
     RCA SB 6740
1381 MIDSUMMER NIGHT'S DREAM
     M. MacLiammoir. SPOWRD SW 131-
     33 (3 pd); also LIST SKP 1003
     (3 pd), also CX103 (2 ac)
1382 MIDSUMMER NIGHT'S DREAM
     Pippa Guard as Hermia; Nicky
     Henson as Demetrius; Robert
     Lindsay as Lysander; Cherith
     Mellor as Helena; Brian Glover
     as Bottom; Phil Daniels as Pack;
     Helen Mirren as Titania; Peter
     McEnery as Oberon. TIMLIF
     V 6024 D (2 vc 3/4)

1383 MIDSUMMER NIGHT'S DREAM
     James Cagney; Dick Powell;
     Joe E. Brown; Mickey Rooney;
     Olivia de Havilland. UAE
     (16mm film)
1384 MIDSUMMER NIGHT'S DREAM (in French
     as LE SONGE D'UNE NUIT D'ÉTÉ)
     M. Casarès; J.-P. Moulinot;
     C. Nicot; J. Vilar. VEG TNP 10
1385 MIDSUMMER NIGHT'S DREAM (exc.)
     Ann Todd. In anth. AMBER 7101
1386 MIDSUMMER NIGHT'S DREAM (exc.)
     Marlowe Soc. In anth. ARGO
     PLP 1122, also DA 2
1387 MIDSUMMER NIGHT'S DREAM (exc.)
     BERG ATTS 007
1388 MIDSUMMER NIGHT'S DREAM (exc.)
     BFA (16mm film, also vc 3/4)
1389 MIDSUMMER NIGHT'S DREAM (exc.)
     John Gielgud as Oberon. In
     anth. COLUMB OL 5550
1390 MIDSUMMER NIGHT'S DREAM (exc.)
     Maurice Evans. In anth.
     GOLDEN AA 58
1391 MIDSUMMER NIGHT'S DREAM (exc.)
     Sarah Churchill as Helena;
     Stanley Holloway as Bottom.
     LIVSHA SND 19A-20A
1392 MIDSUMMER NIGHT'S DREAM (exc.)
     PROTHM (ac)
1393 MIDSUMMER NIGHT'S DREAM (exc.)
     Moira Shearer as Titania;
     Robert Helpman as Oberon;
     Stanley Holloway as Bottom.
     RCA LM 1863
1394 MIDSUMMER NIGHT'S DREAM (exc.)
     Paul Rogers. In anth. SPOA 723
1395 MIDSUMMER NIGHT'S DREAM (exc.)
     Eithne Dunne; Eve Watkinson.
     SPOA 882 (pd), also 8013 (ac);
     also AUDIVS 8013 SC
1396 MUCH ADO ABOUT NOTHING
     Rex Harrison as Benedick;
     Rachel Roberts as Beatrice;
     Alan Webb; Charles Gray;
     Robert Stephens; Newton Blick;
     Charles Heslop; Peter Gilmore;
     Lee Montague; P. G. Stephens;
     Graham Crowden; Ronald Fraser;
     Jerry Verno; Douglas Muir;
     Michael Lewis; Eric Jones;
     Zena Walker; Eileen Atkins;
     Patricia Routledge. CAED SRS
     206 (3 pd), also CDL 5206 (3ac);

Shakespeare, cont'd.
       MUCH ADO ABOUT NOTHING, cont'd.
       also EAV B1RR086 (3 pd)
  1397 MUCH ADO ABOUT NOTHING
       Leslie Howard; Rosalind
       Russell. LIVSHA 89866 (5 pd);
       also YESTER 15287 (at)
  1398 MUCH ADO ABOUT NOTHING
       William Squire as Don Pedro;
       Patrick Creean as Don John; Ga-
       ry Watson as Claudio; John Giel-
       gud as Benedick; Michael Hor-
       dern as Leonato; Donald Layne-
       Smith as Antonio; Peter Pears
       as Balthazar; Peter Orr as Bo-
       rachio; Cyril Luckham as Friar
       Francis; Clive Swift as Conrade;
       Peter Woodthorpe as Dogberry;
       Ian Holm as Verges; Josephine
       Stuart as Hero; Peggy Ashcroft
       as Beatrice; Gillian Webb as
       Margaret; Janette Richer as
       Ursula. LONDON 4362 (3 pd),
       also OSA 1362; also ARGO RG 300
       /2, also ZRG 5300/2, also ZPR
       183/5; also Cass. 183/5 (3 ac),
       also K70K32, also SAY 36
  1399 MUCH ADO ABOUT NOTHING
       Albert Finney; Maggie Smith;
       Franck Finlay. RCA VDS 104 (3
       pd)
  1400 MUCH ADO ABOUT NOTHING
       Hilton Edwards; Michael MacLiam-
       moir; Patrick Bedford; Dennis
       Brennan; Christopher Casson;
       David Basil Gill; Daphne Carroll;
       Coralie Carmichael. SPOWRD SW
       141-3 (3 pd)
  1401 MUCH ADO ABOUT NOTHING
       TIMLIF V 6034 F (vc 3/4)
  1402 MUCH ADO ABOUT NOTHING (exc.)
       Christopher Plummer; Geraldine
       McEwen. In anth. ARGO SAY 41
  1403 MUCH ADO ABOUT NOTHING (exc.)
       John Gielgud as Don Pedro. In
       anth. COLUMB OL 5550
  1404 MUCH ADO ABOUT NOTHING (exc.)
       Ellen Terry. In anth. DELTA
       DEL 12020
  1405 MUCH ADO ABOUT NOTHING (exc.)
       IFB (vc 3/4)
  1406 MUCH ADO ABOUT NOTHING (exc.)
       Richard Johnson as Benedick;
       Pauline Jameson as Beatrice.

       LIVSHA SWA 21A-22A
  1407 MUCH ADO ABOUT NOTHING (exc.)
       MICHMED 9704 (16mm film, also
       vc)
  1408 MUCH ADO ABOUT NOTHING (exc.)
       Ellen Terry. In anth. RCA
       64191
  1409 MUCH ADO ABOUT NOTHING (exc.)
       Eithne Dunne; Christopher
       Casson; Watkinson. SPOA 883
       (pd & ac)
  1410 OTHELLO
       Richard Johnson; Anna Calder-
       Marshall; Peggy Ashcroft;
       Frank Duncan; David King;
       Denis McCarthy; Gary Watson;
       George Rylands; Ian Holm;
       Peter Woodthorpe; Peter Ged-
       des; Clifford Rose; Lisa Har-
       row. ARGO ZPR 204/7 (4 pd),
       also KZPC 204/7 (4 ac), also
       K49K43, and also SAY 64
  1411 OTHELLO
       Frank Silvera as Othello; Cy-
       ril Cusack as Iago; Anna Massey
       as Desdemona; Celia Johnson as
       as Emilia; Ernest Thesiger;
       Abraham Sofaer; James Hayter;
       David Dodimead; Alan Bates;
       Robert Stephens; Ronald Ibbs;
       Wallas Eaton; Donald Eccles;
       Laurence Hardy; Norman Mit-
       chell; Margaret Whiting. CAED
       225 (3 pd), also CDL 5225 (3 ac)
  1412 OTHELLO
       Paul Robeson as Othello; Uta Ha-
       gen as Desdemona; Jose Ferrer as
       Iago; Edith King as Emilia;
       Alexander Scourby; Jack Manning;
       Ainsworth Arnold; Philip Huston;
       Grace Coppin. COLUMB SL 153
       (3 pd)
  1413 OTHELLO
       Marshall as Othello; Robinson;
       Claire; Donegan. FOLKW 9618
       (2 pd)
  1414 OTHELLO
       The Canadian Players. In anth.
       LC T 2609 (at)
  1415 OTHELLO
       Richard David as Duke of Venice;
       John Barton as Brabantio; John
       Wilders as Gratiano; Anthony
       White as Lodovico; Tony Church

as Othello; Gary Watson as Cassio; Donald Beves as Iago;
George Rylands as Roderigo; John
Arnott as Montano; Peter Woodthorpe as Clown; Wendy Gifford
as Desdemona; Irene Worth
as Emilia; Mary Fenton as
Bianca. LONDON A 4414 (4 pd),
also ARGO RG 121/4

1416 OTHELLO
Laurence Olivier as Othello;
Frank Finlay as Iago; Maggie
Smith as Desdemona; Joyce Redman as Emilia; Michael Roth-
well as Roderigo; Derek Jacobi
as Cassio; Edward Hardwicke
as Montano. RCA VDM 100 (4
pd), also RE 5520/3

1417 OTHELLO
TIMLIF V 6018 D (vc 3/4)

1418 OTHELLO (Silent German UFA film)
Emil Jannings; Lya de Putti;
Werner Krauss. PENGUIN (vc)

1419 OTHELLO (exc.)
L. Olivier; Dorothy Tutin;
Sybil Thorndike. In anth.
ARGO NF 4

1420 OTHELLO (exc.)
Marlowe Soc. In anth. ARGO
PLP 1120, also in DA 1

1421 OTHELLO (exc.)
Read by Edwin Booth. In anth.
AUDIOR 2465

1422 OTHELLO (exc.)
BERG ATTS 006

1423 OTHELLO (exc.)
Edwin Booth. In anth. DELTA
12020

1424 OTHELLO (exc.)
IFB (vc 3/4)

1425 OTHELLO (exc.)
John Gielgud as Othello; Ralph
Richardson as Iago; Barbara
Jefford as Desdemona; Coral
Browne as Emilia. LIVSHA
7A-8A

1426 OTHELLO (exc.)
In anth. MICHMED 9701 (16mm
film, also vc)

1427 OTHELLO (exc.)
MICHMED 9705 (16mm film, also
vc)

1428 OTHELLO (exc.)
PROTHM 1ES 9 (ac)

1429 OTHELLO (exc.)
Laurence Olivier; Frank Finlay; Maggie Smith; Joyce Redman. RCA VDM 108

1430 OTHELLO (exc.)
In anth. SPOA 766

1431 OTHELLO (exc.)
M. MacLiammoir. SPOA 783 (pd),
also 7109 (ac)

1432 OTHELLO (exc.)
M. MacLiammoir; Hilton Edwards.
In anth. SPOA 836/7

1433 OTHELLO (exc.)
M. MacLiammoir; Hilton Edwrads.
In anth. SPOA 7005

1434 OTHELLO (in Italian as OTELLO)
V. Gassmann. In anth. CETRA
CLC 0826

1435 OTHELLO (exc., in Russian)
A. Ostuzhev. In anth. MK
013603-4

1436 PERICLES
Paul Scofield; Felix Aylmer;
Judi Dench; John Laurie; Mi-
riam Karlin; Charles Gray;
Jack Gwillim; Daniel Thorn-
dike; Arthur Hewlett; Jack May;
George Howe; David Dodimead; Ja-
mes Mellor; Norman Mitchell;
Edward Hardwicke; Tarn Bassett;
Christopher Guinee; Aubrey Woods.
CAED SRS 237 (3 pd), also CDL 5
237 (3 ac)

1437 PERICLES
Frank Duncan as Antiochus;
William Squire as Pericles; To-
ny Church as Gower; John Tydeman
as Thaliard; Michael Bates, Phi-
lip Strick, and Norman Mitchell
as Fishermen; Yvonne Bonnamy as
Lychorida; David King as Cleon;
Margaret Rawlings as Dionyza;
Denis McCarthy as Helicanus;
Michael Hordern as Simonides;
Peter Orr as Cerimon; Margaretta
Scott as Diana; Peter Woodthorpe
as Pandar; Patrick Wymark as
Boult; David Buck as Leonine;
Gary Watson as Lysimachus; Jan-
ette Richer as Thaisa; Prunella
Scales as Marina; Richard Mar-
quand and David Jones as
Gentlemen; Patsy Byrne as Bawd.
LONDON 4377 (3 pd), also S 1377;

Shakespeare, cont'd.
      PERICLES, cont'd.
         also ARGO RG 411/13; ZRG 5411/13,
         also ZPR 248/50
   1438 PERICLES
         Mike Gwilym; Patrick Godfrey;
         John Woodvine; Robert Ashby; An-
         nette Crosbie; Valerie Lush;
         Patrick Allen; Amananda Redman;
         Edward Petherbridge; Juliet
         Stevenson.   TIMLIF V 6035 F
         (2 vc 1/2)
   1439 ROMEO AND JULIET
         Keith Michell as Romeo; Vir-
         ginia McKenna as Juliet; Flora
         Robson as Nurse.   AUDIBK
         TLS 17 (at)
   1440 ROMEO AND JULIET
         Claire Bloom as Juliet; Albert
         Finney as Romeo; Edith Evans as
         Nurse; Kenneth Haigh; Donald
         Eccles; William Hutt; Michael
         Alexander; Anthony Nicholls;
         Wallas Eaton; Jeremy Spenser;
         Christopher Guinee; Hilton Ed-
         wards; Peter Bayliss; Ronnie
         Stevens; Yvonne Coulette;
         Catherine Lacey.   CAED SRS 228
         (3 pd), also CDL 5228 (3 ac);
         also EAV B3RR474 (3 pd), and
         B1KK365 (3 ac)
   1441 ROMEO AND JULIET
         Olivia Hussey; Leonard Whiting;
         Milo O'Shea.   CAPITOL SWDR 289
         (4 pd)
   1442 ROMEO AND JULIET
         Tom McDermott as Montague;
         Thayer David as Capulet; Ion
         Berger as Romeo; Joe Bova as
         Mercutio; Ed Winter as Benvolio;
         Sidney Walker as Friar Laurence;
         Kathleen Widdoes as Juliet.
         FOLGER WSP 130/3 (4 pd)
   1443 ROMEO AND JULIET
         Laurence Harvey; Susan Shentall;
         Flora Robson; Sebastian Cabot;
         Aldo Zollo; John Gielgud.
         LEARNC (2 vc 3/4, also 16mm film)
   1444 ROMEO AND JULIET
         Hilton Edwards; Michael MacLiam-
         moir.   LIST SKP 1002 (4 pd),
         also CX 102 (3 ac)
   1445 ROMEO AND JULIET
         Terrence Hardiman as Escalus;

Corin Redgrave as Paris; Toby
Robertson as Capulet; Richard
Marquand as Romeo; Anthony White
as Mercutio; John Barton as Ben-
volio; David Jones as Tybalt;
Tony Church as Friar Lawrence &
Musician; George Rylands as
Friar John & Musician; Anthony
Arlidge as Sampson; Clive Swift
as Gregory; Donald Beves as Peter; Julian Curry as Apothecary;
Margaretta Scott as Lady Capulet;
Janette Richer as Juliet; Vivienne Chatterton as Nurse;
Denis McCarthy as Chorus.
LONDON 4419 (4 pd), also OSA
1407; also ARGO RG 200/3 (4 pd),
also ZRG 5200/3, also ZPR 208/11,
also KZPC 208/11 and SAY 37
(4 ac)
   1446 ROMEO AND JULIET
         William Devlin as Escalus; John
         Warner as Paris; Rupert Harvey
         as Montague; John Phillips as
         Capulet; Alan Badel as Romeo;
         Claire Bloom as Juliet; Lewis
         Casson as Friar Lawrence; Peter
         Finch as Mercutio; William
         Squire as Benvolio.   RCA LM 6110
         (3 pd), also LVT 3001; also LFP
         7068 (ac)
   1447 ROMEO AND JULIET
         Olivia Hussey; Leonard Whiting;
         Michael York.   RCA (2 vc)
   1448 ROMEO AND JULIET
         Eamonn Andrews Studio.   SPOWRD
         147-50 (4 pd)
   1449 ROMEO AND JULIET
         Celia Johnson; Michael Hordern;
         Joseph O'Conor; Anthony Andrews;
         Patrick Ryecart; Rebecca Saire;
         John Gielgud.   TIMLIF V 6003 A
         (3 vc 3/4)
   1450 ROMEO AND JULIET (exc.)
         AIMS (16mm film)
   1451 ROMEO AND JULIET (exc.)
         Marlowe Soc.   In anth. ARGO
         PLP 1120, also in DA 1
   1452 ROMEO AND JULIET (exc.)
         Dorothy Tutin.   In anth. ARGO
         SAY 41
   1453 ROMEO AND JULIET (exc.)
         Eva LeGallienne; Richard Waring;
         Dennis King. ATLANT 401 (2 pd)

1454 ROMEO AND JULIET (exc.)
     Jane Cowl; E. H. Southern;
     Julia Marlowe. In anth. AUDIOR
     2465
1455 ROMEO AND JULIET (exc.)
     AUDIVS 8010 SC
1456 ROMEO AND JULIET (exc.)
     BERG ATTS 002
1457 ROMEO AND JULIET (exc.)
     BFA (16mm film, also vc 3/4)
1458 ROMEO AND JULIET (exc.)
     Olivia Hussey as Juliet;
     Leonard Whiting as Romeo; Mila
     O'Shea; Michael York; John Mc-
     Enery; Pat Heywood; Natasha
     Parry; Robert Stephens.
     CAPITOL ST 2993
1459 ROMEO AND JULIET (exc.)
     John Gielgud as Romeo; Pamela
     Brown as Juliet. In anth.
     DECCA DL 9504
1460 ROMEO AND JULIET (exc.)
     Ellen Terry. In anth. DELTA
     12020, also in IRCC 3
1461 ROMEO AND JULIET (exc.)
     Laurence Harvey as Romeo; Su-
     san Shentall as Juliet; Flora
     Robson. EPIC LC 3126
1462 ROMEO AND JULIET (exc.)
     John Barryman; Leslie Howard;
     Norma Shearer. FI (16mm film)
1463 ROMEO AND JULIET (exc.)
     Blanche Yurka. In anth. FOLKW
     FL 9841/2
1464 ROMEO AND JULIET (exc.)
     In anth. IER W3RG94500 (4 pd),
     also in W3KG94500 (4 ac)
1465 ROMEO AND JULIET (exc.)
     IFB (16mm film, also vc 3/4)
1466 ROMEO AND JULIET (exc.)
     Keith Michell as Romeo;
     Virginia McKenna as Juliet;
     Flora Robson as Nurse. LIVSHA
     SRJ 33A-34A
1467 ROMEO AND JULIET (exc.)
     MICHMED 9698 (16mm film, also
     vc)
1468 ROMEO AND JULIET (exc.)
     In anth. MICHMED 9706 (16mm film,
     also vc)
1469 ROMEO AND JULIET (exc.)
     NGS (16mm film, also vc 3/4)
1470 ROMEO AND JULIET (exc.)
     PROTHM 1ES3 (ac)

1471 ROMEO AND JULIET (exc.)
     Edith Evans. In anth. RCA
     LRL1-5037
1472 ROMEO AND JULIET (exc.)
     Claire Bloom as Juliet; Alan
     Badel as Romeo. RCA LM 2064
1473 ROMEO AND JULIET (exc.)
     Geraldine Brooks; Blanche Yur-
     ka; Hurd Hatfield. RCA LM
     6028
1474 ROMEO AND JULIET (exc.)
     J. Gielgud; I. Worth. In
     anth. RCA SB 6740
1475 ROMEO AND JULIET (exc.)
     Read by Paul Rogers. In anth.
     SPOA 723
1476 ROMEO AND JULIET (exc.)
     In anth. SPOA 766
1477 ROMEO AND JULIET (exc.)
     London Swan Theatre. SPOA 812
     (pd), also 7008 and 8010 (ac)
1478 ROMEO AND JULIET (exc.)
     E. Martin Browne; Henzie Rae-
     burn. In anth. SPOA 901
1479 ROMEO AND JULIET (exc.)
     In anth. THEATCL (ac)
1480 ROMEO AND JULIET (exc., in
     German)
     Käthe Gold; Will Quadflieg.
     In anth. DEUTGR 40 009
1481 ROMEO AND JULIET (exc., in Ital-
     ian as ROMEO E GIULIETTA)
     V. Gassmann. In anth. CETRA
     CLC 0826
1482 ROMEO AND JULIET (exc., in Italian
     as ROMEO E GIULIETTA)
     V. Gassmann; Valentina Fortuna-
     to. In anth. CETRA CLC 0855
1483 ROMEO AND JULIET (exc. in Russian)
     M. Babanova; A. Lukyanov. In
     anth. MK D 013603-4
1484 TAMING OF THE SHREW
     Mary Pickford; Douglas Fair-
     banks; Edwin Maxwell; Joseph
     Cawthorn. BLACKH (vc)
1485 TAMING OF THE SHREW
     Trevor Howard as Petruchio;
     Margaret Leighton as Kate; Miles
     Malleson; Hugh Manning; Peter
     Bayliss; Patricia Somerset; Mi-
     chael Meacham; Eric Jones; Au-
     brey Woods; Gerald James; Paul
     Daneman; Willoughby Goddard;
     Edgar Wreford; Ronnie Stevens;

Shakespeare, cont'd.
    TAMING OF THE SHREW, cont'd.
    Newton Blick; James Culli-
    ford; David Dodimead; Elvi Hale;
    Avril Elgar. CAED SRS 211
    (3 pd), also CDL 5211 (3 ac);
    also EAV B3RR473 (3 pd)
1486 TAMING OF THE SHREW
    EMBASSY (2 vc)
1487 TAMING OF THE SHREW
    Shakespeare Students Co. FOLKW
    9621 (2 pd)
1488 TAMING OF THE SHREW
    Hilton Edwards; Michael Mac-
    Liammoir. LIST SKP 1005 (3 pd),
    also CX 105 (2 ac)
1489 TAMING OF THE SHREW
    Sian Phillips as Katharina;
    Peter O'Toole as Petruchio.
    LIVSHA STS 11A-12A
1490 TAMING OF THE SHREW
    Frank Duncan as Lord; Tony
    Church as Sly; Beatrix Lehmann
    as Hostess; V. C. Clinton Badde-
    ley as Baptista; Dudley Jones
    as Vincentio; Peter Orr as Lu-
    centio; Derek Godfrey as Pe-
    truchio; Donald Layne Smith as
    Gremio; David King as Hortensio;
    Gordon Gardner as Tranio; Phil-
    ip Strick as Biondello; Michael
    Bates as Grumio; Peggy Ashcroft
    as Katharina; Janette Richer as
    Bianca; Freda Dowie as Widow.
    LONDON 4367 (3 pd), also S1367;
    also ARGO RG 348/50 and ZRG 5348
    /50 and ZPR 135/7 (3 pd); also
    KZPC 135/7 and SAY 65 (3 ac)
1491 TAMING OF THE SHREW
    Elizabeth Taylor; Richard Bur-
    ton; Michael York. RCAVID (2 vc)
1492 TAMING OF THE SHREW
    Hilton Edwards; Michael MacLiamm-
    moir; Dennis Brennan; Paul Far-
    rell; Anna Managhan; Milo O'Shea;
    David Basil Gill; Patrick Mc-
    larnon; Coralie Carmichael.
    SPOWRD SW 151-3 (3 pd)
1493 TAMING OF THE SHREW
    Richard Burton; E. Taylor.
    TIMLIF F 7061 G (16mm film)
1494 TAMING OF THE SHREW
    John Cleese; Sarah Badel.
    TIMLIF V 6015 C (2 vc 3/4)

1495 TAMING OF THE SHREW
    Edward G. Robinson; Frieda
    Inescort; Charles D. Brown.
    YESTER 15289 (at); also in
    anth. LIVSHA 898667 (5 pd)
1496 TAMING OF THE SHREW (exc.)
    Ann Todd. In anth. AMBER
    7101
1497 TAMING OF THE SHREW (exc.)
    John Gielgud as Biondello.
    In anth. COLUMB OL 5550
1498 TAMING OF THE SHREW (exc.)
    IFB (16mm film, also vc 3/4)
1499 TAMING OF THE SHREW (exc.)
    Performed by puppets. NIT (vc)
1500 TAMING OF THE SHREW (exc.)
    In anth. SPOA 766
1501 TAMING OF THE SHREW (exc.)
    Christopher Casson; Eve
    Watkinson. SPOA 884 (pd),
    also 7111 (ac)
1502 TAMING OF THE SHREW (exc.)
    Anew McMaster. In anth. SPOA
    6048 (ac)
1503 TAMING OF THE SHREW (exc., in Ger-
    man)
    Maria Wimmer. In anth. DEUTGR
    140 011
1504 TAMING OF THE SHREW (exc., in
    German as DER WIDERSPENSTIGEN
    ZÄHMUNG)
    Hilde Krahl. In anth. TELEF
    STSC 13445
1505 TAMING OF THE SHREW (exc., in
    Italian as LA BISBETICA DOMATA)
    V. Moriconi; A. Ninchi; G.
    Mauri; C. Enrici. In anth.
    CETRA LPZ 2064
1506 TAMING OF THE SHREW (exc., in Rus-
    sian)
    L. Dobrzhanskaya; A. Ivanov;
    V. Blagoobrazov. In anth.
    MK D 013603/4
1507 TEMPEST
    Michael Redgrave as Prospero;
    Hugh Griffith as Caliban; Van-
    essa Redgrave as Ariel; Anna
    Massey as Miranda; Edward Ati-
    enza as Alonso; Peter Woodthorpe
    as Sebastian; Robert Hardy as
    Antonio; John Hurt as Ferdinand;
    Cyril Luckham as Gonzalo; Bryan
    Stanyon; William Marlowe; Ron-
    nie Barker; Alec McCowen; Frank

Wood; Patience Collier; Elizabeth Sprigs; Miranda Connell.
CAED SRS 201 (3 pd), also CDL
5201 (3 ac); also EAV B4RR
658 (3 pd)

1508 TEMPEST
Maurice Evans; Richard Burton;
Roddy McDowall; Lee Remick; Tom
Poston. ENTER (2 vc 3/4)

1509 TEMPEST
Arnold Moss. LC T 2568 (at)

1510 TEMPEST
Hilton Edwards; Michael Mac-
Liammoir. LIST SKP 1007 (3
pd), also CX 107 (2 ac)

1511 TEMPEST
Donald Wolfit as Prospero;
Rosalind Iden as Miranda;
Mai Zetterling as Ariel.
LIVSHA STEMP 23A-24A

1512 TEMPEST
Terrence Hardiman as Alonso;
Ian Lang as Sebastian; Michael
Hordern as Prospero; Denis
McCarthy as Antonio; Ian Lang
as Ferdinand; Denys Robertson
as Gonzalo; Derek Jacobi as
Adrian; Patrick Wymark as
Caliban; Philip Strick as Ca-
liban; Clive Swift as Boats-
wain; Natasha Parry as Miranda;
Miles Malleson as Trinculo;
Margaret Field-Hyde as Ariel;
Jill Daltry as Iris; Margaretta
Scott as Ceres; Ena Mitchell as
Juno. LONDON 4346 (3 pd), also
OSA 1318; also ARGO RG 216/8,
also ZRG 5216/8, also ZPR 251/3;
also KZPC 251/3 and SAY 69 (3
ac)

1513 TEMPEST
Raymond Massey as Prospero; Hurd
Hatfield as Ferdinand; Lionel
Stander as Caliban; Lee Grant as
Ariel; Oliver Clift as Sebastian;
Bruce Gordon as Antonio; Robert
Harrison as Gonzalo; Martin King-
sley as Stephano; Dayton Lummis
as Master of Ship; David Orrick
as Trinculo; Margaret Phillips
as Miranda. POLYMU PRLP 5001/2
(2 pd)

1514 TEMPEST
Stratford-upon-Avon Festival Co.
ROYALE LP 1440

1515 TEMPEST
Daphne Carroll; Christopher
Casson. SPOA 8014 (ac)

1516 TEMPEST
Hilton Edwards. SPOWRD
137/9 (3 pd)

1517 TEMPEST
Pippa Guard; Michael Hordern;
David Dixon; Warren Clarke.
TIMLIF V 6010 B (3 vc 3/4)

1518 TEMPEST
Alexander Scourby. In anth.
TRINIT

1519 TEMPEST (exc.)
Ann Todd. In anth. AMBER
7101

1520 TEMPEST (exc.)
John Gielgud. In anth. ARGO
NF 4

1521 TEMPEST (exc.)
John Gielgud. In anth. ARGO
SAY 18

1522 TEMPEST (exc.)
Donald Sinden; Barbara Leigh-
Hunt. In anth. ARGO SAY 41

1523 TEMPEST (exc.)
Richard Burton. In anth. ARGO
SAY 47

1524 TEMPEST (exc.)
Marlowe Soc. In anth. ARGO
PLP 1122, also in DA 2

1525 TEMPEST (exc.)
Christopher Casson; Daphne
Carroll. AUDIVS 8014 SC

1526 TEMPEST (exc.)
M. Redgrave. In anth. CAED
TC 1170

1527 TEMPEST (exc.)
John Gielgud. CONTF ISBN
0-699-00459-4 (16mm film)

1528 TEMPEST (exc.)
Maurice Evans. In anth. GOL-
DEN AA 58

1529 TEMPEST (exc.)
IFB (vc 3/4)

1530 TEMPEST (exc.)
In anth. LONGMAN 3

1531 TEMPEST (exc.)
MICHMED 9710 (16mm film, also
vc)

1532 TEMPEST (exc.)
NATCTR 0226-37/8 (ac)

1533 TEMPEST (exc.)
Daphne Carrol; Christopher Casson. SPOA 886 (pd), also 8014
(ac)

Shakespeare, cont'd.
1534 TEMPEST (exc.)
      E. Martin Browne; Henzie
      Raeburn. In anth. SPOA 901
1535 TEMPEST (exc.)
      Moss. THEAMA GRC 2431
1536 TEMPEST (exc., in Italian as
     LA TEMPESTA)
      V. Gassmann. In anth. CETRA
      CLC 0826
1537 TIMON OF ATHENS
      William Squire as Timon;
      Corin Redgrave as Sempronius;
      Donald Beves as Lucullus;
      David Rowe-Beddoe as Lucius; Mi-
      chael Burrell as Ventidius;
      Anthony White as Alcibiades;
      Peter Woodthorpe as Apemantus;
      John Wood as Flavius; Derek
      Jacobi as Poet; Peter Foster
      as Painter; Philip Strick as
      Jeweller and Servilius; Tre-
      vor Nunn as Merchant; David
      Coombes as Flaminius; Antho-
      ny Arlidge as Lucilius; John
      Sharp as Caphius; Gary O'Connor
      as Philotus; Eric Rump as Titus;
      Tom Bussmann as Hortensius;
      Richard Kay as Page; Jill Daltry
      as Phrynia; Elizabeth Proud as
      Timandra. LONDON 4350 (3 pd),
      also OSA 1322; also ARGO RG 253
      /5, also ZRG 5253/5 (4 pd);
      also ARGO ZPR 212/4 (3 pd)
1538 TIMON OF ATHENS
      Jonathan Pryce as Timon; John
      Welsh as Flavius; John Shrap-
      nel as Alcibiades. TIMLIF
      V 6016 C (3 vc 3/4)
1539 TITUS ANDRONICUS
      Anthony Quayle; Maxine Audley;
      Michael Hordern; Colin Blakely;
      Charles Gray; Jack Gwillim;
      Alan Howard; John Moffatt; Judi
      Dench; Michael Meacham; Ri-
      chard Brooke; Stephen Moore;
      James Cairncross; Christopher
      Guinee; John Dane; Rosalind
      Atkinson; Trevor Martin. CAED
      SRS 227 (3 pd), also CDL 5227
      (3 ac)
1540 TITUS ANDRONICUS
      Dennis Arundell as Saturninus;
      John Tydeman as Bassianus;

William Devlin as Titus An-
dronicus; Tony Church as Mar-
cus Andronicus; Frank Duncan
as Lucius; Gordon Gardner as
Quintus; Richard Marquand as
Martius; Roger Clissold as
Mutius; Jean England as Young
Lucius; Bob Jones as Publius;
Roger Croucher as Aemilius;
David Rowe-Beddoe as Demetrius;
Anthony Jacobs as Chiron; Pe-
ter Orr as Aaron; Peter Wood-
thorpe as Clown; David King,
Philip Strick, and George Rylands as Romans and Goths; Jill
Balcon as Tamora; Susan Maryott
as Lavinia; Barbara Lott as Nurse. LONDON 4371 (3 pd), also
S 1371; also ARGO RG 357/9 and
ZRG 5357/9, also ZPR 215/7
1541 TITUS ANDRONICUS
      TIMLIF V 6036 F (vc 3/4)
1542 TROILUS AND CRESSIDA
      Michael Pennington as Troilus;
      Maureen O'Brien as Cressida;
      Nigel Stock as Pandarus; Norman
      Rodway as Ulysses; John Rye as
      Achilles. BBC ECN 142 (4 ac)
1543 TROILUS AND CRESSIDA
      Jeremy Brett as Troilus and
      Deiphobus; Diane Cilento as Cre-
      ssida; Cyril Cusack as Thersites;
      Max Adrian as Pandarus; John
      Bennett as Priam; Edward De
      Souza as Hector; Alan Howard as
      Paris; Daniel Thorndike; Graham
      Crowden; Richard Goolden; David
      William; Derek Godfrey; Peter
      Bayliss; Eric Porter; Walter
      Hudd; Alec McCowen; Christopher
      Guinee; Patricia Routledge; Ann
      Bell; Dona Martyn; Jeremy Geidt;
      Rodger Sheperd. CAED SRS 234
      (3 pd), also CDL 5234 (3 ac)
1544 TROILUS AND CRESSIDA
      Roger Livesey as Pandarus;
      Anna Massey as Cressida.
      LIVSHA STC 51A-52A
1545 TROILUS AND CRESSIDA
      John Sheppard as Priam; Gary
      Watson as Hector; Anthony White
      as Troilus; Julian Pettifer as
      Paris; John Barton as Margare-
      lon and Nestor; David Gibson as

Aeneas; Clive Swift as Calchas;
Donald Beves as Pandarus; John
Wilders as Agamemnon; Noel Annan
as Menelaus; James Taylor-
Whitehead as Achilles; Tony
Church as Ajax; George Rylands
as Ulysses; John Arnott as Dio-
medes; David Buck as Patroclus;
Peter Woodthorpe as Thersites;
Anthony Jacobs; Wendy Gifford as
Helen; Christine Baker as An-
dromache; Dorothy Mulcahy as
Cassandra; Irene Worth as Cres-
sida. LONDON 4413 (4 pd); also
ARGO RG 128/31, also ZPR 236/9

1546 TROILUS AND CRESSIDA
NBC ISBN 0-699-30151-3 (16mm
film)

1547 TROILUS AND CRESSIDA
Anton Lesser; Suzanne Burden.
TIMLIF V 6019 D (3 vc 3/4)

1548 TROILUS AND CRESSIDA (exc.)
Paul Hardwick. In anth.
ARGO SAY 41

1549 TROILUS AND CRESSIDA (exc.)
John Gielgud as Troilus. In
anth. COLUMB OL 5550

1550 TROILUS AND CRESSIDA (exc.)
In anth. MICHMED 9701 (16mm
film, also vc)

1551 TROILUS AND CRESSIDA (exc.)
Folio Theatre Prod. SPOA 892
(pd and ac)

1552 TWELFTH NIGHT
John Rowe; Robert Middleton;
Oz Clarke; Eileen Atkins;
John Savident; Ronnie Stevens;
Robert Eddison; Louise Purnell;
Michael Dennison; Kenneth Gil-
bert; Jeffrey Daunton; John
Cording. ARGO SAY 39 (ac)

1553 TWELFTH NIGHT
Maggie Smith as Viola; Brenda
Bruce as Olivia. AUDIBK TLS 8
(at)

1554 TWELFTH NIGHT
Siobhan McKenna as Viola; Paul
Scofield as Malvolio; John Ne-
ville as Aguecheek; Vanessa Red-
grave as Olivia; Robert Hardy;
Tom Criddle; James Hayter; Ron-
ald Ibbs; Christopher Guinee;
Willoughby Goddard; Richard
Goolden; Norman Rossington; Mir-
iam Karlin. CAED SRS 213 (3pd)

also CDL 5213 (3 ac); also EAV
B3RR473 (3 pd, also B1KK2823
(2 ac)

1555 TWELFTH NIGHT
Old Vic Repertory Theatre.
DEANE ISBN 0-699-30283-8
(16mm film)

1556 TWELFTH NIGHT
Arnold Moss. LC T 3317 (at)

1557 TWELFTH NIGHT
Derek Godfrey; Dorothy Tutin;
John Barton; Jill Balcon;
Prunella Scales; Tony Church;
Patrick Wymark; Robert Eddison;
David Combes; Peter Pears;
Patrick Garland; Peter Orr;
Ian Lang; Tony Whitehead.
LFP 7081 (ac)

1558 TWELFTH NIGHT
Hilton Edwards; Michael Mac-
Liammoir. LIST SKP 1006 (3 pd),
also CX 106 (2 ac)

1559 TWELFTH NIGHT
Claude Rains; Thomas Mitchell;
Walter Abel; Reginald Denny;
Morris Ankrum. In anth. LIVSHA
898667 (5 pd)

1560 TWELFTH NIGHT
Peter Pears as Feste; Jill Balc-
on as Olivia; Dorothy Tutin as
Viola; Prunella Scales as Maria;
Robert Eddison as Aguecheek;
Tony Church as Malvolio; Derek
Godfrey as Orsino; Patrick Gar-
land as Sebastian; Peter Orr as
Antonio; John Barton as Sea
Captain; Ian Lang as Valentine;
Tony Whitehead as Curio; Pat-
rick Wymark as Belch. LONDON
4354 (3 pd); also ARGO RG 284/6,
also ZRG 5284/6, also ZPR 186/8,
also KZPC and K16K32 (3 ac)

1561 TWELFTH NIGHT
Dennis Brennan; Patrick Bed-
ford; Paul Farrell; David Basil
Gill; Patrick McLarnon; Coralie
Carmichael; Finola O'Shannon;
Hilton Edwards; Michael Mac-
Liammoir. SPOWRD 116/8 (3 pd)

1562 TWELFTH NIGHT
Alec McCowen; Robert Hardy;
Felicity Kendall; Annette Cros-
bie; Sinead Cusack; Trevor Pea-
cock; Clive Arrindell. TIMLIF
V 6011 B (3 vc 3/4)

Shakespeare, cont'd.
1563 TWELFTH NIGHT (exc.)
        Richard Johnson; Patrick Wy-
        mark; Derek Godfrey; Dorothy
        Tutin: In anth. ARGO SAY 41
1564 TWELFTH NIGHT (exc.)
        Donald Sinden. In anth. ARGO
        SAY 60
1565 TWELFTH NIGHT (exc.)
        Marlowe Soc. In anth. ARGO
        PLP 1122, also in DA 2
1566 TWELFTH NIGHT (exc.)
        John Barrymore. AUDIOR 2204
1567 TWELFTH NIGHT (exc.)
        BERG ATTS 005
1568 TWELFTH NIGHT (exc.)
        BFA (vc 3/4)
1569 TWELFTH NIGHT (exc.)
        Michael Redgrave. In anth.
        CAED TC 1170
1570 TWELFTH NIGHT (exc.)
        Maurice Evans. In anth.
        GOLDEN AA 58
1571 TWELFTH NIGHT (exc.)
        Maggie Smith as Viola; Bren-
        da Bruce as Olivia. LIVSHA
        STN 15A-16A
1572 TWELFTH NIGHT (exc.)
        MICHMED 9707 (16mm film, also
        vc)
1573 TWELFTH NIGHT (exc.)
        PROTHM 1ES2 (ac)
1574 TWELFTH NIGHT (exc.)
        SEABRN ISBN 0-699-30284-6
        (16mm film)
1575 TWELFTH NIGHT (exc.)
        Eithne Dunne; Eve Watkinson;
        Christopher Casson. SPOA 887
        (pd), also 7112 (ac)
1576 TWELFTH NIGHT (exc.)
        Foch; Rolf; MacGrath. THEAMA
        GRC 2431
1577 TWO GENTLEMEN OF VERONA
        Peter Wyngarde; Edward DeSouza;
        Johanna Dunham; John Laurie;
        Douglas Muir; Christopher Gui-
        nee; Aubrey Woods; James Mellor;
        Murray Melvin; Colin Blakely;
        Jerry Verno; Elvi Hale; Caroline
        John. CAED SRS 202 (3 pd), also
        CDL 5202 (3 ac)
1578 TWO GENTLEMEN OF VERONA
        John Barton as Duke of Milan;
        David Gibson as Valentine; Rich-

ard Marquand as Proteus; Terrence Hardiman as Antonio;
George Rylands as Thurio; Toby
Robertson as Eglamour; Roderick Cook; Donald Beves; Clive
Swift; David Buck as Host; John
Tracy-Phillips and Chris Renard
as Outlaws; Olive Gregg as Julia;
Janette Richer as Sylvia; Pe-
nelope Balchin as Lucetta.
LONDON 4344 (3 pd), also OSA
1315; also ARGO RG 172/4, also
ZPR 126/8
1579 TWO GENTLEMEN OF VERONA
        SPOWRD 173/5 (3 pd)
1580 TWO GENTLEMEN OF VERONA
        Tessa Peake-Jones; Tyler Butter-
        worth; John Hudson; Nicholas
        Kaby; Joanne Pearce; Frank Barr-
        ie; Paul Daneman. TIMLIF
        V 6030 E (2 vc 1/2)
1581 TWO GENTLEMEN OF VERONA (exc.)
        Patrick Wymark. In anth. ARGO
        SAY 41
1582 TWO GENTLEMEN OF VERONA (exc.)
        Folio Theatre Prod. SPOA 893
        (pd), also 7114 (ac)
1583 WINTER'S TALE
        John Gielgud as Leontes; Peggy
        Ashcroft as Paulina; George Rose;
        Miranda Connell; Robert Hardy;
        Ernest Thesiger; Barry Foster;
        Christopher Burgess; William
        Squire; Alan Bates; William Mar-
        lowe; Nigel Stock; Alec McCowen;
        Paul Vieyra; Tony Robertson;
        Tony White; Rachel Gurney;
        Judith Scott; Renee Asherson;
        Prunella Scales; Derek Godfrey.
        CAED SRS 214 (3 pd), also CDL
        5214 (3 ac); also EAV B2RR166
1584 WINTER'S TALE
        Eric Portman as Leontes; Dia-
        na Wynyard as Hermione; Wendy
        Hiller as Paulina. LIVSHA SWT
        47-48
1585 WINTER'S TALE
        William Squire as Leontes and
        Time; Denis McCarthy as Camillo;
        Terrence Hardiman as Antigonus;
        Corin Redgrave as Dion; Toby
        Robertson as Polixenes; Anthony
        White as Florizel; George Ry-
        lands as Archidamus; John Barton

as Old Shepherd; Michael Ba-
tes as Autolycus; Margaretta
Scott as Hermione; Mary Con-
roy as Perdita; Joan Hart as
Paulina; Jill Daltry as Emilia;
Janette Richer as Mopsa; Clive
Swift as Gaoler; Ian McKellen,
Richard Marquand, and Donald
Beves as Gentlemen. LONDON
4420 (4 pd), also OSA 1408;
also ARGO RG 204/7, also ZRG
5204/7; also SAY 81 (4 ac)

1586 WINTER'S TALE
Jeremy Kemp; Anna Calder-
Marshall; Debbie Farrington;
Margaret Tyzack. TIMLIF V 6017
C (2 vc 3/4)

1587 WINTER'S TALE (exc.)
Judi Dench; Peter McEnery.
In anth. ARGO NF 4

1588 WINTER'S TALE (exc.)
Eric Porter; Paul Hardwick;
Elizabeth Sellars. In anth.
ARGO SAY 41

1589 WINTER'S TALE (exc.)
Old Vic Repertory Theatre.
DEANE ISBN 0-699-32375-4
(16mm film)

1590 WINTER'S TALE (exc.)
Ellen Terry. In anth. DELTA
12020

1591 WINTER'S TALE (exc.)
PROTHM (ac)

1592 WINTER'S TALE (exc.)
Ellen Terry. In anth. RCA 64193

1593 WINTER'S TALE (exc.)
Folio Theatre Players. SPOA
894 (pd and ac)

1594 Miscellaneous exc.
Robert Harris; Christopher
Hassell; Dylan Thomas; John
Laurie. In anth. ALPHA

1595 Miscellaneous exc.
In anth. AMERH

1596 Miscellaneous exc.
Marlowe Soc. In anth. ARGO
DA1-4

1597 Miscellaneous exc.
Humphrey Bogart; Walter Huston;
Brian Aherne; Burgess Meredith;
Grace George; Claude Rains;
Thomas Mitchell. In anth. ARIEL
SHO 1/4

1598 Miscellaneous exc.
T. Bankhead; O. Welles; C.
Hardwicke; Rosalind Russell;
Leslie Howard; Edward G. Robin-
son; Frank Morgan; Elissa Lan-
di. In anth. ARIEL SHO 5/8

1599 Miscellaneous exc.
J. Barrymore. In anth. AUDIOR
2280/1

1600 Miscellaneous exc.
BFA (16mm film)

1601 Miscellaneous exc.
John Gielgud. In anth. CAED
SRS 200

1602 Miscellaneous exc.
Cornelia Otis Skinner. In
anth. CAMDEN 190

1603 Miscellaneous exc.
David Allen. In anth. CMS 541

1604 Miscellaneous exc.
John Gielgud. In COLUMB OL
5390

1605 Miscellaneous exc.
John Gielgud. In anth. COLUMB
OL 5550

1606 Miscellaneous exc.
Edith Evans; John Gielgud;
Margaret Leighton. In anth.
COLUMB OL 7020, also in OS
2520 and PT 11458

1607 Miscellaneous exc.
In anth. COLUMB 19232/3

1608 Miscellaneous exc.
In anth. CONTF ISBN 0-699-
00459 - 4 (16mm film)

1609 Miscellaneous exc.
In anth. CONTF ISBN 0-699-
00460-8 (16mm film)

1610 Miscellaneous exc.
Peggy Ashcroft; John Gielgud.
In anth. DECCA KCSP 573

1611 Miscellaneous exc.
In anth. GRYPHON GR 900

1612 Miscellaneous exc.
Arnold Moss. In LC T 3990 (at)

1613 Miscellaneous exc.
Maurice Evans. LC T 4332 (at)

1614 Miscellaneous exc. In anth. PH
K 065

1615 Miscellaneous exc.
In anth. PH K 077

1616 Miscellaneous exc.
In anth. RCA VDM 115

Shakespeare, cont'd.
1617 Miscellaneous exc.
        In anth. RCA SB 6740
1618 Miscellaneous exc.
        Paul Rogers. In anth. SPOA 723
1619 Miscellaneous exc.
        MacLiammoir; Edwards. In anth.
        SPOA 836/7
1620 Miscellaneous exc.
        Beverly Canning; James Rees;
        Linda Sternberg; Ray Irwin.
        SYRAC (2 pd)
1621 Miscellaneous exc., in French
        D. Seyrig; E. Riva; S. Favre;
        C. Maffei; G. Wilson; S. Pi-
        toëff; L. Terzieff; J. Fabbri.
        ADÈS ALB 56
1622 Miscellaneous exc., in French
        In anth. HACH ES 320E905/7

Shange, Ntozake
1623 FOR COLORED GIRLS WHO HAVE CON-
        SIDERED SUICIDE WHEN THE RAINBOW
        IS ENUF
        BUD 95007

Shaw, George Bernard
1624 ANDROCLES AND THE LION
        Read by Robert Shaw. CMS
        560/3 (3 pd)
1625 APPLE CART (exc.)
        Noël Coward; Margaret Leighton.
        In anth. CAED TC 1094
1626 APPLE CART (exc.)
        Edith Evans. In anth. RCA
        LRL 1-5037
1627 ARMS AND THE MAN
        The Canadian Players. LC
        T 3884 (at)
1628 ARMS AND THE MAN
        Ralph Richardson; Vanessa
        Redgrave; John Gielgud.
        TALK TTC/GBS 01 (ac)
1629 CAESAR AND CLEOPATRA
        Claire Bloom as Cleopatra;
        Max Adrian as Caesar; Judith
        Anderson as Ftatateeta; Lau-
        rence Hardy as Britannus; Jack
        Gwillim as Rufio; Harold In-
        nocent as Pothinus; Gerald Row-
        lands as Ptolemy; Llewellyn
        Rees; Colin Redgrave; Michael
        Godfrey; Robin Lloyd; P. G.
        Stephens; Peter Bayliss; Te-
        rence Bayier; Richard Leech;

James Grout; Patricia Somerset; Annette Robertson. CAED
TRS 304 (2 pd), also CDL 5304
(2 ac)
1630 BACK TO METHUSELAH
        Arnold Moss. LC T 4816 (at)
1631 DOCTOR'S DILEMMA
        Robert Shaw. CMS 559
1632 DOCTOR'S DILEMMA (exc.)
        INDU ISBN 0-699-07881-4
        (16mm film)
1633 DON JUAN IN HELL
        Charles Boyer as Don Juan;
        Charles Laughton as Devil;
        Cedrick Hardwicke as Commander;
        Agnes Moorehead as Dona Ana.
        COLUMB SL 166 (1 pd)
1634 GETTING MARRIED
        Read by Robert Shaw. CMS 564
1635 HEARTBREAK HOUSE
        Jessica Tandy as Hesione Husha-
        bye; Tony Van Bridge as Capt.
        Shotover; Frances Hyland as Lady
        Utterword; Bill Fraser as Boss
        Mangan; Paxton Whitehead as Hec-
        tor Hushabye; Eleanor Beecroft
        as Nurse Guiness; Diana Leblanc
        as Elie Dunn; Patrick Boxill;
        James Valentine; Kenneth Wickes.
        CAED TRS 335 (3 pd), also CDL
        5335 (3 ac)
1636 JOHN BULL'S OTHER ISLAND
        Anthony Brown; Christopher Ben-
        jamin; Patrick Duggan; Edward
        Petherbridge; P. G. Stephens;
        Denis O'Neill; Anna Cropper;
        Will Leighton; Patrick McAlin-
        ney; Marjorie Hogan; Dermot Kel-
        ly; Ivan Beavis; John Drake;
        Charles Kinross; Bert Lean; Jim
        O'Connor; Gary Taylor. CAED
        TRS 346 (4 pd), also CDL 5346
        (4 ac)
1637 MAJOR BARBARA
        Maggie Smith as Barbara; Ro-
        bert Morley as Undershaft;
        Celia Johnson as Lady Britomart;
        Alec McCowen as Cusins; War-
        ren Mitchell as Bill Walker;
        Gary Bond as Stephen; Pinkie
        Johnstone; Graham Crowden; Mur-
        ray Melvin as Snobby Price;
        Hazel Hughes as Rummy; Geor-
        gina Patterson; George Benson;
        Wynne Clark; Daniel Thorndike.

CAED TRS 319 (4 pd), also
CDL 5319 (4 ac)

1638 MAJOR BARBARA
Read by Robert Shaw. CMS 562

1639 MAN AND SUPERMAN
The Canadian Players. LC
T 2609 (at)

1640 MAN AND SUPERMAN
Alec McCowen; Anna Massey.
In anth. MINN 29130/5 (6 pd)

1641 MISALLIANCE
Matthew Long; Gareth Forwood;
Delia Lindsay; Elizabeth
Bradley; Anthony Sharp; Bill
Fraser; Jeremy Child; Caro-
line Blakiston; John Tordoff.
CAED TRS 365 (3 pd), also CDL
5365 (3 ac)

1642 MISALLIANCE
Read by Robert Shaw. CMS 563

1643 MRS. WARREN'S PROFESSION
TIMLIF (vc 3/4)

1644 PYGMALION
Diana Rigg; Alec McCowen; Sarah
Atkinson; Margaret Ward; Den-
nis Handby; Anthony Naylor;
Jack May; Simon MacCorkindale;
Hilda Fenemore; Bob Hoskins;
Ellen Pollock; Melanie Peck.
ARGO ZSW 550/1 (2 pd), also
SAY 28 (ac)

1645 PYGMALION
Michael Redgrave as Higgins; Mi-
chael Hordern as Pickering;
Donald Pleasence as Doolittle;
Lynn Redgrave as Eliza; Felicity
Kendal; Pauline Jameson; Ed-
ward Hardwicke; Megs Jenkins;
Ruth Dunning; Gaye Brown; Ed-
ward Atienza; Rosamund Greenwood;
Frank Gatliff; James Mellor;
Peter Armitage; Robert Oates.
CAED TRS 354 (3 pd), also CDL
5354 (3 ac)

1646 PYGMALION
Leslie Howard; Wendy Hiller;
Wilfrid Lawson. LEARNCO (16mm
film)

1647 SAINT JOAN
Barbara Jefford as Saint Joan;
Alec McCowen as Dauphin; Max
Adrian; Mark Gignam; Barry
Foster; Michael Hordern; Derek
Jacobi; Cyril Luckham; Wil-

liam Squire. ARGO ZPR 119/21
(3 pd), also SAY 42 (ac); also
RG 470/72 and ZRG 5470/2 (3 pd)

1648 SAINT JOAN
Siobhan McKenna; Donald Plea-
sence; Felix Aylmer; Robert
Stephens; Jeremy Brett; Alec
McCowen; Nigel Davenport; Ed-
ward De Souza; Julian Glover;
Willoughby Goddard; Peter Bay-
liss; Stephen Moore; Arthur Hew-
lett; Murray Melvin; Emrys
James; Graham Crowden; James
Cairncross; Ronald Ibbs; Gerald
James; Gerald Rowlands; Michael
York; Jane Evers. CAED TRS 311
(4 pd), also CDL 5311 (4 ac)

1649 SAINT JOAN
Read by Robert Shaw. CMS 566

1650 SAINT JOAN
Siobhan McKenna as Joan; Ian
Keith as Peter Cauchon; Earle
Hyman as Dunois; Fredric Tozere
as Archbishop of Rheims; Mi-
chael Wager as Dauphin; Thay-
er David as Inquisitor; Earl
Montgomery as Stogumber; Dick
Moore as Ladvenu; Dennis Pat-
rick as Baudricourt; Bryant
Haliday as Warwick. RCA LOC
6133 (3 pd)

Sheridan, Richard Brinsley

1651 CRITIC; OR, A TRAGEDY REHEARSED
Noël Coward; Mel Ferrer.
DECCA 9154, also 79154

1652 RIVALS
Edith Evans as Mrs. Malaprop;
Pamela Brown as Lydia; Michael
MacLiammoir as Lucius O'Trigger;
James Donald as Capt. Absolute;
Vanessa Redgrave as Julia; John
Laurie as Anthony Absolute; Ro-
bert Eddison; Alec McCowen;
Alan Bates; Gerald James; Pau-
line Jamieson; Laurence Hardy.
CAED TC 2020 (2 pd), also CDL
52020 (2 ac)

1653 RIVALS
David Thorndike; Barbara McCough-
hey. SPOA 971/2 (2 pd), also
8049/50 (2 ac)

1654 RIVALS
TIMLIF (vc 3/4)

Sheridan, Richard Brinsley, cont'd.
1655 RIVALS (exc.)
        Edith Evans as Mrs. Malaprop;
        Anthony Quayle as Capt. Absolute.
        In anth. ANGEL 35213; also in
        EMI HLM 7108
1656 RIVALS (exc.)
        In anth. FOLKW 9841/2
1657 RIVALS (exc.)
        Walter Hampden; Donald Burr;
        Bobby Clark; Philip Bourneuf.
        HARVOC 1000/3 (2 pd 78)
1658 RIVALS (exc.)
        Robert Culp. LIST 4004 (pd),
        also 404 CX (ac)
1659 SCHOOL FOR SCANDAL
        Edith Evans; Claire Bloom;
        Cecil Parker; Baliol Halloway;
        Peter Halliday; Alec Clunes;
        Harry Andrews; Athene Seyler.
        ANGEL 3542/5 (3 pd), also LFP
        7028 (ac)
1660 SCHOOL FOR SCANDAL
        Alec McCowen as Surface; Sarah
        Badel; Jill Balcon; Nigel Stock.
        BBC ECN 101 (2 ac)
1661 SCHOOL FOR SCANDAL
        John Gielgud as Surface;
        Ralph Richardson; Geraldine Mc-
        Ewan; Gwen Ffrangcon-Davies;
        Meriel Forbes; Laurence Nais-
        mith; Malcolm Keen; Richard
        Easton; David Evans; Pinkie
        Johnstone; Charles Lloyd Pack;
        Peter Barkworth; Howard Goor-
        ney; Donald Pickering; Martin
        Friend; Jonathan Newth; Michael
        Kent; Betty Bowden. COMREC
        RS 33 13002 (3 pd); also CAED
        305 (3 pd), also CDL 5305 (3 ac)
1662 SCHOOL FOR SCANDAL
        Swan Players. SPOA 968/70
        (3 pd), also 7142/44 (3 ac)
1663 SCHOOL FOR SCANDAL
        Joan Plowright; Felix Aylmer.
        YESTER (2 vc)
1664 SCHOOL FOR SCANDAL (in Russian)
        Moscow Art Theatre. MK D
        06247/54 (4 pd)
1665 SCHOOL FOR SCANDAL (exc.)
        Edith Evans as Lady Teazle.
        In anth. ANGEL 35213
1666 SCHOOL FOR SCANDAL (exc.)
        Max Adrian; Claire Bloom;

        Anthony Quayle. In anth. CAED
        TC 4002, also in CDL 54002
1667 SCHOOL FOR SCANDAL (exc.)
        Edith Evans. In anth. EMI
        HLM 7108
1668 SCHOOL FOR SCANDAL (exc.)
        Robert Culp. LIST 4014R (pd),
        also 414 CX (ac)

Sherwood, Robert E.
1669 ABE LINCOLN IN ILLINOIS (exc.)
        Read by Raymond Massey. RCA
        M 591 (3 pd 78)

Ship, Reuben
1670 INVESTIGATOR
        John Drainie; Reuben Ship.
        DISC 6834

Skelton, John
1671 MAGNYFYCENCE (exc.)
        James McKechnie as King.
        In anth. DOVER 99714/6

Skinner, Cornelia Otis
1672 LOVES OF CHARLES II
        Performed by the author.
        SPOA 813

Smith, Betty
1673 TREE GROWS IN BROOKLYN
        Hallmark Playhouse Radio
        Broadcast. MARK 56645

Smith, Winchell, and Bacon,
Frank
1674 LIGHTNIN'
        Read by Frank Bacon. In anth.
        AUDIOR 2465

Sophocles
1675 AIAS (in French as AJAX)
        Dacqmine. In anth. HACH
        320E899
1676 ANTIGONE (In Greek)
        FOLKW 9912
1677 ANTIGONE (In English)
        Dorothy Tutin as Antigone;
        Max Adrian as Creon; Jere-
        my Brett as Haimon; Eileen
        Atkins as Ismene; Geoffrey
        Dunn as Teiresias; Arthur
        Hewlett; June Jago as Euri-
        dice; Willoughby Goddard,

Douglas Muir, and Richard Golden
as Chorus; Thomas Kempinski
as Guard; Stephen Moore as Messenger. CAED TRS 320 (2 pd),
also CDS 5320 (2 ac)
1678 ANTIGONE (In English)
McGill University Students.
FOLKW 9861
1679 ANTIGONE (exc., in English)
MICHMED 9366 (16mm film, also
vc)
1680 ANTIGONE (exc., in French)
Chamarat; Rignault; Dacqmine;
Nerval. In anth. HACH 320E899
1681 ELEKTRA (In English)
Jane Lapotaire as Electra;
Michael Pennington as Orestes.
BBC ECN 171 (2 ac)
1682 ELEKTRA (In French as ÉLECTRE)
Francis; Monfort. CHA TH5
1683 ELEKTRA (exc., in Modern Greek)
Katina Paxinou; Alexis Minotis.
In anth. CAED TC 1127, also in
CDL 51127
1684 ELEKTRA (exc., in English)
Blanche Yurka. In anth. FOLKW
FL 9841/42
1685 ELEKTRA (exc., in English)
MICHMED 9371 (16mm film, also
vc)
1686 OIDIPOUS EPI KOLONOI (In French
as OEDIPE À COLONE)
Rignault. In anth. HACH
320E899
1687 OIDIPOUS TYRANNOS (In English as
OEDIPUS REX)
Douglas Campbell as Oedipus;
Eric House as Priest of Zeus;
Robert Goodier as Creon; Don-
ald Davis as Teiresias; Ele-
anor Stuart as Jocasta; Tony
Van Bridge; Douglas Rain; Wil-
liam Hutt. CAED TC 2012 (2 pd),
CDL 52012 (2 ac)
1688 OIDIPOUS TYRANNOS (In English as
OEDIPUS TYRANNUS)
FI (vc 3/4)
1689 OIDIPOUS TYRANNOS (In English as
OEDIPUS REX)
John Sommers as Oedipus. FOLKW
9862
1690 OIDIPOUS TYRANNOS (In English as
OEDIPUS KING)
MILCAM

1691 OIDIPOUS TYRANNOS (In French as
OEDIPE ROI)
Deschamps; Rignault; Cha-
marat. In anth. HACH 320E899
1692 OIDIPOUS TYRANNOS (In German as
KÖNIG OEDIPUS)
ARIOLA ATHENA 70578 (ac)
1693 OIDIPOUS TYRANNOS (exc., in Modern
Greek)
Katina Paxinou; Alexis Minotis.
In anth. CAED TC 1127, also in
CDL 51127
1694 OIDIPOUS TYRANNOS (exc., in Eng-
lish as OEDIPUS THE KING)
MICHMED 9365 (16mm film, also
vc)
1695 Miscellaneous exc.
Read by John F. C. Richards.
In anth. FOLKW 9984

Steinbeck, John
1696 LONG VALLEY
Matinee Theatre. LC T 8389 (at)

Stoppard, Tom
1697 ARTIST DESCENDING A STAIRCASE
Stephen Murray; Peter Egan;
Dinsdale Landen. BBC ECN 043(ac)
1698 EVERY GOOD BOY DESERVES FAVOUR
Philip Locke; Ian McKellan;
Ian Richardson; Andrew Sheldon;
Elizabeth Spriggs; Patrick
Stewart. RCA RL 12855
1699 PROFESSIONAL FOUL
Peter Barkworth; John Shrapnel.
In anth. In anth. BBC ECN 114
1700 REAL INSPECTOR HOUND
Nigel Anthony; Roger Hammond.
BBC ECN 145 (ac)
1701 ROSENCRANTZ AND GUILDENSTERN ARE
DEAD
Edward Petherbridge; Edward
Hardwicke; Freddie Jones as The
Player; Martin Jarvis as Hamlet.
BBC ECN 124 (2 ac)
1702 SEPARATE PEACE
Christopher Cazenove; Angharad
Rees. BBC ECN 168 (ac)
1703 WHERE ARE THEY NOW?
Timothy West. In anth. BBC
ECN 114

Strindberg, August
 1704 FRÖKEN JULIE (In orig. Swedish)
      Inga Tidblad as Julie; Ulf
      Palmer as Jean; Marta Dorff as
      Kristin; Alf Sjöberg as Regi.
      In anth. GRAMM LT 33137/38
      (2 pd)

Sultanov, Izzat
 1705 IMON (In orig. Uzbek)
      Khamza Drama Theatre. MK
      D 09637/40

Sultanov, Izzat, jt. auth with
Uigun, Rakhmatulla (q. v.)

Synge, John Millington
 1706 IN THE SHADOW OF THE GLEN
          In anth. ARGO RG 223
 1707 IN THE SHADOW OF THE GLEN
          In anth. SPOA 743 (pd), also
          8046 (ac)
 1708 PLAYBOY OF THE WESTERN WORLD
          Siobhan McKenna as Pegeen;
          Eamonn Keane as Christy Mahon.
          BBC ECN 087 (ac)
 1709 PLAYBOY OF THE WESTERN WORLD
          Cyril Cusack as Christy Mahon;
          Siobhan McKenna as Pegeen;
          Thomas Studley as Shawn; Sea-
          mus Kavanagh as Michael; John
          McDarby as Philly; Milo O'Shea
          as Jimmy Farroll; Marie Kean as
          Widow Quin; Maureen Cusack; May
          Craig; Maureen Toal; Harry Bro-
          gan as Old Mahon; Alex Dignam.
          CAED TRS 348 (2 pd), also CDL
          5348 (2 ac); also ANGEL 3547
          (2 pd); also SERAPH IB 6013 (2pd)
 1710 PLAYBOY OF THE WESTERN WORLD
          Siobhan McKenna; Gary Raymond.
          EMI (vc)
 1711 PLAYBOY OF THE WESTERN WORLD
          TIMLIF (vc 3/4)
 1712 RIDERS TO THE SEA
          In anth. ARGO RG 223
 1713 RIDERS TO THE SEA
          Eireann Players. In anth. SPOA
          743
 1714 WELL OF THE SAINTS
          EBEC ISBN 0-8347-1175-3 (film)

Terence
 1715 ADELPHI (exc., in orig. Latin)
          Westminster School. In anth.

CMS 582
 1716 ADELPHI (In French as LES
      ADELPHES)
          Rignault. In anth. HACH
          320E909
 1717 EUNUCHUS (exc.)
          In anth. CMS 582

Testoni, Alfredo
 1718 FINESTRE SUL PO (in orig. Italian)
          E. Macario; F. Bergesio; A.
          Bertolotti; M. G. Cavagnino; C.
          Di Monte; C. Droetto; M. Fur-
          giuele; E. Giovine; M. Martana;
          C. M. Puccini; M. Riccardini;
          P. Rizzo; A. Rossi. CETRA LPB
          35040

Thomas, Dylan
 1719 UNDER MILK WOOD
          Richard Burton as First Voice;
          Hugh Griffith as Capt. Cat;
          Diana Maddox as Polly Carter;
          Sybil Williams as Price; David
          Close-Thomas as Ogmore and
          Bread; Meredith Edwards as Bey-
          non; Philip Burton as Jenkins;
          John Huw Jones as Pugh; Rachel
          Thomas as Mary Ann Sailors, Mrs.
          Nilly, and Rosie Probert; Ra-
          chel Roberts as Mrs. Bread and
          Mae Rose Cottage; Lorna Davies
          as Mrs. Owen; John Glyn-Jones
          as Morgan. ARGO SW 501/2 (2 pd),
          also KSWC 501/2; also WEST WN
          2202, also RG 21-22, also SAY 13
 1720 UNDER MILK WOOD
          D. Thomas; Dion Allen; Nacy
          Wickwire; Roy Poole; Sada Thomp-
          son; Allen F. Collins. CAED TC
          2005 (2 pd), also CDL 52005 (2
          ac)
 1721 UNDER MILK WOOD (exc.)
          DECCA PA 166, also KCPAA 166
 1722 UNDER MILK WOOD (exc.)
          PROTHM 1EP4 (ac)

Tolstoy, Alexei Konstantinovich
 1723 TSAR FYODOR IOANNOVICH (In orig.
      Russian)
          Moscow Art Theatre. MK D
          015375/80 (3 pd)
 1724 TSAR FYODOR IOANNOVICH /exc., in
      orig. Russian)
          I. Moskvin; O. Knipper-

Chekhova; D. Orlov. MK D
06855/6
1725 TSAR FYODOR IOANNOVICH (exc. in
orig. Russian)
I. Smoktunovsky as Tsar; G.
Kirushina as Irina; V. Korshu-
nov as Godunov; Y. Samoilov
as Shuisky; V. Khokhriakov as
Loop-Kleshnin. MELOD 33C10-
05991-92

Tolstoy, Leo
1726 PLODY PROSVESHCHENIYA (In orig.
Russian)
Moscow Art Theatre. MK D
09685-92 (4 pd)
1727 PLODY PROSVESHCHENIYA (In orig.
Russian)
V. Y. Stanitsyn as Zvezdintsev;
L. M. Koreneva as Anna Pavlov-
na; A. I. Stepanova as Betsi;
P. V. Massalsky as Vovo; V. O.
Toporkov as Krugosvetlov; S.K.
Blinnikov as Doctor. SSSR
D 0941/50 (5 pd)
1728 VLAST' TMY (in orig. Russian)
Maly Theatre, Moscow. MK D
09283/8 (3 pd)
1729 ZHIVOY TRUP (In orig. Russian)
Pushkin Drama Theatre, Lenin-
grad. MK D 012391/2

Trenyov, Konstantin
1730 LYUBOV YAROVAYA (In orig. Russian)
Maly Theatre, Moscow. MK D
09519-22 (2 pd)

Udall, Nicholas
1731 RALPH ROISTER DOISTER
Norman Shelley as Roister Doister; Geoffrey Matthews as Mery-
greeke; Mary Law as Custance;
Vivienne Chatterton as Mumble-
crust; Marjorie Westbury as
Talk-a-pace; Denise Bryer as
Alyface. In anth. DOVER 99719-7

Uigun, Rakhmatulla and Sultanov
1732 ALISHER NAVOI (in orig. Uzbek)
Khamza Drama Theatre. MK D
08789-92 (2 pd)

Umari, A., jt. auth. with
Yashen, Kamil(q. v.)

Valentinetti, Emerico
1733 PIGNASECCA E PIGNAVERDE (In
orig. Italian)
Gilberto Govi; Pina Camera;
Nelda Meroni; Claudio
D'Amelio; Ariano Praga; En-
rico Ardizzone; Luigi Dameri.
CETRA LPB 35036 (pd), also
MC 77 (ac)

Van Doren, Mark
1734 LAST DAYS OF LINCOLN
American National Theatre and
Academy. LC T 4580 (at)
1735 LAST DAYS OF LINCOLN (exc.)
Read by the author. LC T 2829
(at)

Van Druten, John
1736 DRUID CIRCLE (exc.)
Read by the author. In anth.
SPOA 718, also in 7145
1737 I AM A CAMERA (exc.)
Read by the author. In anth.
SPOA 718, also in 7145
1738 I'VE GOT SIXPENCE (exc.)
Read by the author. In anth.
SPOA 718, also in 7145
1739 VOICE OF THE TURTLE (exc.)
Read by the author. In anth.
SPOA 718, also in 7145

Varagnolo, Domenico
1740 TANTO PE' A REGOLA (In orig.
Italian)
Gilberto Govi; Enrico Ardizzone; Rina Govi; Nelda Meroni; Ariano Praga; Rudi Roffe;
Jole Lorena; Luigi Dameri;
Anna Caroli. CETRA LPB 35045
(pd), also MC 192 (ac)

Vega Carpio, Lope de
1741 CABALLERO DE OLMEDO (In English
as THE KNIGHT FROM OLMEDO)
LC T 3887 (at)
1742 MELINDRES DE BELISA (In orig.
Spanish)
Nela Conjiú as Belisa; Marta
Gosálvez as Flora; Domingo de
Moral Tiberio; Lola del Pino
as Lisarda; Gabriel Ibañez as
Alguacil; Antonio García Qui-
jada as Felisardo; Victoriano
Evangelio as Carrillo; Anto-

Vega Carpio, Lope de, cont'd.
   MELINDRES DE BELISA, cont'd.
      nio Moreno as Eliso; Ara-
      celi Fernández Baizán as
      Celisa; José Manuel Martin as
      D. Juan. SPOA 843 (pd), also
      50-4 (ac)
1743 PERIBAÑEZ (exc., in orig. Spanish)
      Joaquín Dicenta Sánchez; En-
      rique Raymat; Victor García;
      Ramiro Benito; Lola Alba; Nela
      Conjiú; Domingo Almendros.
      In anth. ADÈS P 32.158
1744 PERRO DEL HORTELANO (exc.)
      Dicenta Sanchez; Raymat;
      Alba; Conjiú; Almendros.
      In anth. ADÈS P 32.158

Vian, Boris
1745 GOÛTER DES GÉNÉRAUX (exc. in orig.
      French)
      François Maistre; Paul Crauchet;
      Claude Evrard; Odette Piquet;
      André Thorent. In anth. ADÈS
      23.001

Vigny, Alfred de
1746 CHATTERTON (exc., in orig.
      French)
      Perrin; Duchaussoy. In anth.
      HACH 320E898
1747 MARÉCHALE (exc., in orig. French)
      Bouquet; Rignault; Virlojeux;
      Casarès. In anth. HACH 320E908

Voysey, Michael
1748 BY GEORGE
      Max Adrian. ANGEL SB 3721 (2pd)

Walser, Martin
1749 ZIMMERSCHLACHT (In orig. German)
      Heidemarie Hatheyer; Arno Ass-
      mann. DEUTGR 140.034

Webster, John
1750 DUCHESS OF MALFI
      Peggy Ashcroft as Duchess; Paul
      Scofield as Ferdinand. BBC ECN
      122 (3 ac)
1751 DUCHESS OF MALFI
      Barbara Jefford as Duchess; Ro-
      bert Stephens as Bosola; Alec
      McCowan as Ferdinand; Jeremy
      Brett as Antonio; Douglas Wilmer

as Cardinal. CAED TRS 334
(3 pd), also CDL 5334 (3 ac)
1752 DUCHESS OF MALFI
      TIMLIF (vc 3/4)
1753 DUCHESS OF MALFI (exc.)
      Dylan Thomas. In anth. CAED
      TC 1158

Webster, Margaret
1754 NO COWARD SOUL
      Performed by the author. LC
      T 4379 (at)

Weiss, Peter
1755 VERFOLGUNG UND ERMORDUNG JEAN
      PAUL MARATS (In English as
      MARAT-SADE)
      Ian Richardson as Marat; Patrick
      Magee as Sade; Glenda Jackson
      as Charlotte Corday. CAED TRS
      312 (3 pd), also CDL 5312 (3 ac)
1756 VERFOLGUNG UND ERMORDUNG JEAN
      PAUL MARATS (exc., in English as
      MARAT/SADE)
      Read by the author. In anth.
      CAED TC 1131

Wells, H. G.
1757 MAN WHO COULD WORK MIRACLES
      Alec Guiness. ASRD 110

Werfel, Franz
1758 JACOBOWSKY UND DER OBERST (In
      orig. German)
      Ernst Waldbrunn. FOLKW 9917

Wilde, Oscar
1759 IMPORTANCE OF BEING EARNEST
      John Gielgud; Edith Evans;
      Pamela Brown; Roland Culver;
      Celia Johnson; Jean Cadell;
      Aubrey Mather; Brewster Mason;
      Peter Sallis. ANGEL 3504B
      (4 pd), also LFP 7001 (ac)
1760 IMPORTANCE OF BEING EARNEST
      Gladys Cooper; Joan Greenwood;
      Richard Johnson; Alec McCowen;
      Lynn Redgrave. CAED TRS 329
      (2 pd), also CDL 5329 (2 ac)
1761 IMPORTANCE OF BEING EARNEST
      Maurice Evans; Lucille Watson.
      THEAMA GRC 2056 (4 pd)
1762 IMPORTANCE OF BEING EARNEST (exc.)
      COLUMB OL 6090

1763 IMPORTANCE OF BEING EARNEST (exc.)
    In anth. FOLKW 9841/2
1764 LADY WINDERMERE'S FAN
    Robert Culp. LIST 4001R (pd),
    also 401CX (ac)
1765 PICTURE OF DORIAN GRAY
    Ian Hunter as Wotton; David En-
    ders as Gray; Ralph Michael as
    Basil; Eric Lugg as Parker; Roy
    Dean as Singleton; Betty Linton
    as Sibyl Vane; Eric Lugg as
    Victor; Elizabeth London as
    Helen Hallward; Lewis Stringer
    as Narrator. LONDON LLP 472
1766 PICTURE OF DORIAN GRAY (exc.)
    Hurd Hatfiled. CAED TC 1095
    (pd), also CDL 51095 (ac)
1767 PICTURE OF DORIAN GRAY (exc.)
    Peter Egan. LFP 7065
1768 SALOME
    Robert Culp. LIST 4011R (pd),
    also 411CX (ac)

Wilder, Thornton
1769 ALCESTIAD, OR, A LIFE IN THE SUN
    Read by the author. LC T 2351
    (at)
1770 SKIN OF OUR TEETH (exc.)
    Fredric March; Florence El-
    dridge. In anth. DECCA DL 9002

Williams, Tennessee
1771 GLASS MENAGERIE
    Montgomery Clift; Julie Harris;
    Jessica Tandy; David Wayne.
    CAED TRS 301 (2 pd), CDL 5301
    (2 ac)
1772 GLASS MENAGERIE
    MAJOR SR4M-3085/6
1773 GLASS MENAGERIE (exc.)
    Read by the author. In anth.
    CAED TC 1005
1774 ROSE TATTOO
    Maureen Stapleton; Harry
    Guardino; Maria Tucci; Christo-
    pher Walker. CAED TRS 324 (3
    pd), also CDL 5324 (3 ac)
1775 STREETCAR NAMED DESIRE
    Rosemary Harris as Blanche;
    James Farentino as Kowalski.
    CAED TRS 357 (3 pd), also
    CDL 5357 (3 ac)
1776 STREETCAR NAMED DESIRE
    Brando; Karl Malden. MARK
    56654

Wodehouse, P. G.
1777 JEEVES
    Terry Thomas as Bertie; Roger
    Livesey as Jeeves; Miles Malle-
    son as Uncle George; Judith
    Furse as Aunt Agatha; Rita Webb
    as Maudie; Avril Elgar as
    Florence; Diarmid Cammell as
    Edwin; Laurence Hardy as Uncle
    Willoughby. CAED TC 1137 (pd),
    also CDL 51137 (ac)

Wolff, Ruth
1778 Miscellaneous exc.
    Read by the author. In anth.
    PAC (2 ac)

Wolinski
1779 ROI DES COUS (In orig. French)
    Julien Guiomar; Michel Muller.
    ADÈS 11.502

Yashen, Kamil
1780 YIULCHI YULDUZ (In orig. Uzbek)
    Khamza Drama Theatre. MK D
    014117-20 (2 pd)

Yashen, Kamil and Umari, A.
1781 KHAMZA (In orig. Uzbek)
    Khamza Drama Theatre. MK D
    08727-30 (2 pd)

Yeats, William Butler
1782 ACTORS AND MUSICIANS
    In anth. ARGO 5468/9, also RG
    468/9
1783 AT THE HAWK'S WELL
    Arthur O'Sullivan as Old Man;
    Jim Norton as Young Man. In
    anth. ARGO PLP 1091
1784 AT THE HAWK'S WELL
    In anth. ARGO RG 468-9
1785 CAT AND THE MOON
    Chris Curran as Narrator; Cait
    Lanigan and Jane Carty as Mu-
    sicians; Arthur O'Sullivan as
    Beggar; Eamonn Keane as Lame
    Beggar; Ronnie Walsh as Saint.
    In anth. ARGO PLP 1092
1786 CAT AND THE MOON
    In anth. ARGO 5468/9, also in
    RG 468/9
1787 CAT AND THE MOON
    Cyril Cusack; Siobhan McKenna.
    In anth. CAED TRS 315

Yeats, William Butler, cont'd.
1788 COUNTESS CATHLEEN
       Siobhan McKenna as Countess
       Cathleen; John Neville as Aleel;
       Tom Clancy as Merchant; Liam
       Gannon as Merchant; Aline Mac-
       Mahon as Oona; Bryan Doyle as
       Shemus Rua; Pauline Flanagan;
       Liam Clancy as Teigne Rua; Der-
       mot McNamara; Helena Carroll.
       TRADIR TLP 501
1789 COUNTESS CATHLEEN (exc.)
       Eve Watkinson; Patrick Nolan.
       In anth. SPOA 752, also in
       7147
1790 DEIRDRE (exc.)
       Eve Watkinson; Patrick Nolan.
       In anth. SPOA 752, also in
       7147
1791 DREAMING OF THE BONES
       Eamonn Keane as Young Man;
       Gerard Victory as Stranger;
       Daphine Carroll as Dervorgilla.
       In anth. ARGO PLP 1091
1792 DREAMING OD THE BONES
       In anth. ARGO 5468/9, also in
       RG 468/9
1793 ONLY JEALOUSY OF EMER
       Siobhan McKenna; Joyce Redman;
       Patrick Magee; Finuala O'Shannon;
       Christopher Casson; Cyril Cusack.
       In anth. CAED TRS 315
1794 ONLY JEALOUSY OF EMER
       Reed College, Oregon. ESOT 506
1795 POT OF BROTH
       Cyril Cusack; Siobhan McKenna; M.
       Kean ; O'Higgins; Sackler.
       In anth. CAED TC 315
1796 PURGATORY
       Cyril Cusack; Siobhan McKenna.
       In anth. CAED TC 315
1797 RESURRECTION
       Jane Carty and Cait Lanigan as
       Musicians; Ronnie Walsh as Hebr-
       ew; Eamonn Keane as Greek; Jim
       Norton as Syrian. In anth. CAED
       PLP 1092
1798 WORDS UPON A WINDOW PANE
       Siobhan McKenna; Patrick Magee;
       Sackler; Cyril Cusack; Marie
       Kean. In anth. CAED TRS 315
1799 Miscellaneous exc.
       Eve Watkinson; Patrick Nolan.
       SPOA 752 (pd), also 7147 (ac)

Zorilla, José
1800 DON JUAN TENORIO (In orig.
       Spanish)
       Francisca Ferrández as Doña
       Ines de Ulloa; M. Calzada as
       Buttarelli; Miguel García as
       Ciutti; Rafael Calvo as D. Gon-
       zalo de Ulloa; Emilio Menendez
       as Don Diego Tenorio; Alejandro
       Ulloa as Don Juan Tenorio;
       José Poveda as Avellaneda;
       Enrique Cerro as Capitan Cen-
       tellas; Pedro Gil as D. Luis
       Mejia; F. Comacho as Gaston;
       R. Delatorre as Doña Ana de Pan-
       toja; A. Vera and P. Calis as Al-
       guaciles; P. Olivos as Lucia;
       L. Bove as Madre Abadesa;
       Luis Torner as Escultor. CAED
       TC 2002 (2 pd), also CDL 52002
       (2 ac)
1801 DON JUAN TENORIO (In orig.
       Spanish)
       Antonio García Quijara; Pilar
       Quintana. SPOA 980/1 (2 pd)

Zuckmayer, Carl
1802 DES TEUFELS GENERAL (In orig.
       German)
       Read by the author. In anth.
       PREISR PR 3187
1803 HAUPTMANN VON KÖPENICK (In orig.
       German)
       Rudolf Platte; Bruno Fritz;
       Reinhold Bernt; Ilse Fürstenberg;
       Eduard Wandrey; Edity Hancke;
       Erich Fiedler. DEUTGR 44008

              Anonymous Plays

1804 ABRAHAM AND ISAAC
       Frederick Worlock as Abraham;
       Terence Kilburn as Isaac; Frank
       Silvera as God; Cavada Hum-
       phrey as Angel; Thayer David as
       Doctor. In anth. CAED TC 1030
1805 ABRAHAM AND ISAAC
       Howard Marion-Crawford as
       Abraham; John Forrest as Isaac.
       In anth. DOVER 99705-7 L
1806 AUTO DE SAN JORGE (In orig.
       Spanish)
       Alberto Castillo as Rey; Maria

Teresa Navarro as Infanta; Manuel Durán as San Jorge; Eva
Llorens as Reina; Miguel Bui-
sán as Pastor. In anth. SPOA
864

1807 BABES IN THE WOOD
JUP OC 35

1808 BANNS
Frank Silvera. In anth. CAED
TC 1030

1809 BETRAYAL, TRIAL AND CRUCIFIXION
James McKechnie as Pilate;
Derych Guyler as Jesus; Howard
Marion-Crawford; Denis Goacher;
June Tobin; Anthony Jacobs;
Carleton Hobbs. In anth. DOVER
99708-1 L

1810 BUTTERFLY DREAM (A Bej Jing drama
in English)
LC T 3463 (at)

1811 CABBAGE SOUP
GENTW GW 1024 (ac)

1812 CALISTO AND MELIBEA
June Tobin as Melibea; Peter
Howell as Calisto; Manning Wil-
son as Sempronio; Vivienne
Chatterton as Celestina. In
anth. DOVER 99715-4N

1813 CASTELL OF PERSEVERANCE
In anth. DOVER 99711-1M

1814 CORNISH ORDINALIA (exc.)
EMC ISBN 0-699-06351-5 (16mm
film)

1815 CREATION AND FALL OF MAN
Deryck Guyler as Deus; John
Glen as Adam; Mary O'Farrell as
Eve. In anth. DOVER 99705-7L

1816 EVERYMAN
Cyril Luckham; Peter Orr; Gerald
Harper; Gary Watson; David King;
Alarice Cotter; Patricia Brake;
Frank Duncan; Yvonne Bonnamy;
Ann Morrish; Denis McCarthy;
Norman Mitchell; Richard Bebb;
Roy Spencer. ARGO ZSW 552

1817 EVERYMAN
Frederick Rolf as God; Frank
Silvera as Death; Burgess Mere-
dith as Everyman; Terence
Kilburn as Messenger. CAED TC
1031 (pd), also CDL 51031 (ac)

1818 EVERYMAN
Godfrey Kenton as Everyman;
Deryck Guyler as God; Ralph Tru-
man as Death; John Glen;

Carleton Hoobs; Trevor Martin;
June Tobin. In anth. DOVER
99712-XM

1819 HEIKE MONOGATARI (In orig. Japanese)
Gakken ISBN 0-699-32732-6
(16mm film)

1820 HICKSCORNER
In anth. DOVER 99714-6M

1821 JACOB AND ESAY
Cyril Shaps as Isaac; Marjorie
Westbury as Rebecca; Frank Partington as Jacob; Trevor Martin
as Esau. In anth. DOVER 99718
-9N

1822 KAGEKIYO (Noh play, in orig.
Japanese)
In anth. ASH AH 9572

1823 MARY MAGDALENE
Mary Winbush as Mary Magdalene;
Anthony Jacobs as Lechery. In
anth. DOVER 99711-1M

1824 MIND, WILL AND UNDERSTANDING
Carleton Hobbs; John Glen;
June Tobin; Trevor Martin; Godfrey Kenton. In anth. DOVER
99711-1M

1825 MUNDUS ET INFANS (exc.)
In anth. DOVER 99713-8M

1826 NATIVITY
Deryck Guyler as Son of God;
Godfrey Kenton as Gabriel;
June Tobin as Mary; Norman
Shelley as Joseph; Rupert
Davies as Mak; Vivienne
Chatterton as Gill. In anth.
DOVER 99707-3L

1827 NICE WANTON
Joan Sanderson as Xantippe;
John Forrest as Barnabas; De-
nise Bryer as Dalilah; John
Graham as Ismael. In anth.
DOVER 99716-2N

1828 NOAH'S DELUGE
John Heldabrand as God; Frederick Worlock as Noah; Mae
Questel as Noah's Wife. In
anth. CAED TC 1030

1829 NOAH'S FLOOD
John Laurie as Noah; Mary
O'Farrell as Wife; Godfrey
Keaton as Angel; Anthony Jacobs
as Satan; Deryck Guyler as Deus.
In anth. DOVER 99706-5L

Anonymous Plays, cont'd.

1830 PASTORALKA (In orig. Polish)
     BRUNO BR 50093
1831 PAUSE IN THE DISASTER
     COTILLION SD 9031
1832 PLAY OF DANIEL
     Russell Oberlin as Belshazzar's
     Prince; Brayton Lewis as Bel-
     shazzar; Jerold Sion as Wise Man;
     Alan Baker as Wise Man; Betty
     Wilson as Queen. DECCA DL
     79402
1833 PLAY OF THE SACRAMENT
     Howard Marion-Crawford as Sir
     Aristorius; Malcolm Hayes as
     Jonathas the Jew.
     In anth. DOVER 99710-3M
1834 POACHER (In Welsh dialect)
     QUAL BMP 2026
1835 PRIDE OF LIFE
     In anthol. DOVER 99710-3M
1836 QUEM QUAERITIS
     William Hess; John Boyne;
     William Aubin. In anth. CAED TC
     1030
1837 RESURRECTION
     James McKechnie as Pilate;
     Deryck Guyler as Jesus; How-
     ieson Culff as Caiaphas; Cyril
     Shaps as Annas. In anth. DOVER
     99709-XL

1838 ROBIN HOOD AND THE FRIAR
     Darren McGavin as Robin Hood;
     Frank Silvera as Friar Tuck.
     In anth. CAED TC 1030
1839 SECOND SHEPHERD'S PLAY
     Joss Ackland, Peter Bay-
     liss, and Diarmid Cammell as
     Shepherds; Robert Stephens as
     Mak; Avril Elgar as Gill;
     Owen Wynne as Angel; Patricia
     Somerset as Mary. CAED TC 1032
     (pd), also CDL 51032 (ac)
1840 SECOND SHEPHERD'S PLAY
     FFHS (16mm film)
1841 SHIDOHOGAKU (Kyogen play in orig.
     Japanese)
     In anth. ASCH AH 9572
1842 YANGJU SANDAE NORI (In orig.
     Korean)
     WASHU ISBN 0-699-32805-5 (16mm
     film)
1843 Miscellaneous exc.
     Sarah Bernhardt; Constant
     Coquelin; Ernest Coquelin.
     In anth. ANNA 1044
1844 Miscellaneous exc.
     Johnston Forbes-Robertson;
     Sarah Bernhardt. In anth.
     ROCOCO 4003

Title Index

Lumpazi Vagabundus (Nes-
troy) 727

Luther (Osborne) 759

Luv (Schisgal) 963

Lysistrate (Aristophanes)
48

Lyubov yarovnaya (Tren-
yov) 1730

Macbeth (Shakespeare)
1294-1332

Macbird! (Garson) 302

Machine infernale (Coc-
teau) 154-156

Macht der Gewohnheit
(Bernhard) 88

Mad money see Beshenye
den'gi (Ostrovsky)

Magnyfycence (Skelton)
1671

Maids see Bonnes (Genet)

Main de César (Roussin)
906

Maître de Santiago (Mon-
therlant) 691

Major Barbara (Shaw)
1637, 1638

Mal-aimés (Mauriac) 540

Malade imaginaire (Moli-
ère) 633-644

Man and superman (Shaw)
1639, 1640

Man for all seasons (Bolt)
96, 97

Man who came to dinner
(Hart) 389

Man who could work mir-
acles (Wells) 1757

Mañana del Sol (Alvarez
Quintero) 34

Mancebo que caso con mujer
brava (Casona) 121

Manezzi pe' maiâ na
figgia (Bacigalupo) 56

Mann ist Mann (Brecht) 104

Man's a man see Mann ist
Mann (brecht)

Maquerida (Benavente)
86

Marat-Sade see Verfol-
gung und Ermordung Jean
Paul Marats (Weiss)

Märchen: eine kitschige
Begebenheit (Goetz) 347

Maréchale (Vigny) 1747

Maria Magdalene (Hebbel)
395

Maria Stuart (Schiller)
949-953

Mariage de Figaro (Beau-
marchais) 68-73

Maribel y la extraña fa-
milia (Mihura) 547

Mariés de la tour Eiffel
(Cocteau) 157, 158

Mariette ou comment on
écrit (Guitry)

Marius (Pagnol) 772, 773

Marlborough s'en va-t-
en guerre (Achard) 3

Marmite see Aulularia
(Plautus)

Marriage see Zhenitba
(Gogol)

Mary Magdalene (anon.)
1823

Maskarad (Lermontov)
496

Master builder see Byg-
mester Solness (Ibsen)

Measure for measure
(Shakespeare) 1333-1340

Medea see Médée (Anouilh)
or Medeia (Euripides)

Médecin malgré lui (Mol-
ière) 645-655

Médée (Anouilh) 42-44

Médée (Cocteau) 159

Médée (Corneille) 204

Medeia (Euripides) 281-
284

Melindres de Belisa (Vega
Carpio) 1742

Meninas (Buero Vallejo)
111

Merchant of Venice (Shakespeare) 1341-1366

Mermaid see Rusalke (Pushkin)

Merry wives of Windsor
(Shakespeare) 1367-1372

Meshuginer Mosciach
(Schwartz) 976

Meteor (Dürrenmatt) 258

Midsummer night's dream
(Shakespeare) 1373-1395

Mind, will and understan-
ding (anon.) 1824

Minna von Barnhelm (Les-
sing) 497, 498

Mirra (Alfieri) 29

Misalliance (Shaw) 1641,
1642

Misanthrope (Molière)
656-668

Miser see Avare (Molière)

Miserie 'd Monssu Travet
(Bersezio) 90

Miserly knight see Skupy
rykar (Pushkin)

Mithridate (Racine) 843

Mocedades del Cid (Guil-
len de Castro) 373

Monsieur le Trouhadec saisi par la débauche
(Romains) 884

Montserrat (Roblès) 879

Moon for the misbegotten
(O'Neill) 748, 749

More stately mansions
(O'Neill) 750

Morte d'Arthur (Malory)
511

Mot de Cambronne (Guitry)
379, 380

Mouches (Sartre) 934

Mourning becomes Electra
(O'Neill) 751, 752

Mozart (Guitry) 381

Mozart i Salieri (Push-
kin) 800

Mrs. Warren's profession
(Shaw) 1643

Much ado about nothing
(Shakespeare) 1396-1409

Mundus et Infans (anon.)
1825

Murder in the cathedral
(Eliot) 266-272

Mutter Courage und ihre
Kinder (Brecht) 105

Na dne (Gorky) 361-363

Nathan der Weise (Lessing)
500-502

Nativity (anon.) 1826

Nègres (Genet) 306

Nelkenburg (Pick) 780

Nice Wanton (anon.) 1827

Nicomède (Corneille)
205-207

No coward soul (Webster)
1754

No exit see Huis-clos
(Sartre)

No man's land (Pinter)
783

Noah's deluge (anon.) 1828

Noah's flood (anon.) 1829

Actor Index

Naylor, Anthony, 1644
Negroni, Jean, 143, 180,
    196, 675, 806, 840,
    847, 860
Neil, Martin, 1177
Nelligan, Kate, 1337
Nelson, Kenneth, 230
Nerval, Natalie, 47,
    148, 144, 147, 150, 277,
    657, 669, 695, 807, 835,
    839, 860, 920, 934, 1680
Nesbitt, Cathleen, 223, 260,
    268, 430
Nettleton, John, 1007, 1193,
    1246
Neugebauer, Alfred, 372
Neville, John, 1022, 1032,
    1554, 1788
Neville, Margaret, 566
Nevins, Claudette, 253
Newton, John, 550
Newton, Robert, 1175
Newth, Jonathan, 1661
Nicholls, Anthony, 268,
    1294, 1367, 1378, 1440
Nichols, Dandy, 48
Nicholson, Nora, 296
Nicoletti, Susi, 345
Nicolle, Pierre, 682
Nicot, C., 673, 677, 1384
Niehaus, Ruth, 107
Ninchi, A., 448, 1505
Nivette, S., 693, 697
Nocher, 670
Noël, 624
Noël, Bernard, 184, 193,
    198, 814, 835, 869, 893
Noël, Denise, 194, 690
Noël, H., 893
Noëlle, 447
Noëlle, Paula, 603
Noerden, Joseph, 103
Noesen, 577
Noiret, Philippe, 179
Nolan, Patrick, 1789, 1790,
    1799
Nollier, C., 185, 813
Noro, L., 693
Norris, Mary, 1193
Norton, Jim, 1797, 1783
Nunn, Trevor, 1044, 1060,
    1174, 1196, 1200, 1379,
    1537
Nyasa, Jill, 1301
Nye, Gene, 751

Oates, Robert, 1645
Oberlin, Russell, 1832
Obonya, Hanns, 401, 863
O'Brien, Edmond, 1134
O'Brien, Maureen, 1542
O'Callaghan, Richard,
    368, 1268, 1369
O'Casey, Sean, 732, 735
O'Connor, Gary, 1537
O'Connor, Jim, 1636
O'Conor, Joseph, 1449
O'Dea, Joseph, 83
O'Dwyer, Frank, 83
O'Farrell, Mary, 1301,
    1815, 1829
Offenbach, Joseph, 1064
Oger, C., 601
Ogier, 610
O'Hara, Jenny, 545
O'Higgins, 1795
Olivier, Laurence, 131,
    129, 170, 1006, 1009,
    1062, 1086, 1094, 1173,
    1175, 1191, 1270, 1281,
    1416, 1419, 1429
Olivier, Marie, 927
Olivier, Pierre, 715, 1800
Ollivier, Pierre, 847
Olmo, Lauro, 736
Olson, James, 508
O'Neill, Denis, 1636
Orlovitz, Gil, 757
Orduna, Luis, 86
Orr, Peter, 986, 991,
    1005, 1028, 1044, 1060,
    1107, 1174, 1193, 1196,
    1198, 1200, 1245, 1269,
    1289, 1368, 1398, 1437,
    1490, 1540, 1557, 1560,
    1816
Orrick, David, 1513
O'Shannon, Finuala, 1561,
    1793
O'Shea, Milo, 1441, 1458,
    1492
Ostushev, A., 803, 1435
O'Sullivan, Arthur, 83,
    1783, 1785
O'Sullivan, Michael, 253
O'Toole, Peter, 1489
Ott, Elfriede, 966
Oumansky, André, 143,
    186, 189
Ousey, Timmy, 427

Page, 205, 208
Page, Geraldine, 517, 590,
    624, 656, 709, 710, 753
Page, Malcolm, 1198
Page, William, 1368
Palau, P., 585
Palmer, Robin, 1043
Palmer, Ulf, 1704
Pankin, Stuart, 550
Paolieri, Germana, 785
Parédès, J., 50, 51, 454,
    572, 590, 624, 626,
    644, 649, 670, 719,
    793, 794, 855, 858,
    859
Parfitt, Judy, 1287
Parigot, Guy, 856
Parker, Cecil, 1659
Parker, Joy, 1374
Parkes, Andrew, 1044,
    1174
Parry, Natasha, 1458, 1512
Partington, Frank, 1821
Partridge, Ian, 1005
Party, Robert, 600, 715
Paryla, Nikolaus, 954
Pasco, Richard, 267,
    1014, 1034, 1120, 1178,
    1245, 1305
Pascual, Asunción, 85
Passeur, R., 375
Patrick, Dennis, 1650
Patrick, Gail, 1015
Patten, M., 82
Patterson, Georgina, 1637
Paturel, 65, 581, 792
Paulin, Michel, 494, 839,
    845
Pavelko, John, 530
Paxinou, Katina, 17, 276,
    1683, 1693
Payen, Marie-Thérèse, 683
Peyton-Wright, Pamela,
    550
Peacock, Trevor, 1194,
    1562
Peake-Jones, Tessa, 1580
Pearce, Joanne, 1580
Pearlman, Stephen, 744
Pears, Peter, 1046,
    1398, 1557, 1560
Peck, Melanie, 1644
Peckins, Hiram, 132, 357
Pedi, Tom, 554, 744
Pedley, Anthony, 1038

List of Anthologies

ADÈS
    TS25LA526. Molière: Dépit & Étourdi. 1 pd.
    TS30LA522. Hommage à Gérard Philipe. 1 pd.
    TS30LA552. Jean Vilar: Ses grands roles. 1 pd.
    7003/4. Hommage à Charles Dullin. 2 pd.
    7007/8. Hommage à Louis Jouvet. 2 pd.
    7016/17. Jules Renard: Pain de Ménage-Plaisir de Rompre-Poil de Carotte. 2 pd.
    10.034. Milosz: Pages Choisies. 1 pd.
    13.030. Musset: On ne badine pas avec l'amour (and) Les Caprices de Marianne. 1 pd.
    13.031. Molière: Amphitryon and other exc. 1 pd.
    13.032. Giraudoux: Guerre de Troie n'aura pas lieu and other exc. 1 pd.
    19 013-14. L'Inoubliable Gérard Philip. 1 pd.
    19 015/16. Giraudoux: La Guerre de Troie n'aura pas lieu and other exc. 1 pd.
    23.001. Boris Vian. 1 pd.
    P 32.158. Siglo de Oro - Teatro. 1 pd.
    P 32.162. Siglo XIX - Teatro. 1 pd.

AGUILAR   GPE 11 102. Seis dramaturgos leen sus obras. 1 pd.

ALPHA   Master Recordings in English Literature. 4 pd.

AMBER   7101. Anthology: Ann Todd. 1 pd.

AMERH   Scenes from Shakespeare. 1 pd.

ANGEL   ANG 35213. Eighteenth-Century Comedy Album. 1 pd.

ANNA   1044. Sarah Bernhardt. 1 pd.

ARGO
    DA 1-4. Scenes from Shakespeare.
    NF 4. Homage to Shakespeare. 1 pd.
    SAY 18. Your favorite poems.
    SAY 33. R. Donat reads favourite poems at home. 1 pd.
    SAY 41. Excerpts from Shakespeare. 1 ac.
    SAY 47. Rime of the ancient Mariner and other works.
    SAY 60. The poet speaks. 1 ac.
    172-174. Two Gentlemen of Verona (and) Lover's Complaint/Shakespeare.

ARGO   223.   Synge: In the Shadow of the Glen (and) Riders to the Sea.
            ZPR 236/9.   Shakespeare: Coriolanus (and) Troilus & Cressida.
                4 pd.
            RG 544/5.   Milton: Comus (and) Samson Agonistes. 2 pd.
            PLP 1059.   Robert Donat reads selected poetry. 1 pd.
            PLP 1064.   Robert Donat reads favorite poems. 1 pd.
            PLP 1072.   The Barrow Poets. 1 pd.
            PLP 1091.   William Butler Yeats: Noh Plays, v.1. 1 pd.
            PLP 1092.   William Butler Yeats: Noh Plays, v.2. 1 pd.
            PLP 1120.   Scenes from Shakespeare's Plays: The Tragedies,
                v.1. 1 pd.
            PLP 1121.   Scenes from Shakespeare's Plays: The Tragedies,
                v.2. 1 pd.
            PLP 1122.   Scenes from Shakespeare's Plays: The Comedies. 1 pd.
            PLP 1123.   Scenes from Shakespeare's Plays: The Histories. 1 pd.
            PLP 1206/7.   Poems of T. S. Eliot. 2 pd.
            ZRG 5307-10.   Shakespeare: Antony and Cleopatra (and) Timon of
                Athens. 4 pd.
            5468-9.   Yeats: At the Hawk's Well, Dreaming the Bones, Cat and
                the Moon, Actors and Musicians. 2 pd.

ARIEL   SHO 1/4.   Shakespeare in Hollywood, v.1. 4 pd.
            SHO 5/8.   Shakespeare in Hollywood, v.2. 4 pd.

ASCH   Noh and Kyogen Plays. 2 pd.

AUDIDR   3085.   Tribute to Eugene O'Neill.

AUDIOR   LPA 2280/81.   John Barrymore reads Shakespeare. 2 pd.
            2465.   Golden Age of the Theater. 1 pd.

BANNER   BAS 1008.   Maurice Schwartz: Monologues. 1 pd.

BBC   ECN 114.   Tom Stoppard.

BFA   Great Scenes from Shakespeare. 16mm Film.

BRUNO   BR 50196.   Bauman: Yiddish Scenes.

CAED   SRS 200/CP 200.   Shakespeare: Ages of Man. 2pd / 2 ac.
            TRS 315.   Yeats: Five One-Act Plays. 3 pd.
            TC 1005.   Tennessee Williams reading from his own works. 1 pd.
            TC 1012/CDL 51012.   Sean O'Casey reading from his works. 1 pd/1 ac.
            TC1020/CDL51020.   Colette reads Colette. 1 pd/1 ac.
            TC 1030/CDL 51030.   Wellsprings of drama. 1 pd/1 ac.
            TC 1045/CDL 51045.   T. S. Eliot reading (his own works). 1 pd/1 ac.
            TC 1067/CDL 51067.   Poesia y Drama de Lorca. 1 pd/1 ac.
            TC 1069/CDL 51069.   Noel Coward & Margaret Leighton performing
                (works by Noel). 1 pd/1 ac.
            TC 1083/CDL 51083.   Jean Cocteau reading. 1 pd/1 ac.
            TC 1094/CDL 51094.   Noel Coward reading his poems. 1 pd/1 ac.
            TC 1127/CDL 51127.   Greek Tragedy. 1 pd/1 ac.
            TC 1131/CDL 51131.   Peter Weiss reading from his works. 1 pd/1 ac.
            TC 1134/CDL 51134.   Selected works of Jean Genet. 1 pd/1 ac.
            TC 1158/CDL 51158.   Dylan Thomas reading from King Lear and
                Duchess of Malfi. 1 pd/1 ac.

CAED   TC 1170. Shakespeare: Soul of an Age. 1 pd.
            TC 1198/CDL 51198. Sean O'Casey reading (from his works). 1 pd/1ac.
            TC 1259/CDL 51259. Poetry of John Milton. 1 pd/1 ac.
            TC 2019/CDL 52019. Seami: Noh Plays. 2 pd/2 ac.
            SWC/TC 2042/CDL 52042. James Agee: A Portrait. 2 pd/2 ac.
            TC 4002/CDL 54002. Eighteenth-Century Poetry & Drama. 4 pd/4 ac.

CAMDEN   CAL 190. Scenes from Shakespeare. 1 pd.

CETRA   CLC 0824. Teatro di Vittorio Gassmann. 1 pd.
            CLC 0826. William Shakespeare. 1 pd.
            CLC 0855. Serata d'Onore con Eschilo a Shakespeare. 1 pd.
            CLC 0856. Le voci di Irma e Emma Gramatica. 1 pd.
            LPZ 2058. Vittorio Alfieri, da Saul, Mirra (and) Oreste. 1 pd.
            LPZ 2064. Jonesco, Jacques o la Sottomissione (and) Shakespeare,
                La Bisbetica Domata. 1 pd.

CMS   541. The great sonnets and soliloquies of Shakespeare. 1 pd.
            582. Latin readings, v.2. 1 pd.

COLUMB   ESJF 1. Jules Romain: Knock (and) Marcel Achard: Jean de la Lune.
                1 pd (45).
            91A02048/OL 7020/OS 2520/PT 11458. Homage to Shakespeare: Lincoln
                Center World's Fair Festival. 1 pd/1 ac.
            91A02055/PT 11460. One Man in his Time, v.1. 1 pd/1 ac.
            91A02057/PT 11461?. One Man in his Time, v.2. 1 pd/1 ac.
            ML 4758. William Saroyan talking ans trying to read from some of
                his novels, plays and stories. 1 pd.
            OL 5390. Ages of Man: Shakespeare anthology. 1 pd.
            OL 5900. Dramatic readings from Eugene O'Neill's plays. 1 pd.
            TV 19232/3. Scenes from Shakespeare. 1 pd.

CONTF   ISBN 0-699-00459-4. Ages of Man, Part 2: Adulthood (Shakespeare).
                16mm film.
            ISBN 0-699-00460-8. Ages of Man, Part 3: Maturity (Shakespeare).
                16mm film.

DECCA   SPA/KCSP 573. Shakespeare: Scenes and poetry. 1 pd/1 ac.
            DL 9002. Anta Album of Stars, v.1. 1 pd.
            DL 9009. Anta Album of Stars, v.2. 1 pd.
            DL 9504/DL 9041. Shakespeare: Scenes from Romeo and Juliet (and)
                Hamlet. 1 pd.
            DL 38026. Parnassus series sampler. 1 pd.
            99.070/74. Molière: Malade Imaginaire - Médecin Malgré Lui - Mis-
                anthrope.

DELTA   DEL 120 20. Great Actors of the Past. Shakespeare, v.1. 1 pd.

DEUTGR   40 006. Amphitryon - Prinz Friedrich von Homburg - Kätchen von
                Heilbronn. 1 pd.
            40 008. Maria Becker spricht. 1 pd.
            40 009. Käthe Gold spricht. 1 pd.
            42 004. Die Grosse Szene: Friedrich Schiller. 1 pd.
            42 013. Kleist: Prinz Friedrich von Homburg (and) Kätchen von
                Heilbronn. 1 pd.

DEUTGR   43 002. Berühmte Monologe. 1 pd.
          43 048. Kleist: Liebesszenen. 1 pd.
          140 011. Maria Wimmer spricht. 1 pd.
          140 013. Ernst Deutsch spricht. 1 pd.
          140 025. In Memoriam. 1 pd.
          168 094. Ein Bertolt Brecht Abend mit Therese Giehse. 1 pd.
          2570-013. Elisabeth Flickenschildt in memoriam. 1 pd.
          2571-011/3321 011. Therese Giehse spricht Dürrenmatt und Brecht.
             1 pd/1 ac.
          2571 107. Sire, geben Sie Gedankenfreiheit: Szenen aus Schillers
             Dramen. 1 pd.
          2755 005. Therese Giehse und Gisela May: Brecht. 7 pd.

DOVER   99705 through 99722. First Stage. Boxes L, M, N, and O.

EIA   DSM 110-208. Antologia Sonora della letteratura Italiana, Serie I:
             48 pd.

EMI   063-028511. Curt Goetz: Miniaturen. 1 pd.
          2C 154-14.344. Si Sacha Guitry m'était conté. 3 pd.
          HLM 7108. Eighteenth Century Comedy Album. 1 pd.

FEST   FLD 49. Paul Claudel vous parle. 1 pd.
          FLDX 70. Jean Cocteau vous parle. 1 pd.
          FLDX 73. Montherlant vous parle. 1 pd
          FLDX 74. François Mauriac vous parle. 1 pd.
          FLDX 150. Jean Giono vous parle. 1 pd.
          FLD 166. De François Villon à Alfred de Vigny. 1 pd.
          FRL 1530. Jean Cocteau, his works and his voice. 1 pd.
          FRL 1531. Paul Claudel, his works and his voice. 1 pd.
          FRL 1536. Selections from the Works of Jules Romains. 1 pd.

FOLKW   9572. Noh Plays of Japan. 2 pd.
          FL 9841-42. Dear Audience.
          9984. Ancient Greek Poetry. 1 pd.

GAKKEN   ISBN 0-699-32732-6. World of Heike Monogatari. 16mm film.

GENTW   GW 1024. Children's Radio Theater. 1 ac

GMS   D 7013. Phèdre and Andromaque (Racine). 1 pd.
          D 7065. Les plus beaux poèmes de la langue française. 1 pd.
          7084. Jean Cocteau vous parle. 1 pd.
          7095/96. Ionesco: Cantatrice Chauve (and) Leçon.
          DISC 7125. Schiller: Kabale und Liebe (and) Wallensteins Tod.
             1 pd.

GOLDEN   AA 58. Maurice Evans' introduction to Shakespeare. 1 pd.

GRAMM   LT 33137/38. Fröken Julie (and) Chrysaetos. 2 pd.

GRYPHON   GR 900. Selections from Shakespeare. 1 pd.

HACH   LAE 3.310. Le Héros Cornélien. 1 pd.
          ES 190 E 979. Françoise Sagan: Pages choisies. 1 pd.

HACH   320 E 058.   Visages de Musset. 1 pd.
            320 E 812.   Dix-septième siècle de la lit. française. 1 pd.
            320 E 836.   Le Héros Racinien. 1 pd.
            ES 320.859 ESH.   Victor Hugo: Pages choisies. 1 pd.
            ES 320 E 866.   Excerpts from Vers d'exil (Claudel). 1 pd.
            ES 320 E 869.   Jean-Paul Sartre: Pages choisies. 1 pd.
            ESH 320.872.   André Gide: Pages choisies. 1 pd.
            ES 320 E 874.   Cocteau: Pages choisies. 1 pd.
            ES 320 E 875.   Jean Giraudoux: selections. 1 pd.
            ESH 320.878.   Mauriac: from Génitrix and other works. 1 pd.
            ESH 320.885.   Montherlant: Pages choisies. 1 pd.
            ES 320 E 892.   Victor Hugo: Pages choisies. 1 pd.
            320 E 898.   Théatre Romantique. 1 pd.
            320 E 899.   Les tragiques grecs. 1 pd.
            ES 320 E 905.   Shakespeare: Comédies. 1 pd.
            320 E 906.   Drames et Tragédies Romaines. 1 pd.
            ES 320 E 907.   Shakespeare: Tragédies. 1 pd.
            320 E 908.   Poèmes antiques et modernes (Vigny). 1 pd.
            320 E 909.   La Comédie Antique. 1 pd.
            320.914.   Tirades et Monologues Célèbres du Théatre Français. 1 pd.
            ES 320 E 920.   Marcel Pagnol, scènes choisies. 1 pd.
            320.924.   Grandes scènes d'amour du théatre français. 1 pd.
            ESH 320.937.   Pirandello: Pages choisies. 1 pd.
            ES 320.938.   Eugène Ionesco: Pages choisies. 1 pd.
            ES 320 E 969.   Rostand: Aiglon & Cyrano. 1 pd.
            ESH 320.972.   Hommage à Molière. 1 pd.
            460E803/5.   Douze textes français: Jean Deschamps. 3 pd.

HARVOC   D-1018/19.   Lennox Robinson reading his own plays. 1 pd (78)

IER   W3RG94500/W3KG94500.   The Genius of Shakespeare.

INSPRACH   TOW 1027/36.   Friedrich Schiller. 4 pd (45) and 1 pd (33)

IRCC   3.   Shakespeare: Selections.

LEARNC   ISBN 0-699-37095-7.   Curtain up. 16mm film.

LEX   7650/55.   Marlowe: Selections. 1 at.

LIVSHA   898667.   Hollywood Immortals Perform Shakespeare. 1 pd.

LONDON   RG 544-5.   Milton: Comus and Samson Agonistes. 1 pd.
            A 4344.   Two Gentlemen of Verona (and) Lover's Complaint
               (Shakespeare). 1 pd.

LONGMAN   The English Poets. 13 ac

LUM   LD 1.212.   Rostand: Aiglon and Chantecler. 1 pd (45)
            LD 3.240.   Molière: Bourgeois Gentilhomme and Malade Imaginaire.
            LD 3.241.   Molière: Fourberies de Scapin and Médecin malgré lui.
            LD 3.247.   Molière: Femmes Savantes and Le Tartuffe.
            LD 3.248.   Molière: Don Juan and Précieuses ridicules.

LVA   12.   Roussin: Rupture and Tombeau d'Achille. 1 pd.
            13.   Mariés de la Tour Eiffel and Médée (Cocteau). 1 pd.

MK   D 04578-9.   Scenes from Pushkin, Gorky, and others. 1 pd.
               D 7285/6.   Scenes from Gorky, Dostoyevsky and Shakespeare. 1 pd.
               D 9385-6.   Scenes from dramas by Pushkin. 1 pd.
               D 10597-8.   Scenes from Gogol, Ostrovsky, Chekhov. 1 pd.
               D 013603-4.   Scenes from Shakespeare. 1 pd.
               D 00015187-8.   Scenes from Dostoyevsky and Chekhov. 1 pd.

MAGICT   CTG 4007.   Dryden: All for love (and) World well lost. 1 pd.

MELOD   12133-34.   Ostuzhev: Tvorcheskiy portret. 1 pd.

MICHMED   9701.   Shakespeare's world.
               9706.   Shakespeare's art.

MINN   29121-25.   Doll's House and other plays. 5 pd
               29126-31.   Macleish: J. B.; Rattigan: Cause celèbre; a.o. 3 pd.

NORTON   23114.   Paul Roche: Rank Obstinacy of Things. 1 ac.

PAC   Six women playwrights. 2 ac.

PAT   MCF 1-13.   Molière: anthologie. 13 pd.
               C 47-1.647.   Aimer Molière.
               2C 161-11.311-13.   Théatre de toujours (Cocteau)
               C 61-12.189.   Molière en 1930.

PEARL   SHE 525.   Merry-go-down. 1 pd.
               SHE 539. Anthology.

PH   K 065.   Scenes from Shakespeare. 7 ac.
               P 76.715 R.   Jean Cocteau: selections.
               K 077.   Scenes from Shakespeare. 6 ac.

PREISR   PR 3187.   Als wärs ein Stück von mir (and) Des Teufels
                    General (Zuckmayer). 1 pd.
               PR 3238.   Nelkenburg (and) Evakathel und Schnudi. 1 pd.

RCA   Victor VDM 115.   Scenes from Shakespeare.
               Victor LCT 1156.   Noel and Gertie. 1 pd.
               Victor LM 1924.   Olivier in Scenes from Hamlet and Henry V. 1 pd.
               LSB 4104.   Hamlet and Henry V.
               LRL1-5037.   Edith Evans reads poetry and prose. 1 pd.
               SB 6740.   Shakespeare: selections. 1 pd.
               Victor 64 194.   Scenes from Shakespeare.

ROCOCO   4003.   Actors and actresses: famous voices of the past. 1 pd.

RODALE   RO 3.   Article 3330 (and) Pain de Ménage. 1 pd.

SAGA   PSY 30003.   Samuel Beckett: selections. 1 pd.

SCOT   SR 123.   The Real Macrae; Man of the Theatre. 1 pd.

SMC   1032.   Hora de la Comedia. 1pd/1 ac.

```
SPOA      LVA 9.  Photo du Colonel.  1 pd.
          LVA 28.  Piéton.  1 pd.
          704.  Arthur Miller speaking and reading from his plays.  1 pd.
          715.  Golden Treasury of French Drama.  1 pd.
          SA 717.  Cradle will rock (Blitzstein).  1 pd.
          718.  John Van Druten speaking on and reading from The Art of
             Playwriting a.o.  1 pd.
          719.  Paul Green discussing and reading from his works.  1 pd.
          723.  Paul Rogers presents soliloquies from Shakespeare.  1 pd.
          725.  Moss Hart reading from his plays.  1 pd.
          743.  Synge: Riders to the Sea (and) Shadow of the Glen.  1 pd.
          751.  Yeats: selections.
          752.  Plays and memories: Yeats.  1 pd.
          766.  Scenes from Shakespeare.  1 pd.
          767.  Scenes from Shakespeare.  1 pd.
          779.  The Art of Ruth Draper, v.3.  1 pd.
          786.  Georges Courteline: La paix chez soi (and) Peur des Coups.
             1 pd.
          793.  Molière: Femmes Savantes (and) Tartuffe.  1 pd.
          794.  Molière: Bourgeois Gentilhomme (and) Malade Imaginaire.  1 pd.
          798.  The Art of Ruth Draper, v.2.  1 pd.
          799.  The Art of Ruth Draper, v.1.  1 pd.
          800.  The Art of Ruth Draper, v.4.  1 pd.
          805.  The Art of Ruth Draper, v.5.  1 pd.
          822.  Golden Treasury of French Literature.  1 pd.
          836/7.  Soliloquies and scenes from Shakespeare.  2 pd.
          862.  Treasury of Spanish Drama, 1.  1 pd.
          863.  Treasury of Spanish Drama, 2.  1 pd.
          864.  Treasury of Spanish Drama, 3.  1 pd.
          901.  Love scenes from Shakespeare.  1 pd.
          924.  Jean Vilar: ses grands rôles.  1 pd
          985.  Morceaux choisies de la littérature française.  1 pd.
          6048.  Scenes from Shakespeare's plays.  1 pd.
          7005/8006.  Selected sonnets (and) soliloquies.  1 pd/1 ac.

SUPERSC   I 141.  Ancient Greek Drama.  1 ac.

SYRAC     1.  The Worlds of Shakespeare.  2 pd.

TELEF     6.41003 AS.  Heinrich George: Portrait eines Schauspielers.  1 pd.
          6.48073.  Ein Portrait: Ernst Deutsch.  2 pd.
          STSC 13445.  Portrait of an actress: Hilde Krahl.  1 pd.
          STSC 13.454.  Büchner: Steckbrief 2493 a.o.  1 pd.

THEAMA    GRC 2431.  An evening with William Shakespeare.  2 pd.

THEATCL   Cymbeline (and) Romeo and Juliet.  1 ac.

TIKVA     T 28.  The World of Sholom Aleichem.  1 pd.

TONO      X 25033.  Ibsen: Peer Gynt (and) Björnson: Bergliot.  1 pd.

TRINIT    The two sides of Shakespeare.  5 ac.

YALE      TV 19232/33.  Shakespeare's pronunciation.  1 pd.
```

Directory of Recording Companies

A & M. A. & M. Records, 1416 North La Brea, Los Angeles, CA 90028

ADÈS. Disques Adès SA, 54, rue Saint-Lazare, 75009 Paris, France

AFRTV. Armed Forces Radio and Television Service (current status not known)

AGUILAR. Discos Aguilar, Juan Bravo, 38, Madrid, Spain

AIMS. Aims Media, Inc., 626 Justin Av., Glendale, CA 91201

AL. Unidentified label

ALLEGRO. Pickwick International, Inc., Edgware Road, London NW 2, England

ALLMEDIA. All-Media Dramatic Workshop, Chicago, IL (current status unknown)

ALP. Unidentified label

ALPHA. Unidentified label

AMADEO. Amadeo, Österreichische Schallplatten Aktiengesellschaft, Maria-
    hilfer Gürtel 32, Wien, Austria

AMBER. Amber Records, Ltd., Wyastone Leys, Monmouth, Gwent NP5 3Y2, U. K.

AMERH. American Heritage Press, Inc., 10 Rockefeller Plaza, New York, NY
    10019

ANGEL. Capitol Records, 1750 North Vine St., Hollywood, CA 90028

ANNA. Unidentified label

ARGO. London Records, 539 West 25th Street, New York, NY 10001

ARIEL. Unidentified label

ARIOLA. Ariola-Eurodisc, G.m.b.H., Steinhauserstr. 3, 8000 München, West
    Germany

ASCH. Folkways Records, 43 West 61st Street, New York, NY 10023

ASRD. American Society of Recorded Drama (current status not known)

ATHENA. Ariola-Eurodisc, G.m.b.H., Steinhauserstr. 3, 8000 München, West
    Germany

ATLANT. Atlantic Records, 75 Rockefeller Plaza, New York, NY 10019

AUDIBK. Audio Book Co., 301 Pasadena St., Pasadena, CA 91030

AUDIDR. Audio Drama (current status not known)

AUDIOR. Audio Rarities, 770 11th Av., New York, NY 10019

AUDIVS. Audio-Visual Productions, Hocker Hill House, Chepstow, Gwent, U. K.

BANNER. Banner Records, 1290 Av. of the Americas, Suite 274, New York, NY
    10019

BBC. BBC Study Tapes, 630 Fifth Av., New York, NY 10020

BERG. Ivan Berg Associates, Ltd., 35a Broadhurst Gardens, London, NW6 3QT,
    U. K.

BERLET. Berlet Films, 1646 West Kimmel Rd., Jackson, MI 49201

BFA. Phoenix/BFA Films & Video, Inc., 468 Park Av. South, New York, NY 10016

BLACKH. Blackhawk Films, 1235 West 5th Street, Davenport, IA 52808

BLUE. Blue Thumb Records (current status not known)

BOR. Bordas, 189, av. du Maine, 75014 Paris, France

BRUNO. Bruno Records (current status not known)

BRUNSW. Brunswick (current status not known)

BUD. Buddah Records, 810 Seventh Av., New York, NY 10019

BUDGET. Budget Video, 1534 North Highland Av., Suite 108, Hollywood, CA
    90028

CA. Current Affairs, P. O. Box 398, Wilton, CT 06897

CAED. Caedmon Records, 1995 Broadway, New York, NY 10023

CAMDEN. Pickwick International, Inc., Hyde Industrial Estate, London,
    NW9 6JU, U. K.

CAPITOL. Capitol Records, 1750 North Vine St., Hollywood, CA 90028

CDM. Chant du Monde, 64, rue Ampère, 75017 Paris, France

CENT. Center for Cassette Studies, 8110 Webb Av., North Hollywood, CA
    91605

CETRA. Fonit-Cetra, Via G. Meda, 45, Milano, Italy

CHA. André Charlin, 15, av. Montaigne, 75008 Paris, France

CMS. CMS Records, 14 Warren St., New York, NY 10007

CNI. Canetti/Discodis, 32, rue François 1er, 75008 Paris, France

COLUMB. CBS Records Group, 51 West 52nd Street, New York, NY 10019

COMREC. Command Records, 1501 Broadway, New York, NY 10036

CONTF. Contemporary Films, 55 Greek St., London, W1V 6DB, U. K.

CONTIN. Continental Records (current Status not known)

COTILLION. WEA Musik G.m.b.H., Arndtstr. 16, 2000 Hamburg 76, West Germany

COTTA. Ernst Klett Vlg., P. O. Box 809, 7000 Stuttgart 1, West Germany

CRAF. Crawley Films, Ltd., 19 Fairmont Av., Ottawa, Ont., Canada

CREDO. Credo Records (current status not known)

CTP. Unidentified French label

DAGGETT. Daggett Studio (current status not known)

DAVINCI. Davinci Records (current status not known)

DEANE. Ch. Deane Prod. (current status not known)

DECCA. Decca Record Co., Ltd., 9 Albert Embankment, London SE1 7SW, U. K.

DELTA. Delta Records (current status not known)

DEUTGR. Deutsche Grammophon Gesellschaft, P. O. Box 301240, 2000 Hamburg 36,
    West Germany

DISC. Discurio, 9 Shepherd St., London W1, U. K.

DOVER. Dover, 180 Varick St., New York, NY 10014

EAV. Educational Audio Visual, Inc., Pleasantville, NY 10570

EBEC. Encyclopaedia Britannica Educ. Corp., 425 North Michigan Av.,
    Chicago, IL 60611

EIA. Editrice Italiana Audiovisivi, Via Alpi 9, Roma, Italy

EMBASSY. Embassy Home Entertainment, 1901 Av. of the Stars, Los Angeles,
    CA 90067

EMC. Educational Materials Corp., 180 East 6th Street, Saint Paul, MN 55101

EMI. EMI Records, Ltd., 20 Manchester Sq., London W1A 1ES, U. K.

ENTER. Enter-Tel, Inc., 25200 Chagrin Bl., Beachwood, OH 44122

EPIC. CBS Schallplatten G.m.b.H., Bleichstr. 64-66a, 6000 Frankfurt
       am Main, West Germany

ES. Hachette, 25, rue du Gén. Leclerc, 94270 Kremlin-Bicêtre, France

ESOT. Esoteric, Inc., 26 Clark St., East Hartford, CT 06108

EUROD. Ariola-Eurodisc, G.m.b.H., Steinhauserstr. 3, 8000 München 80,
        West Germany

EV/ED. Everett/Edwards, P. O. Box 1060, Deland, FL 32720

EVEREST. Everest Recording Group, 2020 Av. of the Stars, Century City,
          CA 90067

EVERG. Evergreen Records, Dimitri Music Co., 7859 Bastille Pl.,
        Severn, MD 21144

FAMREC. Famous Record Co. (current status not known)

FEST. Festival/Musidisc, 99, rue de la République, 92801 Puteaux, France

FFHS. Films for the Humanities, P. O. Box 2053, Princeton, NJ 08540

FI. Films Inc., 733 Green Bay Rd., Wilmette, IL 60091

FOLGER. Folger Shakespeare Library, 201 East Capitol St., Washington, DC
         20003

FOLKW. Folkways Records, 43 West 61st Street, New York, NY 10023

FON. Fontana, Société Phonographique Philips, 6, rue Jenner, Paris 8e, France

GAKKEN. Gakken Films Co., Gakken Bldg. 4-405, Kamiikedai, Ohta-ku, Tokyo,
         Japan

GENTW. Gentle Wind (current status not known)

GID. Guilde Internationale du Disque, Tour Franklin, 92081 Paris-la-
      Défense, France

GMS. Goldsmith Audiovisuals, 85 Longview Rd., Port Washington, NY 11050

GOLDEN. A A Records, Inc., Golden Records, Educ. Div., 250 West 57th Street,
         New York, NY 10019

GOLDGUI. Golden Guinea, Pye Records, Ltd., 10A Chandos St., London W1, U.K.

GRAMM. Grammofon AB Electra, P. O. Box 1178, 17123 Solna 1, Sweden

GRYPHON. Gryphon Records, 507 Fifth Av., New York, NY 10017

HACH.   Hachette, 25, rue du Général-Leclerc, 94270 Kremlin-Bicêtre, France

HARVOC.   Harvard Vocarium, Cambridge, MA (current status not known)

HERDER.   Herder Fono-Ring, Hermann-Herder-Str. 4, 7800 Freiburg, West Germany

HMV.   His Master's Voice, EMI Records, Ltd., 20 Manchester Sq., London,
     W1A 1ES, U. K.

IER.   Imperial Educational Resources, Inc., 19 Marble Av., Pleasantville,
     NY 10570

IFB.   International Film Bureau, 332 South Michigan Av., Chicago, IL 60604

INDU.   Indiana University Films, A-V Center, Indiana University,
     Bloomington, IN 47405

INSPRACH.   Institut für Deutsche Sprachkunde, Goethe-Universität,
     Frankfurt am Main, West Germany

INTERNAT.   Inter Nationes, Kennedy-Allee 91-103, 5300 Bonn 2, West Germany

IRCC.   (Unidentified label)

JUP.   Jupiter Recordings, 140 Kensington Church Street, London W8, U. K.

KING.   King Features Entertainment, 235 East 45 St., New York, NY 10017

KIWI.   Kiwi Records, 182 Wakefield St., Wellington, New Zealand

LC.   Library of Congress, Archive of Recorded Poetry and Literature,
     Washington, DC 20542

LEARNC.   Learning Corporatoon of America, 1350 Av. of the Americas, New
     York, NY 10019

LEWYCKY.   G. Lewycky, New York (current status not known)

LEX.   Lexington Records, 1 Claremont Av., Thorwood, NY

LF.   Library Films (current status not known)

LFP.   Listen for Pleasure, 417 Center St., Lewistown, NY 14092

LIBED.   Library Editions, Request Records, 66 Mechanic St., New
     Rochelle, NY 10801

LIST.   Listening Library, 1 Park Av., Old Greenwich, CT 06870

LITERA.   Literary Records (current status not known)

LIVSHA.   Living Shakespeare, 100 Av. of the Americas, New York, NY

LONDON.   London Records, 539 West 25th Street, New York, NY 10001

LONGMAN.   Longman Group, Ltd., Longman House, Burnt Mill, Harlow, Essex
     CM20 2JE, U. K.

LUM.   Lumen, 3, rue Garancière, Paris 6e, France

LVA.   La Voix de l'Auteur, 5, rue Cambon, Paris 1er, France

MAGICT.   Magic-Tone Records, 545 Fifth Av., New York, NY 10017

MAJOR.   Major Records (current status not known)

MANT.   Harold Mantell, Inc., P. O. Box 378, Princeton, NJ 08540

MARK.   Mark Educational Recordings, Inc., 4249 Cameron Dr., Buffalo, NY
        14221

MELOD.   Melodiya, 24 Tverskoi Bl., Moskva K-9, U.S.S.R.

MERC.   Mercury Records, Phonogram/Disques Philips, 24, blvd. de
        l'Hôpital, 75005 Paris, France

MGM.   MGM Records, 1540 Broadway, New York, NY 10036

MICHMED.   Michigan Media, University of Michigan, Resources Center,
           400 4th Street, Ann Arbor, MI 48109

MILCAM.   Millers of Cambridge, Sidney Street, Cambridge, U. K.

MILLER.   Miller-Brody Productions, 400 Hahn Bl., Westminster, MD 21157

MINN.   Minnesota Public Radio, St. Paul, MN

MK.   Mezhdunarodnaya Kniga, Moskva G-200, U.S.S.R.

MM.   Major Minor, 58 Great Marlborough St., London W1, U.K.

NACTE.   National Council of Teachers of English, 1111 Kenyon Rd.,
         Urbana, IL 61801

NBC.   National Broadcasting Corp., 30 Rockefeller Plaza, New York, NY 10019

NEALON.   Radio Eireann, Dublin, Ireland

NET.   National Educational Television, Indiana University, Bloomington, IN
       47401

NGS.   National Geographic Society, 17th and M Streets, NW, Washington,
       DC 20036

NIT.   National Instructional Television, Box A, Bloomington, IN 47401

NORTON.   Jeffrey Norton Publ., Inc., Audio Div., 145 East 49th Street,
          New York, NY 10017

ODEON.   I. M. E. Pathé Marconi, 19 rue Lord-Byron, 75008 Paris, France

PAC.   Pacifica Tape Library (current status not known)

PAST.   Pastorale et Musique Unidisc, 31, rue de Fleurus, 75008 Paris,
        France

PAT. I. M. E. Pathé Marconi, 19, rue Lord-Byron, 75008 Paris, France

PEARL. Pearl Records, 56 Hopwood Gardens, Tunbridge Wells, Kent, U. K.

PENGUIN. Penguin Video Productions, 3500 Verdugo Rd., Los Angeles, CA 90065

PERIOD. Everest Recording Group, 2020 Av. of the Stars, Century City, CA
     90067

PH. Prentice-Hall Media, 150 White Plains Rd., Tarrytown, NY 10591

PHIL. Philips, Société Phonographique, 6 rue Jenner, Paris 8e, France

PLÄNE. Verlag "Pläne", G.m.b.H., Braunschweigerstr. 20, 4600 Dortmund 1,
     West Germany

PLEI. Pleiade, Société Industrielle de Reproductions Sonore, 8 rue de Berri,
     Paris 8e, France

POLYMU. Polymusic (current status not known)

PREISR. Preiserrecords, Harmonia Mundi, 19-21 Nile St., London N1 7LR, U. K.

PROTHM. Prothman Associates Inc., 650 Thomas Av., Baldwin, NY 11510

QUAL. Qualiton, 164 Old Brompton Rd., London SW5, U.K.

RB. Unidentified label

RCA. RCA Victor, Educational Dept., 1133 Av. of the Americas, New York, NY
     10036

RCAVID. RCA Videodiscs, P. O. Box 91079, 7900 Rockville Rd., Indianapolis,
     IN 46291

RE. Unidentified label

REGAL. Unidentified label

RIVERS. Riverside Productions, 67 Riverside Dr., New York, NY 10024

ROCOCO. Rococo Records, Toronto, Canada

RODALE. Rodale Books, 33 East Minor St., Emmaus, PA 18049

ROYALE. Unidentified label

SAGA. Saga Records Ltd., 326 Kensal Rd., London W10, U. K.

SCHUMM. Erich Schumm, G.m.b.H., Erich-Schumm-Str. 2-4, 7157 Murrhardt,
     West Germany

SCOT. Scottish Records (current status not known)

SEABRN. Seabourne Enterprises, Ltd. (current status unknown)

SERAPH. Seraphim, 1290 Av. of the Americas, New York, NY 10019

SHAREC. Shakespeare Recording Society, Caedmon Records, 1995 Broadway, New
         York, NY 10023

SMC. Spanish Music Center, 319 West 48th Street, New York, NY 10036

SONOPR. Sonopresse MFM, 35, rue Gabriel-Péri, 92130 Issy-les-Moulineaux,
         France

SPECSERV. Special Services Records (current status not known)

SPOA. Spoken Arts, 310 North Av., New Rochelle, NY 10801

SPOWRD. Spoken Word, Dover, 180 Varick Street, New York, NY 10014

SSB. Selections Sonores Bordas, Bordas, 189, rue du Maine, 75014 Paris,
      France

SSSR. SSSR Aprelevskiy Zavod (current status not known)

SUPERSC. Superscope Library of the Spoken Word (current status not known)

SYRAC. Syracuse University Recordings, Syracuse, NY 13214

TALK. Talking Tape Co., 186 Fulham Rd., London SW10, U. K.

TELEF. TELDEC Schallplatten G.m.b.H., Heussweg 25, 2000 Hamburg 20,
        West Germany

TETRA. Tetragrammaton (current status not known)

THEAMA. Theatre Msterworks, 20 Rockefeller Plaza, New York, NY 10020

THEATCL. Theatre Classics Recital, National Public Radio (current status not
          known)

THORN. Thorn EMI Video, 1370 Av. of the Americas, New York, NY 10019

TIKVA. Tikva Records, 1650 Broadway, New York, NY 10019

TIMLIF. Time-Life Video, 1271 Av. of the Americas, New York, NY 10020

TONO. Unidentified label

TRADIR. Tradition Records (current status not known)

TRINIT. Trinity Tapes, Van Nuys, CA (current status not known)

UAE. United Artists Entertainment, 729 Seventh Av., New York, NY 10019

UNI. Unidisc, 31, rue de Fleurus, 75006 Paris, France

UNIVED. Universal Education, 221 Park Av. South, New York, NY 10003

VANGUARD. 71 West 23rd Street, New York, NY 10010

VEG.   Véga, Société Française du Son, 30, rue Beaujon, 75008 Paris, France

VICTROLA.   Victrola (current status not known)

VOG.   Vogue, Productions Internationales Phonographiques, 82, rue Maurice-Grancoing, 93430 Villetaneuse, France

VSM.   Voix de son Maitre, I. M. E. Pathé Marconi, 19, rue Lord-Byron, 75008 Paris, France

WASHU.   University of Washington Films, Seattle, WA 98105

WEST.   Westminster Recording Co. Inc., 1330 Av. of the Americas, New York, NY 10019

YALE.   Yale University Press, 302 Temple St., New Haven, CT 06520

YESTER.   Radio/Video Yesteryear, Box C, Sandy Hook, CT 06482

Herbert H. Hoffman is the catalog librarian at Rancho Santiago Community
College in Santa Ana, California. He holds a Master of Science in
Library Science degree from the University of Southern California and is
a member of the American Society of Indexers. Hoffman is the author of
Latin American Play Index (Scarecrow, 1983) and co-author, with Rita
Ludwig Hoffman, of International Index to Recorded Poetry (H. W. Wilson,
1983).